A COUP IN TURKEY

A Coup in Turkey

A Tale of Democracy, Despotism and
Vengeance in a Divided Land

Jeremy Seal

Chatto & Windus
LONDON

1 3 5 7 9 10 8 6 4 2

Chatto & Windus, an imprint of Vintage

Chatto & Windus is part of the Penguin Random House group of companies whose addresses can be found at global.penguinrandomhouse.com

Penguin
Random House
UK

First published by Chatto & Windus in 2021

penguin.co.uk/vintage

A CIP catalogue record for this book is available from the British Library

ISBN 9781784741754

Typeset in 11.5/15 pt Ehrhardt MT by Integra Software Services Pvt. Ltd, Pondicherry

Printed and bound in Great Britain by Clays Ltd, Elcograf S.p.A.

The authorised representative in the EEA is Penguin Random House Ireland, Morrison Chambers, 32 Nassau Street, Dublin D02 YH68.

Penguin Random House is committed to a sustainable future for our business, our readers and our planet. This book is made from Forest Stewardship Council® certified paper.

To my three girls, with love

CONTENTS

AUTHOR'S NOTE

Over a number of years, and in the course of several visits to Turkey, I have researched the story which appears in these pages. The book draws upon material including newspaper reports, published memoirs and accounts, state documents, court transcripts, unpublished letters, interviews, photographs and film footage; all these sources are acknowledged in the Notes.

For the sake of narrative clarity, I have reordered the incidents described so that they do not always appear in the sequence, or at the time, that they actually occurred. I have also presumed to speculate, not only upon the unspoken thoughts and motivations of some characters but what might have been said at crucial meetings and encounters known to have taken place where the actual exchanges went unrecorded or otherwise remain undisclosed. Much of the dialogue, then, is my own in a work which is ultimately that of an imagination I've done my best to inform.

I have used the Latin-based Turkish script, introduced by Mustafa Kemal Atatürk, where some of the characters carry diacritics which assign pronunciations. The most common of these are summarised here:

- The Turkish c is pronounced j (**j**ournalism)
- ç is ch (**ch**urch)
- ş is sh (**sh**ower)
- ğ is silent but denotes a lengthening of the preceding vowel, and often performs the function of the English 'w' as in the surname of Turkey's President Erdoğan (Er-dow-an)
- ı is the flat 'schwa' sound, as in show**er**, whereas the dotted i is pronounced as in **i**nk

- ö and ü are hard to render but indicate characteristically Turkish modifications of the typical English vowel sounds

I have chosen to use the Turkish versions where readers may be more familiar with anglicised forms, so that our *pasha* (general) is given here as *paşa*, and *hodja* (teacher) as *hoca*.

Many common Turkish titles, among them Bey (Mr) and Hanım (Mrs, or Madam), are given after the subject's first name. I'm never more delighted than when I'm addressed as Jeremy Bey.

TURKEY

BULGARIA

BLACK

Istanbul
Gebze
Imralı
Bursa

T U R

Thessaloniki

GREECE

ANKARA

Eskişehir

•Kütahya

Izmır

•Uşak •Afyon

•Aydın

Milas •Çakırbeyli
•Kargıcak

Konya•

Denizli

CYPRUS

M E D I T E R R A N E A N S E A

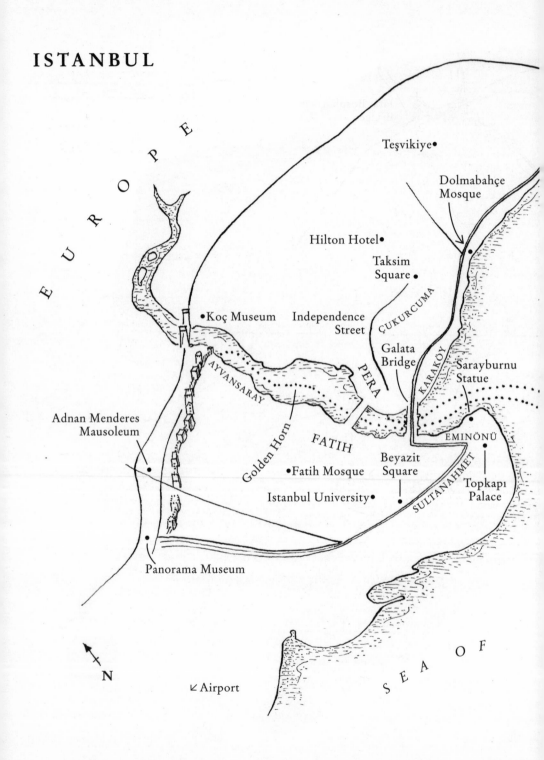

ISTANBUL

EUROPE

Teşvikiye•

Dolmabahçe
Mosque

Hilton Hotel•

Taksim
Square•

•Koç Museum

Independence
Street

ÇUKURCUMA

Galata
Bridge

PERA

KARAKÖY

Sarayburnu
Statue

AYVANSARAY

Adnan Menderes
Mausoleum

Golden Horn

FATIH

•Fatih Mosque

Beyazit
Square

EMİNÖNÜ

Istanbul University•

SULTANAHMET

Topkapı
Palace

Panorama Museum

N

Airport

SEA OF

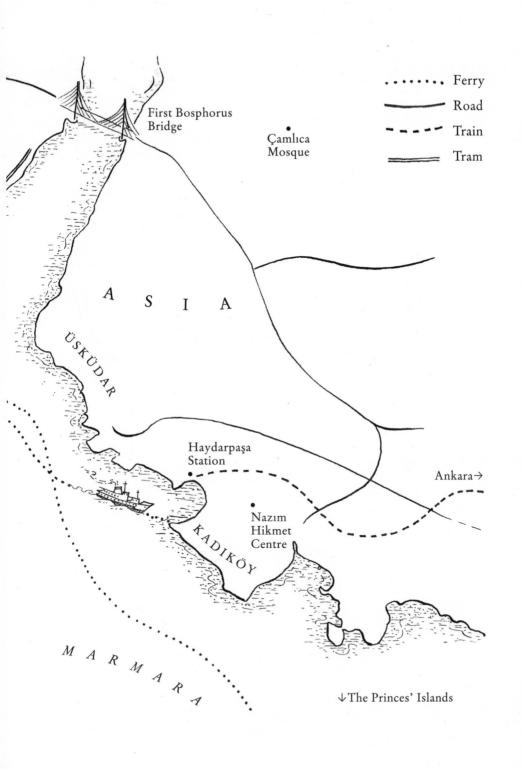

Ferry · · · · · · · ·
Road ———
Train – – –
Tram ====

First Bosphorus
Bridge

Çamlıca
Mosque

A S I A

ÜSKÜDAR

Haydarpaşa
Station

Ankara→

Nazım
Hikmet
Centre

KADIKÖY

M A R M A R A

↓The Princes' Islands

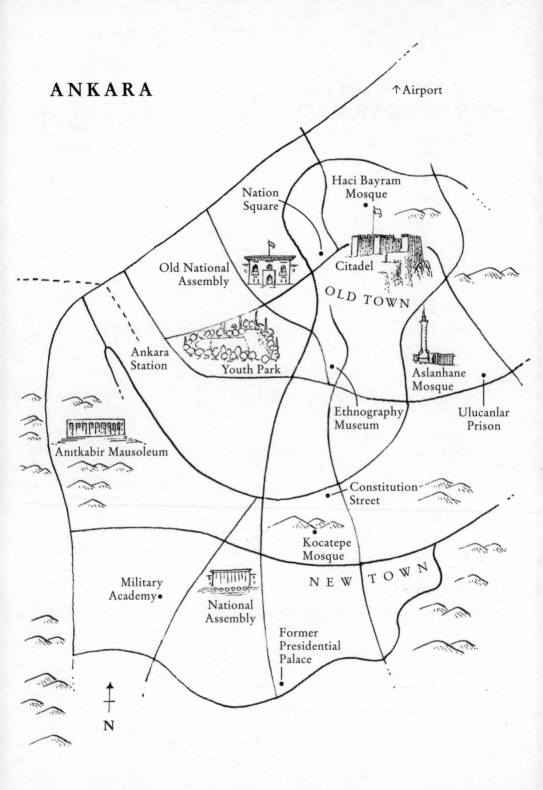

ANKARA

↑ Airport

Nation
Square

Haci Bayram
Mosque

Old National
Assembly

Citadel

OLD TOWN

Ankara
Station

Youth Park

Aslanhane
Mosque

Ethnography
Museum

Ulucanlar
Prison

Anıtkabir Mausoleum

Constitution
Street

Kocatepe
Mosque

Military
Academy

NEW TOWN

National
Assembly

Former
Presidential
Palace

N

ISTANBUL and the
SEA OF MARMARA

BLACK SEA

E U R O P E

I S T A N B U L

A S I A

N

Heybeliada

PRINCES' ISLANDS

Sivriada

Yassıada

Büyükada

S E A   O F   M A R M A R A

Imralı

•Bursa

PROLOGUE

17 February 1959

An aircraft crashes near Gatwick

O n a fog-bound afternoon a few years before my own birth a passenger plane plunged into a wood three miles short of the runway at Gatwick in southern England. Back then, when Kitty Hawk was a living memory and many remembered craning young necks to the sound of engines overhead, those heralds of the new age, and airports were little more than airfields, crashes were commonplace. This one might have been no more exceptional if it were not for the man who walked unscathed out of the wood on that February day in 1959. As it was, the consequences for the country the flight had left hours earlier, amidst high hopes, were to prove unimaginable.

The twenty-four passengers and crew, most of whom were pitched instantly into the final moments of their lives, bore the immediate impact. The plane was into its descent when they felt sudden reverberations beneath their feet, and heard scrabbling sounds which some were yet to recognise as tree crowns brushing against the undercarriage, before leafless beech branches were thrashing at the windows or turning to tinder in the clogged maws of the propellers. Lurching lower still into a cradle of thickening boughs, the Vickers Viscount stalled and crashed into Jordan's Wood.

The fog so muffled the screaming engines and shattering boughs that the noise barely reached the farmhouse on the far edge of the wood where Margaret Bailey was feeding her chickens. Instead a series of concussive thuds caused Margaret to rush inside where she found her husband, Tony, hurriedly pulling on a pair of boots; over the years the couple had heard aircraft overhead often enough to understand not only that one had crashed but that it must be close, for the impact had shaken the farmhouse's fourteenth-century walls and raised seams of dust that had not settled by the time they slammed the door behind them. From the wood store Tony grabbed an axe which he threw into the boot of the car before speeding off down the lane, the two peering anxiously through the gloom. Within seconds Margaret picked out a faint corona which flared among the trees.

'There. Over there,' she exclaimed. Tony brought the car to a halt and the couple made off in the direction of the flames.

It was then that three figures stumbled out of the wood. The men were distressed, muddy and bloodied, but beneath the disorder their olive skins, their well-cut suits and silk ties marked them out. While Tony Bailey continued into the wood, Margaret drove her shaken charges back to the farmhouse. On the way the man in the passenger seat smoothed his lapel, as if crawling from a wrecked aircraft spread with dead friends and colleagues was no excuse for dishevelment, before he thanked his rescuer in elegant but accented English. They were from Turkey, he explained. 'We are here,' he said, gesturing to the older of the men on the back seat, 'with our prime minister.'

Tony Bailey followed the plane's smouldering swathe into the wood. In the gathering dusk the air pulsed with recent violence; it smelt of smoke and kerosene, and the resinous reek of sap. The scoured earth, warm through the farmer's boots, was strewn with mangled pieces of metal, splintered saplings and tree boles, the uprooted stumps uniformly canted as if to point him in the right direction. The plane had left blackened gouges where pieces of plastic twisted out of all recognition lay embedded. But Tony also saw pleated window curtains pristine in their poppered ties, scattered shiny briefcases and document files neatly bound by elasticated corner bands, the pulverisation of the plane's fittings and contents as randomly selective as it was to prove with the passengers.

Tony reached an oak tree hung with the battered tail section of an aircraft, a red Star and Crescent motif visible on the fin. A propeller,

blades crumpled, lay further off where flames skittered across irides-
cent puddles of fuel. The wings had sheared and cartwheeled away.
The fuselage had broken up as it ploughed on. Where it had come to
rest against a tree, the front section smashed beyond recognition,
Tony found three local gardeners clambering over the wreckage.
They were attempting to free the pilot who lay slumped over the
controls, sawing at the jammed safety belt with their penknives. Only
after they had dragged him from the cockpit did they realise that the
pilot was dead. They laid the body at the foot of a tree before returning to the shattered fuselage where a series of moans directed them
to a heap of smoking metal. One man wedged his shoulder under a
panel and pushed, feeling the ferocious heat singe his jacket as
another dragged a casualty clear. It was the air hostess, badly burned.
In their instinctive reticence the men hesitated before tearing at the
woman's smouldering uniform, which came away in clumps of disintegrating fabric. They stripped the air hostess to her underclothes
before gently swaddling her in a curtain ripped from the cabin
wreckage.

Dusk had fallen by the time the rescue services arrived. The
Gatwick firemen hosed down the upturned plane before axing holes
at the windows to reveal the remaining passengers mostly upside
down, still strapped into their seats. As the dead and injured, some
soaked in fuel, were stretchered to the waiting roadside ambulances,
witnesses wondered how it was that there were any survivors to treat.
The plane looked, as a visiting aviation official later put it, 'as if
someone had taken a sheet of foolscap paper and crumpled it up'.

'It is a miracle,' a fire officer added, 'that anyone came out alive.'

Back at the farmhouse Margaret, a trained nurse, was too busy
handing out blankets, dispensing mugs of tea and her father-in-law's
vintage brandy, and helping the men find the telephone number of
the Turkish Embassy in London, to wonder at such things. No time
to marvel that the three men in her care had not merely survived but
walked clear of the wreckage; and that of all the passengers it should
have been the prime minister, though badly shaken, who suffered
nothing more than severe bruising. In the years ahead Margaret

would have good reason to reflect on the remarkable escape that day of Adnan Menderes, and on the bitter irony of what the newspapers hailed the 'Menderes Miracle'.

*

Five days later an aircraft provided by the British authorities flew the victims of Turkish Airlines' first fatal plane crash to the newly upgraded airfield at Ankara. Silent crowds lined the roads of Turkey's snowbound capital, lowering their heads as the cortege of fourteen coffins, draped in the Star and Crescent of their flag, made for the Haci Bayram mosque where the obsequies were to take place.

The dead included the airline's own managing director as well as ministers, MPs, government officials and the prime minister's private secretary. The head of the state Anatolian Press Agency, and a photographer who had made his name covering the recent Korean War, where the Turkish brigades had earned acclaim for their outstanding service, were also killed. The loss of so many distin-guished figures occurred, moreover, at what should have been a moment of national celebration. 'It is particularly sad,' Harold Macmillan, Britain's prime minister, was to say, 'that this tragedy should have fallen upon the Turkish prime minister and his compan-ions while on a mission of peace and reconciliation.' The mood on the flight to London had been one of optimism, even self-congratulation, on account of the historic agreement which Prime Minister Menderes and his foreign minister Fatin Rüştü Zorlu had lately reached with their Greek counterparts over Cyprus. The entourage was on the way to attend the culminating formalities in the agreement over independence from British rule of the troubled Mediterranean island, whose Greek and Turkish communities had lately been at often violent odds. The agreement, which would see Britain cede sovereignty over Cyprus and the Greeks renounce their long-held aspirations for *enosis* (incorporation into the Greek state) in return for the Turks' pledge not to partition the island, was hailed by US president Dwight Eisenhower as an outstanding feat of statesmanship. After years of intractable and repeatedly stalemated negotiations, it appeared that ethnic enmities might be healed and the island's descent into sectarian conflict forestalled. By reconciling Cyprus's warring communities, the agreement held out the prospect of a new era of cooperation between Athens and Ankara.

Then this, the Turkish mission's broken and burned forms strewn across an English wood and the prime minister, physically intact but substantially shaken, reduced to initialling the agreement's cover document in a London hospital bed where he had been advised to rest. The Gatwick disaster disrupted the signing ceremonials; events were to prove that it also portended the agreement's failure, even the grim future – conflict, invasion and partition – which Cyprus was to suffer.

But for Prime Minister Menderes, the crash was to have more immediate implications.

*

A week after grieving the Gatwick dead, the time had come to give thanks for the survivors – one above all, to judge by the vast crowds which gathered on the last day of February to welcome the prime minister on his return to the Turkish capital. On that bitterly cold morning a jubilant throng converged on the station where the prime minister was to arrive, as the national radio repeatedly reminded listeners. Many among the crowds came with a farm animal. From the barns of outlying villages muffled herdsmen in worn boots had driven sheep and goats, cattle, oxen and even camels through the starlit night; some had loaded their beasts at first light onto open trucks painted with appeals to Allah's safekeeping. The city streets unsettled these animals, their nostrils flaring amidst clouds of frozen breath.

To others, these rapturous devotees and their animals constituted an intolerable trespass. Word of the gathering at the station mortified bureaucrats and lawyers, opposition politicians and journalists, teachers, academics and above all army officers who protested that there had been nothing of the sort since Ottoman times. This was the city they considered their own; the city, after all, of the Turks' soldier saviour who had consigned the backward Ottomans to history, whose statue adorned every town square, whose portrait hung behind every desk, whose image the coins and banknotes bore and whose pronouncements – sacred articles of faith to his followers – were picked out in stones on hillsides across the nation's every province and on the walls of his monumental Ankara mausoleum. That man was the founder of modern Turkey, Mustafa Kemal Atatürk, who had made Ankara his capital in the 1920s. To Atatürk's supporters the model city's buildings and institutions, often radically European in style, amounted to an avowal of the future that the great leader had determined for twentieth-century Turkey: ministries, university buildings, a presidential residence, banks, monuments and statues, landscaped parks and broad boulevards, officers' clubs, hospitals and factories, museums, an opera house and railway station, transport hub of a nation sworn to progress by scientific, social and techno- logical advance. This invasion of steaming beasts – destined for an end whose ritual primitivity appeared to confirm the secularists' argument – was rudely retrograde; it returned Ankara to the flea- ridden farmyard it had been under the despised Ottomans, a stew of provincial superstition and torpor, which made a mockery of the new city's ambitions. The greater offence was that these farm workers and blacksmiths, shopkeepers and tea boys, factory workers and porters should have gathered in Atatürk's capital – and resting place – to honour another. For they had come to celebrate the miraculous deliverance of Adnan Bey – Mr Adnan – whom they held as their own saviour.

At the station, its colonnaded facade and rounded Bauhaus-style wings draped in the Star and Crescent, the staff tried to hold back the masses. But the crowds would not be denied; they broke through the cordons and dragged the animals by their ceremonial halters, braided with green and gold thread, up the shallow steps into the high- ceilinged ticket hall and out onto the platform. Those excluded in the thickening crush lined the neighbouring boulevards where their skittish animals, unsteady on the ice, fouled the broken pavement kerbs and tossed horns painted for the occasion.

As the men jostled for space, they traded salutations and village gossip. Allegations circulated; one held that Archbishop Makarios, the Greek Cypriot leader whom many Turks reviled, had paid Gatwick's flight controllers to bring down Menderes's plane. A more universal claim, which the placards reading 'In Allah's Care' confirmed, was of a divine hand at work; some challenged the quieter men among them, taking their reticence for scepticism, to explain how it could otherwise be that just eleven days earlier their leader had emerged from that mangle of metal no worse off than if a grumpy donkey had kicked out to catch him in the midriff. Allah had spared the blessed Menderes for restoring their Islamic faith which the godless bureaucrats had denied them. For almost ten years now this saintly man had striven to reopen their mosques and religious schools. He had legislated that the *ezan*, the call to prayer, could once more be made in Arabic, sacred language of the Prophet. He had provided funds for those wishing to make the pilgrimage to Mecca, mark of the true Muslim. So they loved Adnan Bey – their name for him acknowledged the prime minister's legendary ease with the humble and the uneducated – for backing them in their traditional beliefs. It was surely for this that Allah had preserved their leader from an untimely death among the infidels. The time had come to show their gratitude in the old way.

Those at the platform edge were the first to hear the faint rattling which carried down the tracks. A fevered roar, a blend of Turkish and devotional Arabic, rose from the crush: *Allahu akbar! Allahu akbar! Our beloved leader is near!* The steam train, drawn by a gleaming black and red locomotive, and decked in wilting flowers which government officials had had rushed up from the balmy Mediterranean, drew to a halt along the platform. The crowd surged as station staff and the prime minister's aides fought to clear a space at a carriage door, and a cry of welcome greeted the man – short, dark and impeccably groomed in worsted suit and sunglasses – who appeared at the window.

Of the distressed, disordered and tentative figure whom Margaret Bailey had lately taken into her home there was no trace; the
characteristic confidence and vigour was back. Checking his cuffs
and ordering his brilliantined black hair with a cupped hand, Adnan
Bey smiled broadly and waved before stepping into the rapturous
reception, careless of any discomfort the crush might cause his sore
ribs. Officials and aides ushered the prime minister along the path
they forced through outstretched hands, raised caps and the figures
stooping to kiss the leader's hand. *Maşallah*, the crowd chorused; *to
Allah we make these gifts for sparing our leader.* A man not far from the
prime minister drew a knife.

It was a long knife with a pointed blade which the man, as much
to announce his intentions, tested theatrically against a calloused
finger. Those nearest promptly fell back, creating a compact arena in
which the man and his goat were contained. The man shortened the
halter to run a hand across the flank of the goat, where the whitewashed words FOR ADNAN BEY'S SALVATION were daubed,
then down its muzzle, closing the creature's eyelids as if it were
already dead. He seized the chin and hauled it heavenwards, exposing a milk-white throat into which he rammed the blade point before
driving the pommel deep with a clubbed blow from the base of his
clenched fist. The goat bawled and kicked out, all legs at once, like
the gusted spokes of an umbrella, a last exhalation inflating a blood
bubble at its lips. The man bent to grab a horn which he braced
against his thigh, backhanding the buried blade edge with a lateral
swipe through the goat's windpipe. The man heaved back the horns
of the silenced goat to snap its neck. Then, with bowed head and
bent knee, he laid the twitching form at the feet of his passing leader.

A rising din of bleats and bellows drowned out the pieties and the
chorus of thanks as men set about their slaughter. The people seethed
and swayed, buffeting the object of their adulation, a man known to
relish such displays of attention. This morning, however, even Adnan
Bey found the levels of rapture alarming. 'Have we crossed the
ocean,' he asked an attentive aide, 'only to drown in the river?' On
the aide's advice he lengthened his stride to reach the safety of the

wooden dais erected at the end of the platform. Among the officials, bureaucrats and politicians who had gathered to greet him was the leader of the opposition, the revered Ismet İnönü, whom nobody was about to address as Bey. Here was a man who had attained the highest rank of general in the nation's great army – a *paşa*.

On hearing of the Gatwick crash, the ascetic, bespectacled Ismet Paşa had been quick to cable the prime minister with his commiserations and relief at the news of his escape. Ismet Paşa was not one to begrudge any man his good fortune; but the idea that the man's survival might have been down to anything else incensed him. He was also disgusted to see these displays of ritual butchery, which Menderes did not merely tolerate but appeared to enjoy. The opposition leader could only imagine what the eternal Atatürk would have thought. Ismet Paşa had been the national founder's trusted confidant and his comrade in arms during the 1919–22 War of Independence; it was he who had taken the presidential helm on Atatürk's death in 1938, unwaveringly maintaining Turkey's Western bearing into his own old age. Now that he was seventy-four, hard of hearing, grizzled and wattle-throated, Ismet Paşa might have hoped that his work was done, the national course fixed for good. But this disgraceful exhibition, in Atatürk's own city, of the same superstitious ignorance which he and the great founder had striven all their lives to erase, persuaded him that the fight was far from being won; that under Menderes progress had been checked, all those hard-won victories in danger of counting for nothing.

These were the private thoughts of a shrewd old man. Ismet Paşa had been around long enough to have learned, in war and politics as in his beloved chess, when to make his move. Now was not that time. After surviving so many scrapes he knew what the flashing bulbs now required of him. Steeling himself to a semblance of sincerity, he must commiserate with this crowd-loving populist and political performance artist, not to say shameless libertine, on the loss of so many colleagues. In congratulating Menderes on his remarkable escape, he must betray no sign of contempt for the credulity of the crowds, nor of his deepening disdain for their revered leader. So he offered his good wishes and extended a palm, knowing no more than the prime minister that it was to be the last time the two leaders would shake hands.

Barely had Adnan Bey acknowledged Ismet Paşa and his other well-wishers before aides ushered him out of the station and onto the forecourt where a black Buick awaited. Within seconds of leaving the station, however, the limousine was brought to a halt by the fallen animals and the men who were butchering them. To the blast of car horns and police orders the vehicle nosed between the corpses and the viscera steaming in the freezing air. A bloodied bull camel lurched into the road, two men clinging like balloonists to its flailing halter. The additional weight of another man finally brought down the weakened creature, its limbs folding up at the joints. As the men dodged flailing hooves to fall on the camel's neck, rope-thick pulses of arterial blood spattered the window of the Buick.

To the roar of the crowds – *Allahu akbar!* – the police drew their batons and ordered the camel to be dragged from the road. As the Buick manoeuvred past, one of the camel's butchers, catching the eye of his leader, prostrated himself in a slick of blood. The car drew clear, but not before the prime minister saw the man get to his feet, fix his palms in the sacrificial blood smeared across his coat front, and deliberately wipe it over his face.

'They think you are now untouchable, Prime Minister,' an aide observed. 'Or should I call you *Padişah*?' This was the God-given address reserved for the Ottoman sultan, an office the revolutionary and avowedly secular state had long since proscribed. It was an uneasy jest; and as the Buick gathered speed Adnan Bey responded with a non-committal rub of the ribs. He sat back, reaching for his cigarettes – an elegant lidded pack which carried his name inscribed in gilt – before privately contenting himself with the comfort he took from these expressions of devotion.

For in a democracy – which Turkey had been since 1950, when Adnan Bey first came to power – the devotion of the people was what mattered. Devotion meant votes. The votes which had brought him to power – on three successive occasions – were the only legitimate currency. They were what kept him safe. It reassured him to see so many supporters that morning; through his years in office he had come to depend upon the rallies. For without the multitudes which assembled beneath the balconies of regional party headquarters, governor's residences or town halls to hear him speak, without the roar of their approval, he doubted his own strength to still the anxieties he had battled since childhood; crowds were something he liked to keep close, like his cigarettes and his nerve pills. There was nothing like walking among them, the prow of his sometime fedora pinched between the thumb and forefinger of his waving hand, or, better still, being borne on their strong shoulders to the chorus of his name. The fervour and the placards – 'With Menderes the Good Times Continue', 'Long Live Menderes', 'Great Architect of our Nation', 'Menderes, Tamer of Turkey's Rivers' – were his guarantee. By their very numbers these stalwart farm workers, these tea boys and porters, guarded him against the others.

For there would always be others; they were a fact, however regrettable, of democratic politics. In the privacy of the Buick Adnan Bey recalled Ismet Paşa's cool grip at the station, and wondered what he might have glimpsed in his rival's eyes: the envy of one who had never inspired quite such devotion, despite all he had done for the people? Or the contempt for a mere civilian – a cotton farmer, in Adnan Bey's case – of an illustrious general whose mettle was forged in battle, a national hero who had proved by his own feats that nothing counted but being brave and steadfast? And who believed, moreover, that in the land of Atatürk the unforgivable sin was to court religious reaction and so condemn the country to obscurity and superstition, that half-world of the Ottomans which the great leader had devoted his life to erasing.

This was the current charge – that Menderes had been piling on the piety. In the newspapers and in the National Assembly – Turkey's parliament – journalists and politicians had lately accused the prime minister of rehabilitating, even consorting with, the same holy sheikhs that Atatürk's avowed disciples, the so-called Kemalists, had jailed or exiled back in the 1930s; of larding his speeches with religious references; of castigating the opposition for its godlessness; and of being photographed in mosques which the government had lately restored or alongside architects' models of newly commissioned mosques, all in flagrant pursuit of what the secularists derided as the 'prayer-rug vote'.

The Gatwick incident had stoked the religious temperature, inevitably, by giving rise to the suggestion that divine intervention was responsible for Adnan Bey's survival. This was not a notion the returning prime minister appeared especially willing to dispel, to judge by his decision to give thanks at Eyüp, Istanbul's holiest mosque, before taking the train back to his capital. That these events coincided, by chance, with the run-up to the holy month of Ramadan only deepened the rhetoric. Assembly members of the prime minister's Democrat Party announced that their leader was 'appointed by God and his Prophet'. Pro-government publications hailed Menderes in headlines including 'God has Informed the Nation Very Clearly that He Protects You'. 'It wasn't just a prime minister travelling in that plane,' read an editorial, 'but the outcome of Turkey.' On walls and in shop windows poster portraits of Menderes, lambently light, carried the unambiguous caption: 'God has Saved You for the Sake of a Grateful Nation'. Was it any wonder that his followers should have seized upon the idea that some agency other than chance, something beyond the prime minister's mere choice of seat at the back of the Viscount, had spared him from death in that English wood? An idea which Adnan Bey, prey to perpetual anxieties, may himself have found attractive?

The secularists hit back at these fancies by exposing the prime minister to a harsher light; one rumour bruited about was that the sacrifices at the train station, far from a spontaneous expression of popular gratitude, had in fact been paid for and planned by Democrat activists. Some claimed that the butchered meat had not gone to the traditional recipients, the deserving poor and infirm, but was instead diverted to cold-storage facilities while the cash-strapped government sought buyers by way of recouping an outlay it could barely afford. Further allegations had it that the crash, despite causing Menderes no lasting physical harm, had finally done for a man known to be of pronounced nervous disposition; a man who increasingly appeared to depend on extravagant displays of popular adulation, and ever greater supplies of cigarettes and nerve pills, to stay the tears.

These claims did little to dispel the messianic expressions of devotion which only a generation earlier might have ended, and deservedly in the view of some Kemalists, with the noose. What were they to do with the well-wishers who, not content with the slaughter at Ankara station, sacrificed sixty oxen, one for each of their leader's years, outside the prime minister's residence on 9 March 1959? Or with the father who appeared at a Menderes rally, a knife at the throat of a seven-year-old boy hung with a placard which read 'I am sacrificing my child for your having escaped unharmed from the London airplane accident'? Or with those who swore that the special care of the holy man they so revered, the ailing but influential Said Nursi, was what had protected Adnan Bey? Or with the imams, inflamed to the point of insurrection, who had taken to making public appearances in religious robes and turbans in flagrant violation of the strict secular dress laws? It was as if Menderes's emergence, immortalised, from the Gatwick wreckage had put the righteousness back into Islam – in violation of nothing less than the sacred national vision of Atatürk.

This holy frenzy had deepened the determination of some, though few apart from themselves knew it, to act against the prime minister. For some years now whispered conversations in barracks and training colleges, offices and bars, and significant nods in restaurants, had established common grievances, and the understandings subsequently reached in secret meetings were hardening into plans. Now that this man's followers exultantly proclaimed the divine protection he so patently enjoyed, something must be done to show that the Gatwick miracle had been nothing more than chance, a random choice of seat, and that the man they called Adnan Bey was no less mortal than the rest of them.

*

While in London the prime minister had made a rapid recovery.

Famous for his itinerant energy – 'the despair of his security police-guard', as a commentator wrote, who 'loves to walk alone the crowded bazaar streets of Istanbul, and in Ankara drives home alone at the wheel of his car from late-night parties' – Adnan Bey was soon attending to affairs of state, comforting the bereaved and seeing to it that the injured received the best possible treatment. A week after the crash he was strong enough to travel to Redhill, where his valet was recovering from head injuries and a broken arm in the hospital, before making a courtesy call upon the Baileys. The Baileys invited the prime minister and his aides into the farmhouse where they drank tea and raised glasses of sherry to the future. Then the Turkish entourage took its leave, but not before the prime minister had invited the Baileys to Turkey.

Word of the invitation, which held out the promise of a happy ending in an exotic land far beyond the 1950s horizons of holidaying Brits, energised the accompanying journalists, photographers and film crews. A Pathe newsreel recounted how the crash, though a national tragedy, had at least introduced Turkey's prime minister, himself a farmer, 'to an English farm and two charming people. Anthony and Margaret Bailey have made a friend of Mr Menderes. He has invited them to spend a holiday in Turkey as his guests.'

Barely had the news of the invitation broken before the rest of Turkey followed Adnan Bey's lead. Telegrams and letters flooded in to express the gratitude of municipalities, local party offices, trade organisations and private citizens from every corner of Turkey. These letters were effusive, even on the envelopes, with one addressed to the 'very respected and highly intelligent Mr Bailey and his esteemed wife Mrs Margaret'. 'The first aid help that you have given to our prime minister,' read one letter, 'by taking him into your home and taking care of him, has indebted the Turkish people to such a degree that they will not be able to pay till the end of their lives, and with the will of God, made our prime minister survive.' Another wrote of being 'thankful to Almighty God for having given you the opportunity of nursing and taking care of our beloved prime minister who dedicates his life to his people and who works day and night for our sake'. One correspondent, having addressed 'the very honourable Bailey family', signed off with the words, 'I kiss respectfully the hands of the grown-up members of the family and the eyes of the young people.' 'The nation is so much indebted to you,' another wrote, 'that the name of Baileys is already in our hearts.'

Invitations accompanied many of these notes; as the Baileys had taken Turkey's prime minister into their home, so all Turkey now wished to take the Baileys into theirs. One arrived from Istanbul whose mayor, Kemal Aygün, wrote of being 'profoundly happy to see you this summer among us as our guests and hope that you will do us the honour of accepting this invitation'; cities and towns with exotic names – Bursa, Samsun, Gaziantep, Mersin, Uşak, Kütahya, Bolu, Kırıkkale, Afyon, Manisa, Malatya, Elazığ and Sakarya – also extended official invitations to the Baileys. Letters arrived from Rukuye and Salih Uslu of Ankara who declared that they could think of no greater honour than if the Baileys were to accept their invitation 'to drink our tea and soup together in our modest home, unceremoniously'. From Eskişehir Raife Aksoy wrote that her family would count themselves 'the happiest people in the world in preparing a cup of coffee for you' before sending Margaret, her husband and in fact the 'noble English nation respects and affection of the whole Turkish nation without end'.

Beyond these endearing offers of hot drinks, many resorted – in the Turkish way – to gifts: a box of figs arrived from Turkish State Railways, and one of nuts and apricots from the town council at Bergama; a cushion cover embroidered by the hand of a primary-school teacher in Ankara; angora wool scarves for Mrs Bailey and an antique silver watch chain and a box of Turkish cigars for her husband; candies and other confectionery; hand-woven carpets, one featuring Atatürk's signature from a class of schoolgirls; a set of commemorative spoons engraved with Turkey's renowned whirling dervishes; and a piece of silk brocade. The Union of Fig Cooperatives in Izmir – formerly Smyrna – sent raisins, soaps, olive oil and green olives along with the statutory figs. A samovar arrived from the

Society of Drivers and Automobile Traders of Van Province on Turkey's distant border with Iran. A nursing organisation, by no means first to compare Margaret with another British nurse famously feted for her humanitarian treatment of wounded Turks, sent Mrs Bailey a set of Turkish stamps issued to commemorate the centennial of the stay in Turkey of Florence Nightingale during the Crimean War. An Istanbul branch of Mr Menderes's Democrat Party dispatched an engraved antique copper stove to await collection at the London Embassy whose staff thought to forward the stove's measurements, fearing Tony Bailey might need to borrow a car with a bigger boot.

This torrent of goodwill culminated with the arrival on 4 March of a telegram from the Turkish Red Crescent, the Islamic world's equivalent of the Red Cross. The telegram announced the decision of the Red Crescent's central committee to award the Baileys with 'gold medals as a mark of appreciation for your splendid services. This is the highest distinction which our society can give.'

It was then that Margaret Bailey, who had neither been abroad nor in an aeroplane, realised that this was going to be no ordinary holiday.

CHAPTER ONE

14 May 1950

Adnan Menderes is swept to power

I knew about holidays to Turkey. I'd been writing about them for decades.

In the course of my first job – teaching English to mature students in an Ankara language school in 1984 – I'd fallen headlong for the country. From that fraught moment when I faced my students for the first time, only to discover that many of them had brought gifts – towels, bowls of fruit, slippers, ribbon-tied boxes of baklava – to help their new teacher settle into his apartment, I loved the infinite courtesies of the people. I loved how they welcomed me into their own homes, pointedly placing my shoes, which I'd quickly learned I was to remove at the thresholds of apartments and mosques alike, amidst the family's own pairs to touch me with a sense of belonging which I retain to this day. The most austere of cities, its apartment buildings rusted and gimcrack, its skies foul with the dust of lignite, Ankara at least to me proved the sweetest of places.

I loved the capital's snowbound winters, and falling in with strangers over glasses of rakı, the unforgiving national spirit, in the smoke-filled bar on the night train to Istanbul. I explored at every opportunity, heading for Istanbul or taking buses deeper into the interior. I loved the mountains and the high steppe lands, and the forests of juniper and pine above the pristine Mediterranean coasts. I loved the ruins – the tottering temples of the classical age, the cities of the Hittites, the Byzantine rock chapels of Cappadocia – whose sheer profusion emphasised the land's unimaginably rich history.

The more I learned, the more I came to see the country not merely as a bridge between east and west, as the easy trope would have it, but as a land inspired, and sometimes infected, by its proximity to the grand and diverse cultures on all four sides; Greece and Persia west and east, Russia and Arabia north and south.

For all these reasons Turkey was captivating; and no sooner had the teaching year concluded with my return to England than I found myself itching to be back. I advertised myself as a travel writer – particular patch: Turkey – a country enjoying the timeliest of tourism booms. From the 1990s I returned regularly on assignments. I wrote about hidden beaches where loggerhead turtles nested on summer nights; about hotels in lemon groves, hammocks slung between the boughs of tamarisk trees; about archaeological sites whose aged guardians claimed to remember the howl of wolves from their childhoods; about caravanserais, mosques and museums; about the delights of Turkish food; and about bazaars and hiking trails, all the while considering myself blessed that I was *paid* to enthuse about Turkey. The only requirement seemed to be that I persist in peddling a passionately felt enthusiasm, one which only spurred yet more gifts and favours – restaurant bills, beds for the night, lifts to remote spots which had sparked my curiosity – from insistent Turkish hosts.

On one such assignment I spent a few days walking a newly opened trail in the Aegean region of south-western Turkey. We passed a lake, its islands topped with ruined monasteries, and squeezed between vast boulders whose eroded undersides were variously painted with prehistoric stick figures in faded ochres or with medieval Christian frescoes. Below the shattered ceremonial steps at Labraunda, the sacred hill sanctuary where ancient Carians once dined in honour of Zeus, the path descended through pastures and woods daubed pink with cyclamens and stands of verbena. Dogs slumbered in the lane which led into the village of Kargıcak where an elderly man hailed us from his yard and invited us inside. It was a warm day, but a perpetual chill stalked

Mehmet whose thickly padded feet, custard-coloured toenails poking through unravelling weave, led the way into a timber house teetering on collapse. From the ground floor, which appeared abandoned except for the cats, we trod gingerly up a rotten staircase to arrive in a room which looked like it might at least outlast our visit, one in which a degree not only of structural security but even comfort had been achieved. There were rugs and chairs, and a stove that hazed as Mehmet's wife fed it handfuls of crackle-dry pine cones.

As the tea brewed I took in the photographs pinned to the timber walls. They showed the couple's long-dispersed family; smartly dressed sons about to leave for military service, daughters proudly displaying swaddled babies, grandchildren balanced in tree forks or mounted on push bikes, and a summer lake where dozing forms lay beside a floral cloth scattered with the ruins of a picnic. Many of these photographs, faded from the sun, had scrolled up like cinnamon sticks, but not the one in pride of place and protected by gilt-framed glass. It was a portrait of somebody whom I did not recognise but took to be a public figure. The fact that it did not depict Atatürk, who continued to monopolise the public iconography so many years after his death, was itself startling. Here was a well-groomed man in an outfit – suit, tie and dark glasses, and with brilliantined black hair – that was unmistakably 1950s; and doing something, besides, that Atatürk would never have done. He was directing three colleagues to admire an architect's model of a mosque.

'We have kept that photograph for many years,' Mehmet explained. 'Back in the 1960s and 70s, though, we had to be careful. We would have been in trouble if they had caught us with it.' He lifted the portrait from its place, polished the glass with a worn sleeve and placed it reverently back on its hook.

'The blessed Menderes,' he whispered. 'What they did to him . . .'

We finished our tea and took the sagging staircase back to firm ground. At the edge of the village a road sign bearing the name of Atatürk was dented from what I took to be the toe of a boot.

That night I wrote up my notes in the way I usually did after long walking days; as rapidly as possible so as to get down what I could before sleep overcame me. Only when I got home, and looked back over my almost illegible scribblings, did I notice how little there was about the walking and how much I'd written about my visit to the old couple's house.

*

By 2016 Turkey had descended into despotism as President Recep Tayyip Erdoğan pursued increasingly authoritarian policies. Many Turks despised the regime's restrictive press laws, its ruthless imprisonment of dissident writers and journalists, its brutal deployment of the security forces against peaceful protesters, and the systemic corruption. They deplored the bloody conflict which the army had lately resumed against Kurdish dissidents and which had led to the brutal destruction of entire city neighbourhoods in south-east Turkey. Suicide bombers targeted soldiers, tourists and peace marchers; there were attacks on buses, on stations and airports. The economy was failing and a wave of construction projects – bridges and airports, metro lines, roads, tunnels and high-speed trains, as well as giant mosques and a presidential palace of fatuous dimensions – seemed like nothing less than state-designed distractions. These engineering achievements, though they eased both the levels of unemployment and the traffic, could not disguise the growing unrest – at its most acute among the military, the media and the universities – that was gripping Turkey by the spring of 2016.

As for my own livelihood, demand from the travel pages for my stock-in-trade articles had evaporated. Not many people were taking holidays in Turkey any longer, and no commissioning editor was about to encourage them to do so. Anyway, to persist in writing about the country's holiday options amid the mass imprisonments, judicial abuses, media clampdowns, suicide bombings and brutal army operations would have been to condone a regime I opposed; a regime that had criminalised writers infinitely braver than myself for doing no more than standing by views they truly felt.

It was then that I found myself thinking about another story; the one which I had begun to write years earlier, I now recognised, when I scribbled down my impressions of an old couple in their ramshackle village house and the photograph they patently cherished. Although this story would not take me back to the beaches, hotels and cultural sights, or yield the usual gifts, it was nevertheless time to find out what they had done to Adnan Menderes.

But first I had somebody to see. After more than half a century I recognised from the newspaper photographs the woman who greeted me at her door. Margaret Bailey, widowed and now in her nineties, still lived near Gatwick though she had left the farmhouse and the chickens for a cottage on a nearby residential estate. She invited me in, and over tea told me about that foggy afternoon in February 1959 and about the family's holiday in Turkey.

'We couldn't leave until Tony had got the harvest in,' she explained. 'And then there was school to consider.' It was eventually arranged that the whole family – Margaret and Tony along with nine-year-old Nick and seven-year-old Elizabeth – should fly out to Turkey in late August 1959. They left Heathrow to put down at Amsterdam and Vienna before finally reaching Istanbul late that night. Camera bulbs flashed as a reception committee, among them the prime minister's private secretary and the mayor of Istanbul, welcomed the family with bouquets at the aircraft steps.

'They held a press conference for us at the airport,' said Margaret. 'An endless line of kind people presented us with more flowers. Then we were driven to the Hilton and shown to two suites on the seventh floor overlooking the Bosphorus. Honestly, with all the flowers our suite looked like a film star's.' In the morning more flowers arrived, this time from Mr and Mrs Menderes. 'Pinky mauve lilies,' Margaret recalled, 'with a most exotic perfume.'

In the days that followed, the family were chauffeured around the city while a posse of photographers trailed after them. At the Grand Bazaar a goldsmith invited them to select presents – trinkets for the children, a bracelet for Margaret, a ring for Tony – as tokens of his personal gratitude. There were visits to the beach and days spent with the mayor of Istanbul's family who soon befriended the Baileys. There was an appointment with the governor and a flying visit to Izmır. The Baileys took a ferry across the Sea of Marmara, past the Princes' Islands, to the city of Bursa where the hotel staff showed their visitors to the grand suite usually reserved for Mr Menderes. The bouquets were so numerous that the hotel ran out of vases; and still the gifts – a tablecloth, napkins and bath robes of embroidered local silk – arrived. On their return to Istanbul the family visited more mosques and palaces, and they lunched with the prime minister's wife, Berin. The stream of invitations continued; a delegation of politicians from a Black Sea mining town were insistent even though, as Margaret Bailey wrote in her holiday journal, 'it is ten hours in a boat, and we would have had to stay two days to catch a plane back which takes off in a field!!' At the Red Crescent awards ceremony the air hostess rescued from the wreckage at Gatwick, lately returned from extensive burns treatment in England, was on hand to pin the medals to the Baileys' chests.

It proved a hectic schedule, the more so because the newly formed tourism ministry took every opportunity to shoehorn sightseeing trips between the official engagements. Exotic impressions – the camel trains, the silk farms, the palaces, the ferries and the mosques, the fabled views over the Bosphorus from the hilltop at Çamlıca – so accumulated that the family could barely take it all in. Certainly, they were kept too busy to notice anything of the growing unrest, at its most acute among the military, the media and the universities, that was gripping Turkey by the summer of 1959; the increasingly authoritarian regime's restrictive press laws and its ruthless impris- onment of dissident writers and journalists; the failing economy and a treasury labouring beneath a wave of construction projects – dams, ports, roads, storage depots, refineries, factories and power stations, airfields and mosques – that it could not afford.

The holiday culminated in a visit to the capital. The family took tea with the mayor, attended a cocktail party in their honour at An- kara's Press Club and a gala dinner hosted by the municipality. On the following day the Baileys were driven to the airport, but not before they had stopped to visit a newly opened dam and attend a final cocktail party.

'That was the one time we got to see Mr Menderes,' Margaret remembered. 'With his usual impeccable manners he sympathised that we had had to put up with so many official events and invited us to return the following year for a real holiday. He clearly meant it; his private secretary made a point of repeating the invitation when he saw us off at the airport.' Margaret Bailey paused reflectively. 'We'd have gone like a shot,' she said. 'But by the following year everything had changed, of course, and we were never to see him again.'

Margaret gave me directions to the crash site along with a warn- ing that I should not expect to find anything.

'For years you could clearly make out the shattered treetops from the road,' she said. 'But after all this time they've grown back. There's no visible sign that anything ever happened there.'

I followed a country lane past pubs, timbered barns, stables and cricket grounds. Where the fields gave way to woods, and a gate marked the head of a track, I pulled up. I had cut the engine and was pushing open the car door when a rising roar caused me to duck; an airliner, the landing gear down, passed low overhead on its descent to the airport. It had barely disappeared before another aircraft approached along the same flight path, and behind it another, each an echo of the Viscount once lost to an ill-designed altimeter or to pilot error, as the accident investigators had concluded. They surmised that the pilot had limited experience of fogs like the one which settled over Gatwick that afternoon; a fog so thick that young Elizabeth Bailey, hurrying home from playing at the neighbour's shortly after the crash, struggled to locate the gate to the farmhouse garden.

I followed the track into the woods where I soon understood that Margaret was right; the overhead planes aside, I should expect no reminders of the tragedy that had taken place here more than half a century before. Nothing remained of the metal and plastic scraps that wanderers reported finding in the years after the plane's removal. The jagged gouges that the crash had left in the damp earth had disappeared beneath decades of repairing moss and leaf mould. The trees had recovered, new growth restoring their crowns, and at the feet of the oaks and pines their own seedlings had sprouted and grown to saplings, then to trees, and all the fierce heat of that distant moment had dissipated and the violence was enfolded into healing. Blackbirds sang throughout the wood, heedless of those who had died so far from home, and who had no memorial here.

Later that day, I left Gatwick on a Turkish Airlines flight to Istanbul.

*

Adnan Bey's rapid rise to national prominence occurred at the end
of the Second World War – just as world events caused Turkey's
abrupt turn towards democracy.

At the time the country knew little of the National Assembly
member for the town of Aydın in the Aegean region, and hardly more
of democracy. Earlier attempts to kindle the liberal flame, particularly from the mid-nineteenth century, had guttered before the
prevailing winds of repression. The abolition in 1922 of the Ottoman Empire and the emergence of the Turkish Republic did not
bring the greater freedoms that some dared to anticipate, with the
Republican People's Party ruling Turkey almost without interrup-
tion as a single-party state ever since.

But victory stirred men to imagine a new world, among them
Adnan Bey, who on 7 June 1945 joined three other members of the
ruling party in submitting a motion which called for a radical reform
of the party's values and practices. The motion argued that the time
had come for the Assembly to embrace democracy, particularly as
Turkey had lately committed to upholding the freedoms that
membership of the United Nations, then in the process of formation, would require of it. The four men charged that the guarantees
and liberties embodied in Turkey's constitution, the freedom of the
press included, could no longer be so blithely ignored.

The reaction proved seismic. Ministers and Assembly members
steeped in slavish obedience to the party were outraged that they
should have been subjected to this preposterous calling to account
– and by four of their own. They closed ranks to oppose the motion,
accusing the renegade democrats of grievous betrayal, the more so
when the four took their liberal manifesto to the press – as if the
people should have a say in all this.

The most articulate voice belonged to Adnan Menderes, a popular cotton farmer and politician who had also trained as a lawyer. A
persuasive advocate, Adnan Bey made the case for democracy in the
pages of *Vatan*, a progressive newspaper whose proprietor had been
quick to offer the rebels his support. In a series of articles Menderes
roundly condemned the totalitarian mindset of Turkey's political

class, asserting that 'governments that do their work well should have no reason to be afraid of freedom of the press'. The Assembly members, who viewed such liberties with deep foreboding, expelled Menderes and two colleagues from the party. The fourth member of the quartet soon resigned his seat in solidarity.

The rebels might have found themselves in the political wilderness if they had not already sensed an unlikely ally in the president. Statesman and soldier Ismet Inönü had also concluded that the time had come for the country to adopt democracy, if for a more immediate reason, which was to avoid being pitched headlong into another fight for national independence, this time against neighbouring Russia; rather than take the Western democracies' recent triumph to signal that liberal freedoms might similarly serve his own country's development, Inönü intuited that only by declaring for democracy would Turkey stave off the threat of communist totalitarian takeover by its traditional enemy to the north.

The triumphant Russians had already shown themselves to be in belligerent mood. On 19 March, before war's end, they had unilaterally withdrawn from their long treaty of friendship with the Turks, making it clear that the Soviet Union intended to reclaim two of Turkey's eastern provinces, and secure guarantees over shipping rights through the Bosphorus; these prizes they meant to pressure Turkey into surrendering in recompense for what the Russians judged to be a contemptible war record. Not only had the Turks remained neutral until February 1945, when the war's outcome was already decided, but they had also persisted until 1944 in selling Hitler the vital chrome supplies the Nazis needed to plate their munitions.

The Turks worried that the Western powers, no more impressed than the Soviets by Ankara's recent war record, might stand aside in the event of a Russian attack, the more so as the West would not concede the full extent of Moscow's expansionist intentions until 1946, when Churchill first referred publicly to the Iron Curtain. There was nothing for Turkey's leadership to do but embrace democracy, whatever concerns the president might have that the country was not ready for it, and pledge Turkey to the Western family of nations. Within days of the Soviets' treaty withdrawal President Inönü had begun signalling his readiness to commit the country to democratic principles. That same November Inönü used the occasion of his annual presidential address to formally describe the absence of an official opposition party as a matter of national regret. When freely contested elections were duly mandated, and the formation of independent political parties legalised, the four expelled Assembly members wasted no time in founding their own, the Democrat Party, whose name told of where they meant to take the country.

In its modest but prestigious ranks – the veteran Celal Bayar had served as prime minister under Atatürk – the new party boasted considerable political pedigree. It soon drew high-level defections from the Republicans and enjoyed a burgeoning membership. In no time the Democrats established themselves as a formidable political proposition, one which duly spooked a Republican People's Party machine yet to reconcile itself to democracy's more irksome obligations. In a high-handed move which caught the fledgling Democrats on the hop, the Republicans called elections much earlier than they had promised. Not only did the new party find itself unready to fight more than a limited number of seats but the election results of July 1946 were further skewed by government officials who took their role to be preserving the Republicans' hold on power, and with it their jobs, even if that meant intimidating opposition voters and preventing independent observers from inspecting the vote tallies.

The 1946 elections, widely derided, ended in the Democrats' defeat but nevertheless established them as the official opposition and the coming force in Turkish politics. The party rapidly achieved a broad appeal which many credited to the oratory of their talismanic frontman, Adnan Bey. At rallies in the country's far-flung towns and villages democracy's tireless champion argued that triumph over the autocracies, in 1945 as in 1918, had consigned the Republicans' one-party state to history and ushered in a new age of social justice and freedom. No longer did Turkey's ordinary folk need to remain sunk in poverty and oppression, held in contempt by a remote authority whose baton-wielding agents and officials descended on the villages only to plunder grain stocks, extort taxes or issue conscription orders. Freedom of expression – 'such a strong weapon that the secret type of political administration cannot resist it for long' – was to be taken for granted. Democracy was liberation, granting the people rights and entitlements, not least in choosing their political representatives. They were to think of politicians not as their superiors but servants, whose failures they were encouraged to punish, their successes to reward, at the ballot box. In 'fluent and captivating speeches', which caused 'many a hesitant constituency to go over to the Democrats', Adnan Bey let the people know that they were the masters now.

It proved a message the peasants heeded when elections were held again, for the first time under the 'secret ballot-open count' principle, on 14 May 1950. Turks 'put on their best suits and ran to the polling stations as if they were running to their place of worship'. Some came by donkey or cart, the old and infirm in motorised ve-hicles – in some cases for the first time in their lives – which the contending political parties had laid on. In the rural areas few could write, though most had thumbs, all they needed to ink their support for the party which had beaten democracy's drum so persuasively; the Democrats won the 1950 elections by a landslide, securing 408 of the National Assembly's 487 seats. Celal Bayar, appointed head of state as president, ignored more senior candidates in backing the party's poster boy as prime minister. So it was that a man whose main charge had been of the family farm near Aydın would head the government as Turkey entered the second half of the twentieth century.

*

Times had changed by 2016, not least at Turkish Airlines, which liked to advertise that it flew to more countries than any of its competi-tors. And Istanbul looked nothing like it had in August 1959 when the airport lay far from the city amidst grasslands which it shared with seasonal flocks of migrating storks. These birds put down in plague volumes to feed on an abundance of insects, frogs and snakes, causing chaos. Jeeps patrolled the runway as airport staff in the passenger seats clanged pots and pans to put the flocks to flight. In the hangars engineers laboured to service aircraft, clearing their choked intakes of the compacted stork flesh and feathers that had necessitated emergency landings. On their arrival at the airport an improved road, aid-funded, had whisked the Baileys to their bouquet-strewn suites at the Hilton, but not before traversing a darkness barely stippled by the lights of the few mud and brick shanties which the first pulses of migrants from the villages had thrown up on these plains at the very edge of Europe.

Of these picturesque scenes nothing was visible from the window of the light railway, one of President Erdoğan's much-vaunted infrastructural improvements, which I boarded at the airport on my own journey to the city in the spring of 2016. Istanbul had grown tenfold, swallowing up the airport along with the plains of Thrace, so that I looked out on the drear suburbs of Ataköy. Here were exhibition centres, industrial estates, malls, freight depots, car parks, abbatoirs, yards and apartment blocks relentlessly compacted, all grey as the gulls except where yellow taxis stood in choked streams of traffic. A fitful wind tugged at the vast cloth portraits of the president which hung from the walls of office buildings. At Zeytinburnu, where I took to the tramway, development sites were strewn with rubble and bulldozers. The occasional park was furnished with kitsch lamp posts and hyperactive fountains, and figures disappeared into underpasses before they emerged, closer now, passing through the turnstiles to the platform where our tramcar awaited. We shifted, ourselves compacting, to make room for them as Istanbul itself had done. These shawled women with their bags of vegetables and loaves, these men in their muted and worn greys, worry beads at their fingers, were the children of the villagers who from the 1950s had migrated in their millions to cities like Ankara and Istanbul, where a better kind of living was said to be had.

Only when the tram passed a gap in the ancient land walls, and entered the old city, did the view acquire a patina of age and Ottoman elegance. In the marble kiosks and ornate doorways were glimpses of old Constantinople. Booted porters shouldered stacked trolleys redolent of an earlier world, even if a closer look revealed boxes of Two-Phase hair conditioner or consignments of plastic-wrapped computer printers rather than the signature sacks of sesame, dried mulberries and chickpeas. Around the minarets memorial stones leaned close, their tops carved with the turbans and fezes that had once defined later generations of Ottomans. There were plane trees and pavilions, and the glow of coals in the *nargile* pipes. At Sultanahmet, in the midst of the old city, the vehicles of the tourist police in their blue and white livery were arrayed across the square, though the troubles meant there were currently no tourists to protect. With a clank the tram sloped seawards, slipping into the shadows cast by the high walls of the Topkapı Palace. Beyond a canyon of nineteenth-century apartment blocks, the ground floors bright with the digitally displayed rates of the money changers, we emerged by the water at Sirkeci – the confluence of the Bosphorus and the Golden Horn, the city's waterways, and the old heart of Istanbul. As the tram trundled onto Galata Bridge I observed on every side waterfronts lined by shabby tenements and palace gardens, fish markets and period-piece ferry stations, derelict naval dockyards, mosques and churches, elegant timber mansions, railway stations, restaurants and nightclubs, converted warehouses, domed Turkish baths and neighbourhood squares shaded by giant plane trees.

Beyond the bridge I left the tram and at the turnstile a security guard motioned at my bag, making a pass with his explosives detector as I headed for my hotel.

*

In the 1950 elections Adnan Bey's Democrats had campaigned under the slogan 'Enough! Let the People's Voice Be Heard!', which they now set out to prove. Within weeks of coming into office an amnesty was confirmed for all political prisoners. A lifting of restrictions made for a press, in the words of *Time* Magazine, as 'free as the wind off the Taurus Mountains', while guarantees were given that the national radio station, the country's only broadcaster, should fairly reflect the views of all political parties.

The new administration also cut down on unnecessary expenditure. Turkey's finances were parlous, as the national football team's decision to withdraw from the 1950 World Cup in Brazil, citing flight and accommodation costs, so eloquently expressed. President Bayar ordered his salary and allowances to be 'almost halved' and commended himself, at the expense of his predecessor's reputation, by abandoning the trappings of high office that Ismet Paşa had enjoyed. He gave instructions for the presidential train and yacht to be sold off. To get around Ankara and to attend sessions of the National Assembly, he gave up the usual motorcade and motorcycle escort for a utilitarian jeep in which he sat up front alongside the driver, and was even to be seen on Istanbul's public trams and ferries.

But it was in the countryside, which three-quarters of the newly enfranchised electorate called home, where the new administration made its main play. The uneducated and often illiterate inhabitants of Turkey's 30,000 villages might at first have found the new freedoms confusing – many reportedly mistaking *demokrasi* for the name of an influential interfering foreigner, a type with which Turks were wearily familiar – but they soon came to hail a system whose chief virtue was to have marked them down, astonishingly, as its main beneficiaries.

This contrasted with life under Atatürk's people – the doctrinaire Republicans' own slogan 'For the People, In Spite of the People'. The ruling party had shown little interest in raising Turkey's villagers out of their historic poverty or addressing their material needs. They held that the greatest block to rural progress was in the peasant mind. What constrained the villagers and condemned them to brutish lives, the Republicans reasoned, were narrow horizons and ambitions which rarely extended beyond raising offspring to serve them in old age – plus a moral slate, largely clean, which might give them a tilt at Paradise.

The Republicans had accordingly concentrated their efforts not on infrastructure but on education, creating a rural network of teacher-training schools known as 'village institutes'. Here, where light bulbs in the familiar outline of Atatürk's image announced the entrance, bright young villagers acquired a wide range of practical skills – rudimentary healthcare, progressive techniques in agriculture and beekeeping, livestock husbandry and mechanics, iron- and leatherwork – which they were to pass onto their students. They were also encouraged to learn subjects less immediately applicable, like foreign languages, and to participate in the arts. Many institutes even boasted marching bands and staged Greek dramas. Such initiatives helped evoke a rural utopia where resourceful and enlightened peasants cheerfully endured occasional calorific shortfalls by drawing the necessary sustenance from music and literature.

It took a book, published in 1950, to lift the lid on the realities of peasant life. *Our Village* by Mahmut Makal, a young teacher who was himself a graduate of a village institute, revealed the rife poverty and primitive conditions which prevailed in the villages. Base standards of hygiene, resulting from the widespread lack of piped water, were the cause of dysentery and trachoma. Tuberculosis, diphtheria and malaria were endemic, malnutrition a seasonal fact of life and famine a regular prospect. Women birthed onto earth floors, wiped themselves down and returned to the fields or to collecting the dung that was the only fuel source through the hard winters; men laboured and aged prematurely, spending what remained of their years shuffling between the mosque and the teahouse – if the village ran to one. There was no electricity, more than half of the country's roads were classed as 'passable by cars during the dry season only' and the chief mode of transport remained the *kağnı*, the two-wheeled cart which had hardly evolved since the time of the Hittites. What little the villagers saw of the state were the officials who turned up to seize the wheat or cotton, or at best paid pitiful rates for them, commonly punishing shows of rural recalcitrance with beatings. The villagers, malnourished, flea-ridden and unshod, clearly had greater priorities, whatever the know-best Republicans might think, than correcting any superstition or lack of culture on their own part.

Whatever welcome they might have been led to expect at their remote postings, newly trained teachers like Mahmut Makal in fact encountered the profound alarm, even hostility, of village elders, imams and *ağas* (landlords) who viewed the arrivals as a challenge to their entrenched authority. That these teachers, with their radios, books and revolutionary ideas, and their proud avowals of godlessness, were openly contemptuous of superstition, and insistent that boys and girls be educated alongside each other, struck villagers as tantamount to communism. Many, who were content with knowing only what the elders and imams told them, even fearing the radio as 'the voice of the Devil coming from his deep hiding place', held teachers in profound suspicion. They had ideas of their own about what they needed to know, which rarely ran to the violin part in Schubert's Trout Quintet. If the new supply of state-approved journals and books was welcome, it was because the villagers might stuff ill-fitting windows with their pages against the ferocious Anatolian winters.

In shifting the rural emphasis from enlightenment to material improvement, the Democrats duly won villagers' hearts. It helped that the US, which under the Truman Doctrine had recognised Turkey as a vital bulwark against international communism, rushed financial support to its front-line ally. Adnan Bey's government, flush with development aid and with the national wind firmly at its back, set about delivering on key electoral promises. Drawing on resources the statist Republicans had not yet been able to field, and with an energy the old party had rarely mustered, the Democrats ran piped water supplies to many villages and, with the assistance of advisers from Wyoming's Highways Department, rapidly expanded the network of sealed roads. Villages accustomed to being cut off for months at a time, when even the arrival of wandering shepherds or itinerant sheikhs passed as items of interest, gained a daily bus service. Another world was in the villagers' reach.

With the scrapping of agricultural taxes, and the availability on cheap credit of fertiliser, modern ploughs and even tractors, life in the fields was transformed. The weather helped; successive summer rains – God-given according to the Democrats, merely fortuitous in the view of the Republicans – turned Adnan Bey's good start into a golden one. Through the early 1950s Turkey enjoyed a series of record grain, cotton and tobacco crops. Massive wheat surpluses were racked up as harvests doubled in the space of two years. Many peasants found themselves, for the first time in their hard-scrabble history, with cash in hand. The spare lira often went on much-needed building improvements, with the 'mud hut becoming more and more often a whitewashed cottage'. Extra floors and glazed windows were added. Money was even available for extras such as radios, or bicycles which proud owners might now ride on the new asphalt as far as the nearest town.

So it was that the century's halfway point brought change and widening horizons to the countryside and its grateful inhabitants. The villagers would not forget Adnan Bey, the man who had taken their feet out of rawhide sandals, as the phrase has it, and put them in shoes. They were also impressed in the newspaper offices, in the ministries and universities where admirers spoke of Adnan Bey's 'genial mien, always smiling' and 'of a man endowed with an enormous capacity for work, who truly embodied the best of the nation in the eyes of the masses'. They spoke of his 'great personal magnetism' and rated him as 'probably the most intelligent man in Turkish politics'. The man from *The Times* spoke of Adnan Bey's 'great energy, exuberance, eloquence, and genuine goodwill', the British travel writer and MP Fitzroy Maclean calling him 'a figure of the first magnitude. An energetic, alert man of first-class intelligence and wide experience.'

It was left to Howard Reed, an American educationalist who travelled extensively through Turkey's villages in the early 1950s, to sound a first warning. Reed noted how modest enrichment had turned many peasant farmers into 'daring gamblers'. They appeared to have forgotten the hard-learned lessons of their forebears who, in acknowledgement of Anatolia's patchy rainfall patterns, had trad-itionally used the *saban*, the wooden stick plough expressly designed to expose as little as possible of the soil's precious moisture to the drying sun. Instead, they began to use the new American steel ploughs. These rooted the seeds more securely by turning the soil to create a much deeper furrow, but one which exposed the crop to ruin in the event of prolonged dry weather – when the plateau's thin and carefully husbanded topsoils were liable to disastrous erosion. Reed also noted that many peasant farmers, in a bid to cash in on the favourable market for grains, had begun to plough marginal lands traditionally set aside for livestock grazing; the risk was that this would leave them with nothing to fall back on should their crops fail.

It was a reckless approach, and one which some were minded to liken to government policy. The Democrats had guaranteed the price they would pay Turkish farmers for their wheat, but at levels far in excess, it turned out, of what the crop was fetching on an inter-national market depressed by the wider region's bumper harvests. Enriching the peasants meant beggaring the treasury; courting Turkey's masses turned out to be at the expense of those who did not have wheat to sell at such advantageous prices. When the prime minister characterised any subsequent criticism as that of a few hundred intellectuals disgruntled that their time of special favour was at an end, as he took to doing at rallies and in other public remarks, Turkey's educated and professional classes understood that he had taken sides. And it wasn't theirs.

CHAPTER TWO

6 October 1926

Turkey's first statue is unveiled in Istanbul

On coming to power in 1950 the Democrats were quick to take down the pictures of the old president. In recent years these had become increasingly visible as Ismet Paşa's portraits not only proliferated in municipal offices, town squares and other public spaces but also assumed ever greater dimensions. Atatürk's successor was suspected, apparently under the influence of Europe's wartime fascist leaders, of building a personality cult that would rival, even usurp, that of the national founder. But rather than put up ones of the new man, Celal Bayar, the Democrats either left 'discoloured patches of wallpaper . . . where once the portrait of Inönü had rested' or replaced them with Atatürk. The decision was also taken to make Atatürk a permanent presence on the nation's coins and stamps, where Ismet Paşa had recently installed himself, which further served to belittle the personal ambitions of the Democrats' ousted rival. The general principle, intended to guard Turkey against the subsequent cultivation of such cults by would-be dictators, was established that the national iconography should thenceforth be the exclusive preserve of the great founder.

In another ruling, that only the dead were to be commemorated in carved form, the Democrats forbade the Ismet Paşa statues which the ex-president's Republican supporters had lately commissioned. A colossal equestrian bronze of the general in triumphal martial mode, to have been installed with great fanfare in Istanbul's Taksim

Square, was consigned to storage in a bonded warehouse stacked with barrels of rakı, the anise-flavoured spirit. To complete the humiliation the pedestal, already under construction and inscribed in lavish praise of the man's military achievements, was unceremoniously boarded over.

These proscriptions brought to mind the Ottomans' bans on depictions of the human form. Just as even in the twentieth century some rural Turks regarded foreign books, mixed teaching classes and the radio as the Devil's work, and in their time conservative Ottomans condemned inoculation and quarantining, steamships and passenger trains, the telegraph, insurance, football, constitutional government and even electricity as illegal infidel innovations under Islamic law, so traditionalists viewed portraiture with deep doctrinal misgivings. Muslims looked to calligraphy, geometric abstractions and floral motifs in their aversion to figurative representation, especially of the sultan-caliph, supreme head of the Muslim faith, where it amounted to blasphemy.

But many sultans, perhaps because they found Western ways no less fascinating than Europeans appeared to find those of the Ottomans, were in the habit of sitting for portraits. They even commissioned infidel artists such as Gentile Bellini, who came to Constantinople in 1480 to create a series of portraits of Mehmet the Conqueror. The sultans allowed the circulation of their likenesses in the form of miniature ivory figurines, often in presentation boxes containing the Ottoman dynasty's every ruler. While the display of such images was mostly discreet – the portraits confined to the royal palaces, the figurines rarely circulating beyond a coterie of refined European orientalists and cultivated Ottomans – the more militantly progressive Ottoman leaders went further; in 1829 Mahmud II, impressed by portraits of the tsar and tsarina during an inspection of a Russian warship, had a medallion stamped with his own likeness, and in provocatively Western dress, which he widely disbursed as a mark of imperial favour. In the 1830s he commissioned a portrait which the outraged religious authorities were required to bless before copies were hung in schools, government buildings and army barracks. In 1872 Sultan Abdülaziz, another committed moderniser, went so far as to order an equestrian bronze of himself, only for his conservative-minded mother to have it dumped into the Bosphorus upon its arrival in the city. Mother knew best, it seemed; whatever the reach of their authority, the sultans remained subject to the judgement of an often determinedly traditional populace. In the public sphere the ban on human depiction was rigorously enforced, especially when it came to statues.

All this was to change, of course, under Mustafa Kemal – the leader would not take the surname Atatürk until 1934 – who was also drawn to Western ways; unlike the sultans, however, he meant to adopt them wholesale and without discretion, judging that the independence struggle he finally won in 1922, and the universal devotion he earned in the process, gave him the necessary leeway. Western ways, in the conviction of Mustafa Kemal, were key to the challenge he had set himself, which was to remake the country utterly and without hindrance, banishing all vestiges of the Ottoman past. To this end he determined to introduce his new nation to statues – and of himself – the first of which was unveiled in Istanbul in 1926.

*

The First World War had ended in the Ottomans' defeat which they formally conceded days before their German allies on 30 October 1918, and in surroundings designed to humiliate them. That the surrender took place at Lemnos was a reminder to the Ottomans, former masters of this Greek island, of the degree to which the sultan's domains had shrunk. The message implicit in the venue for the signing ceremony – the British battleship HMS *Agamemnon*, named for the Greek victor of the Trojan Wars – could not have been clearer: West had bested East, as it always did. Two weeks later the Allies twisted the knife when battleships under the flags of Britain, France, Italy and Greece proceeded up the Bosphorus to announce the occupation of the imperial capital.

War had reduced the Ottoman Empire to a smoke-wreathed ruin. In Anatolia demobilised troops returned to find their fields abandoned and their families starving. Disease was rife, the infrastructure shattered and the public finances exhausted. Worse was to follow when word of the Europeans' plan for the empire got out. The little that remained of the imperial domain was to be parcelled out among the Ottomans' former subject peoples, including national homes for the Kurds and Armenians, and with the best bits – the cotton fields of Cilicia, the oil fields of Mosul, the bread basket that was the famously fertile Meander Valley – reserved for the four occupying powers that had already staked claims by installing control officers in these coveted regions.

The Ottoman sultan and the religious leadership acquiesced in the proposal to dismember what remained of their empire; but the spectre of something akin to statelessness outraged many among the main losers, the region's Turkish-speaking Muslims. The sheer extent of the carve-up, to include much of the empire's Anatolian heartlands, soon stirred thoughts of resistance even among the exhausted. By 15 May 1919, when on Britain's say-so Greek armies landed at Smyrna – ostensibly to maintain order, but patently as invaders in pursuit of the romantic dream the Greeks had long cherished of a nation whose bourn encompassed all the lands around the Aegean Sea – the provocation had become intolerable.

It was then that a Turkish army officer, who had served with distinction at Gallipoli four years earlier, made his move. In somehow convincing the Ottoman authorities that he was reconciled to their policy of capitulation, Mustafa Kemal secured a commission to oversee the demobilisation of forces in Anatolia, one which gave him an active command beyond the authorities' reach. He and his retinue left Istanbul by coaster, heading north up the Bosphorus into the Black Sea. He had barely put ashore at the port of Samsun on 19 May 1919 before he set about stoking resistance in the national hearth, as patriots called the Anatolian interior. In the months that followed like-minded nationalists, among them high-ranking army officers including Ismet Inönü, made for the steppe towns of Sivas

and Ankara, Mustafa Kemal's makeshift headquarters, to rally under
his command. Not a year after defeat in the First World War, the
Turks readied themselves to fight another war – this time for their
national independence.

Over the next three years the defiant nationalists increasingly
drew converts to their cause, wresting from their craven adversaries
in the hobbled Ottoman administration any lingering authority they
still retained. With his rabble of militia gangs forged into hardened
army units, Mustafa Kemal duly repeated the trick he had pulled off
at Gallipoli in matching, then seeing off, powerful Western invaders.
After facing down the half-hearted expeditionary forces of the
French and Italians, he then turned on the Greek armies which had
advanced to take possession of swathes of western Turkey. His forces
finally routed them in September 1922, driving the Greeks back to
the same quaysides at Izmır, as the Turks knew Smyrna, where their
enemies had landed three years earlier.

It was a brilliant victory, one that demanded heroic sacrifices of
Mustafa Kemal's fighting forces and the civilian population as well
as of himself. But he also had the Russians to thank; it was ironic that
the Soviets, whose territorial threats would cause the Turks to seek
assistance from the West after the Second World War, had been their
only ally in the fight against the Western powers after the First World
War. Mustafa Kemal made much of ties which bound his nationalists
to their fellow anti-imperialists, and in 1920 even sent a series of
delegations to Moscow. The Bolsheviks responded not only with
enthusiasm but vital materiel, dispatching munitions as well as quan-
tities of gold roubles to the nationalists through Anatolia's Black Sea
ports. A treaty of friendship, signed in the spring of 1921 and which
spoke of 'the common struggle which both peoples have undertaken
against the intervention of imperialism', came hot on the heels of the
opening by the Soviets of an embassy in Ankara, generally agreed to
be the grandest building in town. Soviet support was to play a crucial
role in delivering victory to Mustafa Kemal's nationalists.

For the Ottomans, who had so supinely colluded with the occupying forces, defeat sounded their dynasty's end as surely as it meant

a new national beginning under Mustafa Kemal, who soon made it clear that he was not ready for an early retirement spent polishing his field medals. The great warrior's ambitions apparently extended beyond the battlefield, even if that meant deploying altogether different skills. Both at Gallipoli and in the War of Independence Mustafa Kemal had made his name as an exceptional strategist whose genius was defensive, who trusted in the fabled endurance of his peasant forces as well as in the eventual rupture of the enemy's overstretched supply lines, and who accordingly knew time to be on his side; but in rebuilding the nation, which he regarded as his true destiny, Mustafa Kemal meant to take the fight to those who might oppose his vision. And this, as he well knew, amounted to a challenge of another order altogether.

In this, the experience of the Soviets inevitably came to mind. For while Mustafa Kemal was no communist, whatever the gestures of fraternity he extended to his allies beyond the Black Sea, the parallels between the two movements remained compelling; like the Bolsheviks, Turkey's nationalists now found themselves heirs to a former empire, or at least to its heartlands, which Mustafa Kemal also meant to transform. And like the Bolshevik leadership, Mustafa Kemal was faced with the thorny issue of what to do with the ruling dynasty – if only until the dread prospect of resort, Russian-style, to the royal family's extermination was averted when the last sultan, Mehmet VI, made clandestine arrangements for a British warship to take him, his son and entourage into exile in November 1922.

That left Mustafa Kemal free to begin building a new nation, but one which many Turks were sure to find unpalatable, intolerable even, for its foreign likeness. The new leader was under no illusions as to the resistance he would face, even from some of his brothers in arms, outraged that the victories they had recently won at such cost were to lead to what they could only see as a wholesale adoption of the defeated infidel's hated ways. In Turkey, where Islam was broadly viewed as 'the entire frame of everybody's existence', tradition ran deep; and while the population wholeheartedly celebrated the restoration of their threatened homeland, fewer were willing to accept its social and cultural transformation.

The only thing for it was to act with all speed, before dilution began to do for the devotion, which meant setting about the former theocracy at the double. From the abolition of the sultanate on 1 November 1922, the Ottomans' cherished shibboleths went down in a revolutionary tumble. In October 1923, the new state was declared a republic, with the steppe bastion that was Ankara named the new capital in place of the historic port-metropolis of Istanbul. In 1924 the Topkapı Palace was turned into a museum, and the caliphate, office of the Supreme Head of all Muslims, was abolished, with all remaining members of the old imperial dynasty exiled abroad. In 1925 came the proscription of the Ottoman national fez, a cherished badge of Islamic identity, in favour of Western hats such as the homburg or panama which conservatives widely reviled. In the same year, clerics were banned from wearing the traditional Islamic turban and robes in public. The Ottoman ban on alcohol, which Mustafa Kemal's hard-core coterie of rakı drinkers had long ignored, was officially lifted. Religious orders and sects including the whirling dervishes were closed, and fortune tellers, writers of amulets, magicians and other 'peddlers in superstition' were banned from the streets. People were forbidden from visiting the tombs of revered local saints, with Mustafa Kemal branding it 'a disgrace to seek help from the dead'. In 1926 the religious courts were closed down and replaced by a legal system borrowed from the Italians. Roman numerals were adopted in 1928 when Islam lost its status as the national religion; a law stipulated that any attempt to use religion as a political instrument would constitute high treason. The Western calendar was adopted, obliging Muslims to reckon their history not from the Prophet's flight out of Mecca but from the birth of Jesus Christ. That year also saw the replacement of the Ottoman script, closely modelled on Arabic characters, by a Latin one; citizens were given four months to master the changes before the Arabic script was formally prohibited, a formidable challenge given that the new alphabet was not only unfamiliar but to be written backwards. In

1932 the last school for imams and preachers was closed. A law decreed that the *ezan*, the call to prayer, be made not in Arabic, the language of Islam, but Turkish. It was amidst this avalanche of reforms, in October 1926, that Turkey's first statue was unveiled in Istanbul.

*

If there were any reason to visit Istanbul in the spring of 2016, it was because the tourists who typically crowded the sights – the great basilica of Aya Sofya, the imperial mosques and palaces – were staying away. But for the pitches of desperate guides I might have walked straight into the Topkapı Palace, where I'd often battled the crowds on previous stays in the city.

Topkapı had long intrigued me; the old seraglio, home for hundreds of years to the Ottoman sultan, was not a palace in the Western sense but an assortment of discrete, low-built pavilions, apartments and other structures arranged within a succession of high-walled courts, each more private, more exclusive, than the last. It was the residence, after all, of those who held themselves remote, as if they were divine invisibles, from their subjects. The sultan passed unseen, even by those closest to him, attending his viziers' deliberations not in person but by a means of a grille – the Eye of the Sultan – which allowed him to spy upon them in the council chamber. Favoured concubines, even as they shared the sultan's bed, were warned on pain of death against looking upon the imperial visage while throughout the palace grounds a sepulchral silence was maintained. Those fortunate enough to gain an audience with the sultan – ambassadors, merchants and emissaries – were subjected to extensive protocols which above all insisted that under no circumstances were they to turn their backs on the sublime presence. Any such lapse would have spelt disaster – for their petitions most certainly, for their broader professional prospects, and even for the lives of those charged with guarding against such eventualities; no surprise, then, that the palace chamberlains preferred not to chance it but dispatched pairs of hefty eunuchs to pinion petitioners and frogmarch them backwards out of the hall as their audience drew to a close.

This morning, however, I was headed not for the palace but for its final symbolic repudiation. I crossed Galata Bridge, the balustrades lined with hundreds of hunched anglers, the retired and the jobless, who in their threadbare coats congregated above these fish-rich waters to feed themselves and their families. The air was thick with their flailing lines, the catches flashing like foil on the hooks and flexing in the yoghurt pots and other makeshift containers at the fishermen's feet. Beyond the bridge, where crowds spilled from the bazaars, I saw more policemen and security vehicles. Pigeons rose in clattering clouds over grey domes and ferries strained at their warps along the Eminönü waterfront, their yellow-painted stacks smoking. I passed through Sirkeci Station, once the terminus of the Orient Express, where the timetables spoke of shrunken ambitions, the few suburban services terminating well short of the city's ever extending periphery. In the high-ceilinged waiting room, all elegant panelling and painted belle-époque glass, broken souls lay prostrate upon the benches. I wandered into Gülhane Park where shawled mothers and their children picnicked among tulip beds beneath the walls of Topkapı. Beyond the sunken train tracks and a busy highway the statue I was looking for rose from a low-walled precinct on Sarayburnu – Seraglio Point.

It was an imposing bronze, larger than life; a man in a civilian suit of a sharply tailored and Western cut, with knotted tie and turned-up trousers. On a high plinth he appeared mid-stride, one hand resting on a hip, all heroic resolution, as if the Austrian sculptor had in mind a barrister striving for justice in a Vienna courthouse; a reporter, a rising star in a Chicago newsroom, pitching a story about corruption to an editor; or a London schoolmaster tirelessly imparting civilising values and ideals to his students. I wondered what Mustafa Kemal's subjects would have made of him.

The statue was unveiled on 6 October 1926, the third anniversary of the city's liberation from British occupation by Mustafa Kemal's triumphant nationalist forces in 1923, and to considerable fanfare, as some surviving silent news footage demonstrates. To mark the lifting of Turkey's 'ancient ban on graven images', to quote the scratchy caption, an official gives a speech from a podium before the sheet at his back is whipped away to reveal the statue. A crowd of men rise to their feet, doffing their new brimmed hats – the Ottoman fez having been outlawed for less than a year – as they break into applause.

Why, then, should that applause have caused my eyes to narrow? Why was I unable to watch the footage without sensing an official, out of shot, flapping his arms to fire up the crowd at that historic inauguration? Because these men were entirely unfamiliar with public statuary; so much so that it seemed to me their outward enthusiasm must mask an unease, even affront, at this transgressive representation of a leader who looked nothing like any they had known before. Who was dressed in clothes no Ottoman, from the bureaucrat in his black *stambouline* frockcoat to the peasant in his baggy *şalvar* trousers, would have dared countenance. Who bore no badge of office or military medal. What were they to do with this unfamiliar thing? Idolise it? Or take instruction from it, dressing themselves in the same way – in cast-offs if made-to-measure proved beyond their threadbare pockets?

And what of the leader's stance, his gaze directed not merely over the Bosphorus but towards the newly declared capital at Ankara? A gaze dismissive of Constantinople, that corrupt and complicit city, and of the Ottoman Empire's signature seraglio, whose skyline domes and turrets, kitchen chimneys, minarets and roofed pavilions showed through the trees at the statue's back. The repudiation was final and unmistakable as Mustafa Kemal, having seen off sultan and princeling caliph in short order, turned his back on the Ottoman past forever.

Within years of this unveiling the leader's image had proliferated, with statues and shoulder busts springing up across the country. State policy was clear: the new leader should be as ubiquitous as the sultans had been invisible, his image a perpetual reminder of the contract that bound them to him, he to them, by representing him in two complementary roles; the warrior statues, which served to remind people of the debt they owed their leader, and the ones in which he was represented as a civilian, embodying the Western values – education over ignorance, scientific enlightenment over religious superstition, graft over sloth, and civilised dress over the robes of Ottoman reaction – that he meant to foist on them.

Or force – as the statue's face made plain. It was as if Mustafa Kemal had discarded the military garb only to double down on the warrior resolve. The sculptor had taken Mustafa Kemal's admired features, fearsomely hawk-like, with a high forehead, strong jaw and penetrating blue eyes, and worked them to a peak of implacable purpose. It was the face of one who meant to wage the peace as he had fought the war, who had won the right and the wherewithal to impose his vision.

As to whether he would succeed was a question which members of the foreign press corps, freer in this respect than their Turkish counterparts, felt safest asking. Months before that first statue's unveiling a correspondent for the London *Times* left Istanbul for the provinces to gauge attitudes towards Mustafa Kemal's revolution. From the Eminönu quayside the correspondent journeyed by steamer up the Bosphorus, past the waterfront mansions, palaces and castles into the Black Sea; the route had acquired a storied quality since Mustafa Kemal himself had travelled it on his way to kick-start the national rebirth seven years earlier. At the port of Giresun the correspondent took in a performance by an acting troupe whom the regime had dispatched 'to propagate the idea that the modern Turkish woman is to be encouraged to take up a career'. A certain number of local women attended, under some compulsion, only to discover that they were supposed to sit with the men. Many did not even enter the theatre while those who stuck with the performance 'were so shocked by the licentious acting and depraved gestures of the performers that they left in a body before the first act was over'. 'Whatever Kemal may do to convert a formerly theocratic state into a completely laicised republic,' the correspondent judged, 'the attacks that he is making on his people's immemorial customs are creating enormous discontent.'

Worse still was the arrival in the town of the 'Tribunal of Independence', a specially convened itinerant court whose function was to enforce 'obedience to Kemal's ordinances by the simple process of hanging reactionaries or sentencing them to imprisonment'. There was, the correspondent concluded, 'a genuine hatred of the whole system which time does not dissipate'.

These tribunals made an especially egregious example of an elderly holy teacher called Atıf Hoca. Atıf Hoca's crime was to have written – that Turkish transgression – a pamphlet called *On Imitating the Francs and the Hat*. In its pages Atıf Hoca fulminated against Western dress along with other corrupting influences like alcohol, prostitution and dance. Despite the fact that the book was published in 1924, more than a year before the Hat Laws even came into force, the assertion of these standard Ottoman orthodoxies was nevertheless deemed deserving of death sentences for the author and his assistant, who were hanged in Ankara on 4 February 1926.

Turkey's revolution certainly had its victims, especially in the 1920s and 30s, though for the majority of those who viewed statues, alcohol, brimmed hats, Western dance and the rest as the flouting of sacred tradition, the result was not the noose but wholesale humiliation. The German traveller Lilo Linke was exploring Turkey in 1935 when she found herself sharing the back of a lorry with three religious teachers. The men, forbidden from wearing the clothes which had traditionally dignified them, were attempting to fashion something approaching their proscribed turbans from old woollen scarves, to the general scorn of their fellow passengers. These passengers, supporters of the reforms, dismissed the teachers as 'ignorant old men' and justified the ban on robes and turbans by claiming that the religious teachers' 'existence must not be pressed continuously on the people's mind'.

Mustafa Kemal's radical reforms, though they might have fast-tracked Turkey's transition, also heaped abuses and indignities upon generations of devout and conservative Turks; and if his first statue was any kind of indicator, these grievances were now, as I looked up at it in 2016, being avenged. It stood among skewed marble slabs in a weed-strewn precinct which stray dogs favoured as their toilet. The brass plaques had been ripped away, either as souvenirs or for their scrap value, and the air was thick with fumes from the highway which ran discourteously close. To the other side a developer's corrugated fence had been erected inches from the leader's nose, depriving the gull-fouled Mustafa Kemal of his Bosphorus views.

It was a sorry sight, and a reminder of the destablising forces that democracy's adoption had unleashed in 1950; a new beginning under a new party – and a man whose mission, many hoped, was to lead them back to the old ways.

*

There were no statues of Adnan Menderes in Istanbul. To find his likeness in the city I'd have to look harder, in out-of-the-way places like Çukurcuma.

The hills rise steep from Istanbul's shorelines, occasionally through parks and woodlands but mostly through close-clustered neighbourhoods like the ones above Tophane where I laboured up narrow-stepped pavements, the high kerbs rough-trimmed in yellow and white paint in the manner of some period racing circuit, and outside their little shops men perched on low wicker stools, smoking and drinking tea from tulip-shaped glasses. The area proved an arresting mix of the workaday and the hip, with a design boutique, its window bare but for an object which I took to be an interesting lamp, next to a greengrocer's fronted by a stack of empty vegetable boxes – a sun-struck cat, snugly rectangular, shoehorned into the topmost carton.

I left the main street for Çukurcuma, all buckled iron gutters and sagging roofs, and timber facades weathered to wafer. Its sunken alleys, arrayed around a green mosque, bore the faint signatures – dust, naphtha and mildew – of Istanbul's attics. I was in the city's antiques quarter where clutter gravitated in search of a second chance. For these cast-offs, these cleared furnishings and fixtures, Çukurcuma meant not the end so much as the possibility of another beginning. Each item had a tilt here at an afterlife, if only someone might sense covetable patina where previous owners had seen only wear. The better antique shops were airy and elegant, with prestigious style magazines left lying casually open, as if to assert an easy equivalence between the pages' contents and the items in the display rooms: high-end pieces – palazzo fountains and chandeliers, decorative mouldings and cornices, Ottoman brocades and chaises, ornate window shutters and walnut-wood doors traced with floral patterns in nacre inlay – artfully arranged to catch the eye of roving designers with luxury hotels and trophy homes to furnish.

For less guarded glimpses of Istanbul's past I headed for the places where it was advisable to move with care for fear of being buried beneath the dusty junk – the preferred term was *nostalja* – which rose in precarious stacks on every side. Here were lanterns, pickle jars, floral dinner services, scent bottles, boxes of tie pins, scabbarded daggers, old cameras and door knockers. There were guitars, globes and hinged rulers, replica weapons, sea charts, a pilot cap from the early years of Turkish Airlines, thermometers and mannequins. There were wristwatches, wicker-fronted radiograms whose frequency dials indicated Daventry and Leipzig, bird cages, weighing scales and old coins. There was a wooden model of HMS *Victory*, all tattered top-gallants and perished rigging, and posters for a low-budget 1970s porn movie whose overweight love interest, Behcet, naked but for black knickers and blacked-out nipples, courted considerable personal danger by attempting a salacious squat over a burning candle. I was drawn to these shop interiors precisely for their lack of guile; not because I meant to buy but in the hope they might provide uncurated glimpses into the city's recent history.

I plunged in and spent the morning poking about in dusty seams which dated from the 1950s, levering free faded albums of postcards, cigarette cards and family photographs; collections which had once meant much to their owners, to judge by the meticulous presentation and the neat captions, if not to those who had taken it upon themselves to dispose of them. I sifted piles of pamphlets and advertisements, but did not find what I was looking for. Every query led to knitted brows, the odd tug at a cabinet or foray into a dusty corner, all to no avail until after hours of fruitless searching one shopkeeper stroked his chin and dropped to his knees, back-swiping a dozing cat out of the way to reveal a stack of old framed pictures. He drew out a large one.

'Our much-loved former prime minister,' he said, dusting the glass with a reverent pass of a sleeve – just as Mehmet had done in the village house – to reveal a head and shoulders portrait, in black and white. The photograph bore the caption *Geçmiş Olsun*, a Turkish

condolence which translates as 'May Your Troubles Be Over'. 'This must have been printed shortly after the air crash in London,' the dealer concluded. 'Though by the miraculous grace of Allah Adnan Bey himself survived, he did lose many good friends and colleagues there.'

He wandered away, leaving me to examine the portrait at my leisure. The man so far glimpsed against a sequence of dramatic backdrops – at the edge of a darkening English wood, backlit by ragged kerosene flames; at the bedsides of stricken associates; on a crowded station platform, shoes steeped in sacrificial blood – appeared here in a contrastingly composed mood; attentive, inclined towards a bow, dark eyes set in an incipient smile. The eyes had it, but rather than blaze with the revolutionary zeal of Mustafa Kemal, they expressed deference. Although Adnan Bey's features were hardly heroic, with one writer even describing him as 'chipmunk-cheeked', they were attractive. His was a face alert with intelligence and energy, but also with unmistakable traces of fragility; the fragility of one whose misfortune it had been to receive more than his share of condolences. All through his life well-wishers had had occasion to express their hope that Adnan Bey's troubles would soon be over.

He was born near the city of Aydın to wealthy landowners in the last year of the nineteenth century. Ali Adnan, as he was known in his childhood, never knew the actual date of his birth. In the late-Ottoman decades, when parents deliberately obscured sons' birth dates to defer military conscription, a dread prospect in that war-ravaged age, this was unexceptional. In this case, though, any such ignorance may have had as much to do with the loss of the boy's parents and only sibling by the age of three.

Prosperity was no protection against the ravages of tuberculosis. The infant's earliest memories, if they clung so young, were of his mother's clammy sternum, bossed like a breast plate, and of the coughs which increasingly convulsed her. Tevfika never recovered – bearing two children while beset by the debilitating disease – and died in 1901, when her boy was two. On Tevfika's death Ali Adnan's grandmother, Fıtnat, moved into the family's Izmır home to tend her ailing son Ibrahim, who also suffered from tuberculosis. The family arranged for Ibrahim to be treated in a Swiss sanatorium. The journey soon proved too much for him and he died in an Istanbul hotel. Barely had Fıtnat returned from her son's funeral before Ali Adnan's only sister, five-year-old Melike, also succumbed to the disease.

The formidable Fıtnat put her remaining energies into saving the surviving member of the stricken family. She moved the emaciated Ali Adnan from the house in Izmır to a suburb on the other side of the bay, where the air was cleaner and there was space for him to play. Here the boy made a gradual recovery and regained weight, but lingering concerns as to his condition's communicability kept him from mixing with other children. In his early years he was largely confined to the company of his grandmother or private tutors, which left him free to brood on the only memory he retained of his immediate family, of a blue-eyed sister whose name would bring tears to his eyes throughout his life. The sufferings left their mark, shaping an emotionally volatile, solitary and highly strung individual even as they suggested a marked knack for survival, at Gatwick as in his childhood, amidst the catastrophic loss of those closest to him.

In the end it did not surprise the Çukurcuma shopkeeper, familiar with time-wasters, to discover there was to be no sale. When I made my excuses, citing hand luggage, he once more put the cat to flight before wordlessly returning the portrait to the stack.

CHAPTER THREE

22 November 1952

A journalist is shot in eastern Turkey

In the 1950 election campaign one of the Democrats' headline pledges was to restore the Arabic *ezan*.

This highly symbolic move reversed the law of 1932 which required that the *ezan*, the call to prayer, be made in Turkish; to facilitate the change, a recording of the Turkish version, made at Istanbul's famed Blue Mosque, had been circulated among muezzins across the country. To Kemalists, the use of Arabic was a bulwark of Ottoman obscurantism; Turks were to practise their religion in the mother language rather than in one so few understood. Many hoped that the 1932 law, in which Mustafa Kemal took a personal interest, presaged the wholesale extirpation of Arabic in Turkish devotion, including the *mevlut*, the funeral obsequies, and even the text of the Quran itself.

But devout Muslims considered it a solemn requirement that all utterances in the service of the faith be made in the language in which the Prophet, peace be upon Him, received the Angel Gabriel's recitation of the Quran. For many, the Turkish *ezan* proved insupportable; indeed, according to one source, 'this one act of government interference in the ritual caused more widespread popular resentment than any of the other secularist measures'. Enduring it was more painful, some peasants claimed, than the bouts of hunger they commonly suffered. And while the muezzins generally fell in with the 1932 law – as officials of the state, they were strictly enjoined to adherence – any presumption that the adoption of Turkish in the people's wider devotions would follow in the natural course of events proved vain. The scenes that Lilo Linke in 1935 witnessed in the mosques – the 'old men, squatting on their heels, swaying forward and backward, touching the ground three times with their foreheads and rising again to their stiff legs', and 'still murmuring the ancient Arabian words' – led the German traveller to doubt that such changes could ever be achieved.

When the Arabic *ezan* was first heard again at dawn on 17 June 1950 it was greeted with undisguised exultation. Those who had gathered to hear it, in great numbers at centres of devotion like Istanbul's Fatih mosque, resting place of Sultan Mehmet the Conqueror, took it as a special sign of divine approval that the Arabic *ezan*'s restoration should have taken place on the first morning of Ramadan, one of the holiest days in the Islamic calendar.

Others vehemently disagreed, pointing out another reason why the restored call was first heard again on so auspicious a day – the Democrats having timed the law's passage accordingly, blatantly stage-managing the event to political advantage. Though Menderes might claim that the new law was about 'the freedom of religion and conscience . . . how we understand the meaning of true secularism', opponents saw the restoration of the Arabic *ezan* as marking the fateful moment when the first of the great Atatürk's reforms fell to the reactionaries.

To the devout, however, it seemed that the stars had aligned and that Adnan Bey was leading them back to God.

*

A sepia photograph shows Adnan Bey – having long since dispensed with Ali – at the time of his marriage.

It is 1928, at the height of the Kemalist reforms, and the young man poses with his seated wife. Berin wears her hair in a fashionable bun, fiercely parted, with a pearl necklace and a large white bloom in the buttonhole of her striped silk jacket. Adnan Bey stoops behind his wife, one hand on her shoulder, the other lodged in the trouser

pocket of his stylish double-breasted suit. He wears a tie and sports a handkerchief in his top pocket, and his parted hair ends in a dandy's wave which mirrors the one worn by the elegant Berin. The couple resemble gilded Europeans; it doesn't take much to imagine cigarette holders and champagne glasses. They are as their revered leader would have them be: modern standard-bearers of Atatürk's social revolution.

The couple had known each other since childhood when Adnan, fully recovered, was finally released from his long quarantine to attend Izmır's prestigious American School. The proud owner of an English Raleigh bike, he was also free to mix with the children of Karşıyaka; it was on the lanes of this exclusive neighbourhood that Adnan first noticed the young girl whom he would eventually court. Though Adnan Bey turned into an impressive young man – intelligent, a talented sportsman, popular and capable – Berin took some persuading as to the match. She was an Evliyazade, an influential

Smyrna family of prosperous merchants, mayors and politicians whose daughters did not tend to marry farmers, not even ones who were sole heir to a cotton farm of some 30,000 acres; and not if it meant leaving Izmır's elegant cafes, salons and concert halls for an out-of-the-way village near Aydın called Çakırbeyli.

Berin was nevertheless taken with her suitor's energy and magnetism, not to mention the turreted chateau-style mansion which Adnan Bey had commissioned Hungarian craftsmen to build, with ample space for Berin's beloved grand piano and her other comforts, amidst spacious grounds in Çakırbeyli. Trusting her suitor to make her happy, provide her with children, and run the farm with the same competence and intelligence that had made it one of the most productive in the Aegean region, she consented.

In fact, it was Berin's pointed hope that farming would continue to satisfy her new husband, whom she meant to keep from politics at all costs. It was a calling she had come to fear, and with reason. Just two years before her marriage a favourite cousin's husband, falsely implicated in a plot against Mustafa Kemal, had been hanged alongside his alleged conspirators in an Ankara prison. Berin went so far as to extract a promise from Adnan Bey that he would never be drawn into politics.

For a while all was as Berin Hanım – Madam Berin – would have wished it. Life in Çakırbeyli was provincial but pleasant enough, and her native city was not so distant as to prevent regular return visits. She bore their first son and raised him while Adnan Bey devoted himself to the farm, rising at dawn to saddle up and ride the cotton fields bordering the banks of the Meander River. But he proved restless; given his abilities and boundless energies it was perhaps inevitable that Adnan Bey eventually outgrew the farm. It appeared that he had bigger ambitions; ignoring the pledge lately made to his wife, he put himself forward as prospective parliamentary member for his home town of Aydin. He was duly elected to Turkey's National Assembly in 1931.

*

A friend, whom I'd texted earlier that day, rang me.

'So you want to talk sedition,' he said cheerfully. 'Then we might as well do it properly.' He proposed the Nazım Hikmet Cultural Centre, a place I did not know from earlier travel assignments, in the Asian suburb of Kadıköy.

Kadıköy is a progressive and liberal neighbourhood, the kind of district that Atatürk no doubt hoped the whole country might come to resemble: cinemas, cafés and an opera house, and cultural centres like the one I found off a quiet lane beyond a high-walled Armenian church. In a garden shaded by limes, pines and mulberry trees I spotted Metin among a congregation of writers, journalists and students. I might have freely described Metin if the risible charges that Turkey's journalists and writers commonly face these days – incitement, insulting the president, propaganda on behalf of a terrorist organisation – did not make it necessary to disguise him, and not only with a false name.

So there he was in his worn peacoat and crumpled trousers, a packet of cigarettes in his constant clasp, every inch central casting's leftist literary dissident, in deep conversation with an attractive young woman. He broke off to embrace me, but not before bidding the woman to stay, which left me with the impression that I had interrupted more urgent matters.

'I should warn you that we don't think much of Menderes here,' he told me, clamping a hand around the young woman's wrist. 'He reminds us too much of Erdoğan. In fact, the parallels are uncanny.' He lit a fresh cigarette.

'Take Erdoğan,' he said. 'Started so well. Seemed like a committed democrat, even a martyr to freedom for doing time; they'd banged him up for reciting a few lines of inflammatory religious poetry back when he was mayor of Istanbul. We journalists and human rights groups were all for him. In the early 2000s he was pro-European, and for a time even EU membership looked possible. The economy was in good shape and he seemed committed to making peace with the Kurds, the same people he's now pounding to pieces. He got things done, like sorting the country's infrastructure, and he even cultivated relations with us journalists. Well, at the time we admired him. Tea, fresh tea! And another for you,' he beseeched the woman, who was now making concerted efforts to free her arm from Metin's grasp. 'Anyhow, he was dynamic, and we wanted to believe in him, and now it's all gone to shit, and we've only ourselves to blame for never noticing the warning signs.'

'The warning signs?' I asked, scribbling notes.

'Oh, that time he compared democracy to a tram: "We ride it as far as we want," he said, "and that's when we get off." Rather than listen, most of us dismissed it as a joke. We only began to understand what we were dealing with when he began his ludicrous vanity projects. I mean that insane presidential palace – 600 rooms! – in Ankara, and the mega-mosque, the biggest in Turkey, that's now going up on the hilltop at Çamlıca. That's all his economic strategy amounts to these days – endless construction projects, especially of mosques. Then there was that development plan he had for Gezi, and the terrible things he said about the protesters there back in 2013 and the violence the police did to them. He's corrupt, and his people are corrupt, and anybody who calls him corrupt soon learns that Erdoğan doesn't do criticism; what we writers and journalists have come to understand is that you're either with him or you're with the terrorists, in which case there's a long prison sentence coming your way.' As I wrote Metin lit up two cigarettes, pressing one upon the woman who eventually accepted it with a reluctant sigh.

'I will be anonymous, won't I?' he asked. I nodded. 'And there's no way they'll know it's me?'

'Different name, full disguise, completely unrecognisable,' I assured him. 'They won't even know you exist.'

'Then let me go on record by saying President Erdoğan has left the tram. He is a dictator, pure and simple, who deserves everything he gets,' he said.

'But doesn't he know what happens to leaders like him in Turkey? Doesn't he know how the story tends to end?'

'Oh, he's smart. For years he's been tackling the main danger, the armed forces, by removing officers he suspects of plotting against him, and replacing them with loyal Islamists. Just as he's purged the army, so he's tamed the media by closing down or taking over every newspaper, magazine, radio or TV station which has dared to criticise him, labelling them terrorist organisations. Now most journalists just toe the line. Those who don't he jails, the same with writers. He's sacked the good judges to leave himself with the bad ones, which pretty much means they hand down the sentences he expects, the same with the prosecutors, and he's thrown out the academics and professors he considers enemies, even if that's for doing nothing more than condemning war and calling for peace with the Kurds. He clearly thinks he's coup-proof.'

'And is he?'

'One can but dream that there's still somebody out there,' said Metin. 'But seriously; would anybody – in 2016?'

With the one arm that was not restraining the young woman Metin embraced me again before I wandered off into the Nazım Hikmet Cultural Centre.

*

Nazım – as he is simply known in Turkey – was the greatest, and most persecuted, of all Turkish writers. A revolutionary poet whom compatriots revere or revile, Nazım lived an extraordinary life in thrall to words, and to women, much of it either in prison or exile.

Adnan Bey's contemporary, if anything but his confrere, Nazım enters our story at dawn on New Year's Day 1921 when, with char- acteristic brio, he surreptitiously boarded a coaster called *The New World* docked beside the Galata Bridge. The eighteen-year-old was on his way to join Mustafa Kemal's resistance movement in Anatolia. The train to Ankara was out of the question – the Ottomans were watching the stations to stem the flood of recruits to the rebels – which left the route via the Black Sea; arduous and chill, no doubt, but resonant in a way that would have thrilled Nazım and his fellow travellers as they slipped aboard, concealing themselves among cotton bales until the Ottoman authorities' Bosphorus lookouts had disappeared beyond the stern. They were embarking on the very journey Mustafa Kemal had made just eighteen months earlier, and to the same end, which was to build a new world.

Not that these nationalists had much idea of what that world would look like. What united this motley confederacy of poets, soldiers, students, doctors, journalists, lawyers, intellectuals, adventurers and the rest was their resistance to occupation, and a contempt for the Ottomans' spineless submission to the Western powers; they knew what they were fighting against, even if any idea of what they were fighting for, beyond freedom, remained poorly defined. Anyway, there was first a war to be won if ever that world was to emerge.

Nazım's journey to Ankara, which took up much of January 1921, was to change all that. The stowaway who left Istanbul, though he might have burned with romantic resentment at the injustice of the occupation and the arrogance of those who administered it, a staunch anti-imperialist, by nature profoundly egalitarian, and always ready with a spirited rendering of 'La Marseillaise', was still to settle upon a pronounced political position; the man that arrived in Ankara, frozen to the bone, stinking and blistered after his trek through snowbound mountains, was in the grip of the communist conviction that would be his life's guiding motive.

For in the course of the journey Nazım fell in with students of the radical left, blooded survivors of the revolutionary movements so brutally suppressed in Germany and elsewhere, who thought to find common cause with the independence fighters of Anatolia. Through all the cant he heard from these idealists about class struggle, radical proletarianism and the hydra that was international capitalism, Nazım divined the essential truth that the age of empire had ignored: that all were truly equal, and the poor and the ordinary were the real heroes, and these were to be the triumphant subjects of his writing life.

Given the solidarity that bound Mustafa Kemal's nationalists to the Russian Bolsheviks, not only the Turks' munitions suppliers but the first foreign power to recognise the outlaw Ankara regime, Nazım's convictions did not appear to put him at odds with Mustafa Kemal. Patriots and irreligious progressives, the two men had in common not only their origins in Ottoman Salonica – a city which seemed to breed more than its quota of dissenters, independents and freethinkers. The poet saw no reason why he should not take his place in the nationalists' ranks as well as in those of the newly formed Turkish Communist Party.

But Mustafa Kemal had become increasingly alarmed at Turkey's burgeoning communist movement. He had no wish to win his country's independence from the Western powers only to lose it to the Russians. He was not about to forget his south-seeking neighbour's historic disregard for the sanctity of Turkey's borders, suspecting the Soviets' magnificent new Ankara embassy might be 'a measure of their designs'; when supping with a Russian, the Turkish saying went, use a long spoon. The only thing for it was to ban Turkey's communist party. When a delegation of leading Turkish communists were subsequently murdered in mysterious circumstances, Nazım took it as his cue to flee, not only fearing for himself but recognising that the Kemalists' cause was no longer his. In the autumn of 1921 he crossed the Black Sea to the Soviet Union.

Nazım's return to Turkey later that decade, without the correct papers, ended in arrest. So began a long acquaintance with the country's courts and prisons, often on charges arising out of his revolutionary poems which, when they were not exploring his spectacularly tangled love life, typically traduced Turkey's venal bosses or championed the rights of Istanbul's taxi drivers. Lengthy prison stays on charges of incitement, the spreading of communist propaganda and insult only spurred Nazım to pour his celebrated spirit into his visionary poetry.

Nazım's prolific output included the acclaimed *The Epic of Sheikh Bedreddin*. The poem, written during an extended 1930s stay in Bursa prison, was inspired by the historical revolt which a medieval religious leader led in protest at the feudal injustices perpetrated by the early Ottomans. For all his own atheism Nazım took inspiration from Sheikh Bedreddin's radical egalitarianism, itself rooted in the Islamic assumption that all property belongs to Allah. The revolt was mercilessly crushed and the sheikh hanged along with some 4,000 of his followers.

Bedreddin was to be the last of Nazım's poems to appear in Turkey during his lifetime. It was published in 1936, by which time Stalin's brutal excesses had done for any lingering fellow feelings that the Kemalists might have had for their former allies. In fact Turkey was now in the grip of anti-Soviet paranoia; the army especially was on the lookout for signs of communist sympathy, not least from influential voices such as Nazım's. The issue was not so much *Bedreddin*'s content, though some considered the poem's powerful braiding of Islamic and communist grievances recklessly inflammatory, as the fact that the poem was said to be turning heads at Istanbul's prestigious Kuleli Military Academy. When a handful of cadets admitted to an enthusiasm for Nazım's work, some having even sought out the poet's company, the spectre of a communist scare in the armed forces – reds not so much under the bed as on the bedside table – was more than the military authorities could take. They set out to quash Nazım's literary insurgency as their forebears had dealt with the sheikh 500 years before. Nazım was arrested in 1938 and subjected to a series of absurd trials. On being found guilty he was sentenced to a total of twenty-eight years and four months on charges of inciting the army to rebellion. He was to spend the next thirteen years in prison.

This historic injustice sparked protests, though not until the late 1940s were concerted efforts made to secure the poet's release. Nazım's failing health, the result of a series of hunger strikes, lent urgency to the campaign which received international backing thanks to his growing fame. The Soviets put Nazım on a stamp and the Bulgarians organised a day of events in commemoration of his fight for freedom. Even in the West protests and petitions were staged on his behalf, with a mass gathering on Rockefeller Plaza, New York. In the poet's beloved Istanbul his aged mother, unsteady and almost blind, left an enduring impression on those who witnessed her stand for hours on Galata Bridge beside a placard denouncing 'My Son's Unjust Imprisonment'.

The Democrats, having committed to an amnesty for all political prisoners, were obliged to order Nazım's release two months after coming to power. They did so with profound misgivings; the recent outbreak of war in Korea, to which Turkish brigades were soon to be dispatched, had only underlined the extent of the red threat and confirmed the anti-communist convictions of the party's leaders. Barely had Nazım walked free on 15 July 1950 before the army, which had never ceased regarding him as a traitor, took the opportunity of inflicting upon the great poet of injustice a final one of their own: it ruled that as Nazım was yet to undertake the national duty required of all Turkish males, he must now present himself for military service, regardless of the fact that he was in his late forties and suffered from a chronic heart condition. Nazım reckoned his chances of surviving the ordeal as minimal, the more so because he was to be posted to an especially remote corner of eastern Anatolia, no doubt selected to place him beyond the protective scrutiny of his admirers. Nazım, recently remarried and with a young child, was left with no choice but again to flee the country he had never ceased to love.

He leaves our story as he first appeared in it thirty years before, slipping out of Istanbul on a boat one June morning in 1951. Without so much as a bag to betray his intentions, Nazım made his way to the Bosphorus village of Tarabya and wandered casually down to the waterfront where a skiff awaited him. What looked like a Sunday jaunt was in fact a planned operation; Nazım's well-connected accomplice had procured the craft only after receiving assurances that it had the beating of anything the authorities could put on the water. The skiff idled out onto the Bosphorus and into the Black Sea where the two men spotted a ship which they identified through their binoculars; she was Romanian and named, in what Nazım took for a good omen, after a prominent Marxist theorist. As they closed on the ship, Nazım hailed the crew in Russian and French. The two men endured an anxious wait as the crew digested the celebrated poet's unexpected request for political asylum. A further delay ensued while the captain radioed the nearby port of Constanza, which contacted Bucharest, which in turn consulted Moscow, before the request was granted. Then, after gratefully embracing his accomplice, Nazım scrambled up the rope ladder the crew had thrown down. Sailors helped him aboard before ushering him to the ship's saloon where officers, stokers and hands crowded round to greet him, pointing to the wall where the poet saw his own photograph above the caption 'Free Nazım Hikmet!'

Weeks later, the Menderes government stripped Nazım of his citizenship, accusing him of initiating a communist propaganda campaign against the country. He was forbidden from ever returning to his homeland, his manuscripts were confiscated, his writings banned from publication, and his family and friends were subjected to years of harassment and official opprobrium.

Yet here he was – with a cultural centre in his name. Much of Nazım's prolific prison output – his poems, plays and verse novels in a wide range of foreign-language editions, along with his own translations of Italian librettos, La Fontaine's *Fables* and Tolstoy's *War and Peace* – lined the shelves of the centre's bookshop. It heartened me that Nazım's writings had survived their suppression and that the country had made peace with its finest poet; and as I was buying a copy of his *Human Landscapes From My Country*, his paean to Anatolia, and admiring his image on the posters and badges, the bags and notebooks arrayed at the counter – handsome and unbowed in that worn peacoat and the crumpled trousers – it struck me that here was the disguise in which I would dress Metin.

*

One November evening in 1952 Adnan Bey, on a series of rallies and dedication ceremonies in Turkey's mountainous eastern interior, was dining with aides and colleagues in the town of Malatya. The dinner, hosted by the mayor, was a convivial affair, with wine from the region's Elazığ vineyards fuelling fervent talk of rural development programmes, transformative dam projects and another excellent

harvest, not least of the town's famed apricots. The dinner was punc-
tuated by toasts to Atatürk, to the NATO alliance which Turkey had
joined earlier that year and to the brave Turkish soldiers battling the
communists in Korea. Glasses were also raised to the commendable
spirit of cooperation in that staunch Republican stronghold –
Malatya, Ismet Paşa's seat, had been one of the party's few 'holds' in
the 1950s elections – between the opposition and the honoured
Adnan Bey's ruling party.

At the dinner was a craggy, cultivated man called Ahmed Emin
Yalman, a veteran newspaper publisher and journalist who had made
his name as an outspoken advocate of a free press. Like Atatürk and
Nazım, the opinionated Yalman was from Salonica where he had
spent his childhood writing news sheets which he copied out by
hand before cajoling family members into buying them. Growing up
in the late nineteenth century under the repressive rule of Abdul
Hamid II, who disdained a free press as an unwelcome Western
innovation, Yalman was quick to distinguish the liars who pretended
'abject homage to the sultan' from those who despised the despot
and 'secretly read books and papers written against him' – and as
quick to know to which of these groups he belonged.

By all accounts an impressionable man – usually adopting 'the
views of the last person to stand him a drink', as one of his critics put
it – Yalman was nevertheless immovable when it came to press freedoms. This uncompromising independence regularly landed Yalman
in trouble; during the War of Independence the British authorities
had exiled him to Malta for publishing his nationalist views. In 1925,
when the dreaded Independence Tribunals charged him with under-
mining the government's authority, Yalman feared he might even
face the gallows.

Under Adnan Bey, however, such worries were safely in the past.
Happening to be in Malatya on an assignment, Yalman found there
was a place for him at the table of the prime minister, with whom he
had a close association. The two shared exceptional levels of energy,
an outspoken admiration of Western democratic values and a correspondingly virulent dislike of communism; back in 1945 it was

Yalman's newspaper, *Vatan*, that had carried the rebel Adnan Bey's scathing attacks on the ruling party's totalitarian tendencies. The paper had served as Adnan Bey's unofficial mouthpiece while he established himself as the opposition Democrats' most persuasive voice. The well-connected Yalman acted as one of the Democrats' 'principal publicists' in the early years, often hosting networking events and maintaining a generally favourable editorial line, even after the Democrats came to power. Adnan Bey valued Yalman's opinions, numbering him among the select handful of ministers, editors, jurors and professors to whom he turned for advice.

Publisher held prime minister in equally high regard, not least for all he had done to ensure a free press; lifting publishing and licensing regulations and seeing to it that the government advertising budgets on which many publications depended were fairly allocated. He applauded the country's NATO membership and Adnan Bey's prompt dispatch of troops to Korea as well as the tough line he had lately taken with Nazım Hikmet. It happened that Yalman had worked for Nazım's cause in 1949 when he argued in *Vatan* for the release of a poet he openly admired and whose devotees were also said to include President Bayar. But after Nazım's flight, and the disparaging comments he had been making about his country since arriving in Moscow, Yalman considered him nothing more than a worthless traitor whom Adnan Bey had been right to condemn.

For all that, the Democrats' impressive record in government was in danger of amounting to nothing, to judge by the signs of religious reaction Yalman had lately noticed in the country. Reaction, in the view of avowed Kemalists like Yalman, was the most grievous threat to the country – more so even than communism – and an affliction to which rural Turks seemed fatally susceptible. Yalman feared that Adnan Bey, in pursuit of the popularity which was democracy's currency, was failing in his sacred duty to guard against any such contagion.

It had begun with the Arabic *ezan*, of course, which secularists likened to leaving ajar a door through which a stream of religious freedoms duly slipped. Among these were the readings from the

Quran which the national radio took to broadcasting, and the decision
of the authorities to reopen more saints' tombs to religious visitors.
The American educationalist Howard Reed observed numerous
signs of an Islamic resurgence: 'private mosque construction and
support; private religious education; pilgrimage to Mecca and to
local shrines; public observance of prayer and the fasting month of
Ramadan; substantial, even crowded, attendance at mosque services;
deferential respect shown to the increased number of those wearing
apparently religious garb; the popularity of religious ejaculations or
phrases in colloquial speech; the use of religious talismans in public
places, especially in conveyances such as buses or taxis'.

These new freedoms only emboldened Turkey's traditionalists
and their Democrat representatives to clamour for the return of
such Ottoman shibboleths as the fez, the old alphabet and polygamy.
Clerics and their students took to wearing religious garb again which
the police, who in earlier decades had been quick to censure such
outfits, now allowed to go unchallenged. Then the attacks on the
Atatürk statues began.

These assaults recalled those of the Byzantine Empire's eighth-
century iconoclasts or the English Puritans; but where the idolatrous
representation of saints otherwise unconditionally revered inspired
those earlier desecrators, the militants who now set upon Atatürk
meant not only to register their disapproval of graven images but to
insult the memory of the man they held responsible for laying waste
to their cherished religious beliefs and practices. They attacked him
at night, in town squares, in the yards of police stations or party
offices, breaking noses and shattering chins, shooting, stoning and
pelting the statues with eggs. Some statues were daubed with paint,
often with messages that insulted infidel ways. Other representations
of Atatürk – busts, bas-reliefs and even framed photographs – regularly had their eyes gouged out or were otherwise defaced. In more
audacious attacks, carried out in daylight, some appeared to confuse
the statues for their living likeness, remonstrating with Atatürk
before laying about him with sledgehammers. In Ankara's Nation
Square, site of the capital's first statue, a protester was seen to

clamber onto the neck of the leader's horse before haranguing the great man at close quarters.

The attacks were not confined to such symbols of secularism. Militant traditionalists took to expressing open disapproval of those who chose to sit with their wives in restaurants, and couples who held hands in public. They began to denounce secular activities such as dance and ballet performances, and inveighed against prominent secularists. Among those in their sights was Yalman, and not only for targeting Turkey's reactionaries in his often outspoken articles. It incensed them that Yalman's newspaper had chosen to cover the Miss Europe beauty contest, publishing photographs of partially clad Turkish entrants alongside a caption they found especially offensive – 'Making Known to the World the Beauty of the Turkish Lady is a National Duty'. On that November night these grievances were about to be expressed; and they would almost cost Yalman his life.

It had been a long evening and the guests were onto the apricots when Yalman excused himself; he had to file tomorrow's editorial – a favourable take, in case Adnan Bey had been wondering, on the regional 'spirit of understanding' between the ruling party and the opposition. Yalman made his way to the town's telephone exchange where he rang in his copy before heading for the nearby hotel. It was then that he 'suddenly had the sensation of being showered with pebbles' – a prank on the part of some errant youths, he briefly assumed – before realising that he was bleeding heavily from arms and legs. Seconds later, he collapsed outside the hotel.

The attempt on Yalman's life – the sixty-four-year-old survived, despite being struck by seven bullets, suffering catastrophic internal bleeding and undergoing several operations – shook a nation which had been free of political violence for more than twenty years. Nobody was more concerned by the attack than the prime minister who with characteristic energy set about doing all he could for Yalman. He immediately arranged for the minister of justice and the director general of security, who both happened to be leading medical experts, to be flown to Malatya by special plane. He organised a second plane to fly the publisher's wife and son from Istanbul. He spent hours at Yalman's hospital bedside, checking on the progress of the stricken patient; and, in Yalman's own appreciative testimony, did not sleep on the night of the attack but at once launched the search for the would-be assassins.

Those assassins, some were tempted to conclude, could only have been encouraged by the government's policies. Yalman himself never expressed anything other than gratitude for the prime minister's efforts in Malatya; but as he lay in his hospital bed, the solicitous Adnan Bey at his side, did it cross the mind of either man that Adnan Bey must take his share of blame for the attack?

*

It was evening by the time I left Kadıköy on the Bosphorus ferry. Squadrons of terns flew low over the water and seagulls hopeful for scraps of bread banked over the ferry's stern. The sun was low and the European side's fabled skyline – Topkapı, Aya Sofya and the Blue Mosque – appeared like graphite, the domes, minarets, towers and cypress trees fading to nacreous ghosts. But along the unsung Asian shore the utilitarian silos, derelict warehouses and sea containers were slicked in gold. The last of the light caught waves which sparkled along the rusted waterlines of moored Romanian freighters. Shiny red and black tugboats, their cabins pushed back like sailors' caps, were tethered to a waterfront slung with lorry tyres, the blistered treads spent on the roads of Anatolia. I looked up to Çamlıca, that former beauty spot in the hills which the Bailey family had visited for the views, where arc lights now illuminated something huge and disturbing. I might have been witness to the dramatic downing of some sci-fi super-arachnid, the jointed legs rising above the carapace in a confusion of ruinous angularity, before the vision resolved into a partially constructed dome amidst a hem of cranes and half-built minarets. This was the mosque Metin had mentioned; Turkey's biggest, and Erdoğan's self-proclaimed gift to his people.

I remembered that first photograph of Adnan Menderes, who had also favoured mosques, one reason for Erdoğan's increasingly overt identification with his revered forebear. It was his God-given mission, the president liked telling the crowds at rallies, to continue the work of Adnan Bey by restoring to right-thinking religious folk the things they wanted, like mosques, while cutting the godless minority, for too long the country's rulers, down to size. Erdoğan's cultivation of the association had been successful, to judge by the proliferation of placards on show at the president's rallies which presented the two leaders, partners in remaking traditional Turkey, alongside each other.

In the course of a recent rally at Aydın, a city which retained a special affection for its most famous son, Erdoğan's references to the man he called Turkey's first democrat acquired a strange and unsettling intensity. To the assembled crowds the president described 14 May 1950 as the beginning of an era of democracy, which was to be cruelly terminated a decade later. Menderes and his friends, said Erdoğan, gave everything for Turkey's future and would always be

remembered. 'Our nation,' he added, 'will not forgive those who betray our democratic and economic achievements, which we have gained through great struggles under extremely difficult circumstances. We would be honoured to end up like Adnan Menderes.'

As the ferry closed on the Eminönü quayside I joined the crowd gathering at the rails, the young men thrusting their way to the front to eye the churning waters beneath the closing gap like herd animals crowded at a Serengeti river crossing. With a long stride these chancers were gone before the ferry came alongside, the heavy warps creaking taut on the bollards as the ferry men in high-vis jackets booted the gangplanks into place, and the rest of us filed obediently across the boards and dispersed into the city. Back at my hotel the young man on the desk told me that he lived in Çamlıca.

'Where they're building the mosque we used to play football,' he said sadly. 'And all to remind us how holy the man is.'

CHAPTER FOUR

29 May 1953

Turkey celebrates the 500th anniversary of the Conquest of Istanbul

I'd often thought it odd that Turks – in many cases even in present times ignorant of their own birthdays – should have dates of national significance at their fingertips, as if the milestones in their personal histories meant less to them than those of the country. I wondered that these dates so readily and repeatedly served as the names of streets, neighbourhoods, universities and schools, convention centres and hospitals, apartment blocks, stadia, bridges, dams and forests; and were celebrated as national holidays, complete with marches, parades, rallies, speeches, firework shows and folk-dance displays.

But with varying degrees of enthusiasm. For while many of the most prominent anniversaries remained well observed – 19 May, the day Atatürk initiated the national resistance in 1919; 29 October, when he declared the Turkish Republic in 1923; and 10 November, at five past nine in the morning, when he died in 1938 – other calendar nods to the great leader did not endure. It seemed telling that defiant rivals, with their conflicting claims to national observance, should have shouldered their way in.

Take 6 October, which for decades was commemorated as the date when Istanbul fell to the forces of Mustafa Kemal in 1923; an anniversary whose significance was further marked with the unveiling in 1926 of that first statue. With its marching bands and twenty-one-gun salutes, so-called Liberation Day became an established annual fixture celebrating the occasion when the Turkish forces made their triumphant entry into Istanbul, finally confirming the new nation's territories after victory in the War of Independence.

On that day in 1923 the troops entered the city amidst a carnival strew of flowers, confetti and streamers. They 'marched between an unbroken avenue of festoons of laurels' stripped, it was often reported, from the gardens and cemeteries of the city's foreign communities and its minorities, among them the Rum people, as the Greek Orthodox were known, whose ill-advisedly overt enthusiasm for the Allied occupation of the city had made them the focus of growing Muslim hostility. When the general in command of the Turks' 1st Infantry Division put ashore at Eminönü – where the poet Nazım had slipped unseen out of the city to join the fight two years earlier – there was unconfined din as 'every ship lying in the harbour,' in the words of the *Times* correspondent, 'played discordant pranks with her siren'. The tumult continued into the afternoon when 'the Anatolian forces made their triumphal march from Stambul across the Galata Bridge up the tortuous streets of Pera to their barracks at Taxim and Harbie'.

These affecting scenes occasioned, as the *Times* man put it, 'pardonably flamboyant rhetoric' in the local press. They set the seal, according to one report, on 'the absolute and crushing victory won by Moslems at the beginning of the twentieth century over the whole Christian world'. The War of Independence had culminated in Istanbul's 'second conquest' – one that many in their excitement rated an even greater achievement than the first one.

Mustafa Kemal's nationalists were to be forgiven for glorying in their military feats, and for belittling the vanquished Ottomans' own record in the process. In truth, however, that October day in 1923 amounted to little more than a prerehearsed pageant. For almost a year – since another of Mustafa Kemal's generals had stepped ashore on 19 October 1922 – the city's governing functions had been in the hands of the nationalists. Only because it took until July 1923 before the treaty was signed at Lausanne did the Allies take so long to leave. Rather than the dramatic culmination of a campaign fought to the death, the outcome uncertain to the last, 6 October 1923 was merely the final act of a carefully scripted handover, and to a timetable scrupulously observed by both sides. Indeed, the Turks waited fully four days after the Union Jack was lowered and folded, and the last enemy contingents were embarked to waiting warships, before staging their entrance into the city.

For all the claims that 6 October commemorated a double liberation – from the Ottomans, after almost 500 years, as well as from the Allies, if only after rather less than five – enthusiasm for the anniversary soon began to flag, most notably among those who felt less than liberated under the new regime. The date only endured as a calendar event because the state insisted upon its continued observance – and with equal vigour suppressed its natural rival in what we might call the conquest stakes.

That rival was 29 May, anniversary of the 'first' Conquest of the city in 1453, indubitably an historic event of the first rank. As Islam's defining triumph over the West the Conquest, which brought over a thousand years of Christian rule in the city to an end, merited the capital C. Possession of the city at the juncture of two continents, the key to the Ottomans' supremacy, crucially improved their hold on both Europe and Asia, enabling their armies to advance ever deeper into the Balkans, southern Russia and Arabia. Possession of the city turned the Ottomans into the greatest power of the age.

Not that the Kemalists were about to acknowledge the sultans' crowning achievement. With the declaration of the Republic, an all-out assault had been launched upon the Ottomans' heritage, expunging laws and institutions, costumes, script and customs, closing palaces and converting mosques. All Ottoman insignia were zealously removed from public buildings, streets commemorating sultans were renamed, and Ottoman archival documents were sold off by the stack to Bulgarian paper recyclers. Citizens were encouraged to dismiss forebears raised to take pride in their Ottoman identity, to condemn even living parents for their association with the torpor, superstition and reaction of the old order. As the Kemalist state had it that Turkey's true birth took place on 19 May 1919, and that studying Ottoman history was a deviant activity, it would have been an omission indeed to have left 29 May – heralding such a significant Ottoman victory – on the commemorative calendar.

But as Democrat rule fostered a new spirit of freedom, the authorities began to tolerate manifestations of interest in the Ottoman past, even to allow a modest pride in it. It was now permissible to perform Ottoman music and to allocate funds for the restoration of Ottoman buildings and mosques. Ceremonial army units took to dressing in Ottoman costume. From around 1950 these interests began to cohere around a historical event, the Ottoman Conquest of Istanbul, and for the excellent reason that an anniversary too important to ignore – the 500th – loomed large. The quincentenary carried such symbolic weight that calls for celebrations grew into a clamour which the Democrats were happy to indulge. The Istanbul Conquest Association was formed and charged with organising a ten-day programme, with flotillas of floodlit ships, fly-pasts by the Turkish air force, wreath-laying ceremonies, athletics meetings, and performances of a new play called *The Conqueror*. The government even ordered a set of commemorative stamps as well as a brand of cigarettes called 'Conquest'. The newspapers prepared special editions lavishly illustrated with historic heroes like Hasan of Ulubat, martyred in the act of planting Mehmet's triumphal standard on the ramparts.

All of which was to give the people what they wanted, even if some saw those who would rehabilitate 29 May – elevating the first Conquest and conqueror, with their combustible and traitorous Islamic associations, over the second – as nothing less than traitors to the vision of Atatürk.

*

Struck by Turks' apparent facility for falling out over questions of ritual and symbolism – statuary, sacrifice, the language of the call to prayer, the observance of one anniversary rather than another – I decided that 29 May merited further investigation. On a bright May

morning I boarded a ferry which headed up the Golden Horn, pushing a viscous bow wave as it zigzagged between the shores of this
unkempt backwater at the city's heart. As the ferry nosed alongside
the landing stations passengers alighted, making their way across the
waterfront parks into tatty shoreline neighbourhoods. In the shallows cormorants perched on old pilings, opening their wings to the
sun, and fig saplings poked through broken windows in the derelict
shipyards. Narrow lanes curtained with washing rose to sagging
roofs and rusty flues beneath a skyline spiked by the minarets of the
great imperial mosques – of Sultans Süleyman, Selim and Mehmet
the Conqueror – which lined the old campaign road into Europe.

I left the ferry on the southern shores of the Golden Horn where
the great fortifications, first raised by the Byzantines, ran down to the
water at Ayvansaray. Just outside the walls I entered a garden containing a mosque and some scattered tombs, and more attention than
this nondescript place appeared to merit. These Turkish visitors
came in coachloads, and the veils which the women all wore, tightly
pinned at the chin, identified them as devout Muslims. They had
come to offer their prayers at the tombs which Atatürk had closed
and Adnan Bey reopened. What drew them to Ayvansaray were the
Sahabeler – Companions of the Prophet – said to lie there.

These Companions – like Christ's disciples, only more numerous
and belligerent – are revered for having known Muhammad (Mehmet
in Turkish) in person, often as his brothers in arms. Of the thirty
said to be buried in Istanbul several lie at Ayvansaray, among them
Sheikh Betul Hudri whom devout Turks revere as the Prophet's
'milk brother', the honoured bond between those suckled by the
same wet nurse. These Companions lie where they were purportedly
martyred during the four-year siege the Arab armies mounted at
Constantinople from AD 674; but as the siege did not commence
until fully forty-two years after the death of the Prophet – by which
time any such Companions can hardly have been in their fighting
prime – the basis for such claims are dubious. The Companions'
tombs are nevertheless sanctified as the resting places of some of the
first martyrs in the long conflict between Islam and Christianity; so

long that these Companions had been dead for the best part of 800
years when Sultan Mehmet II's forces arrived at the foot of these
walls on 5 April 1453, intent on making the thirteenth attempt on
the city by Muslim armies the first to succeed.

From its Arabian outset Islam had regarded Constantinople not
merely as a physical objective – a strategic asset, glittering trophy or
the richest of plunder pots – but as a hallowed goal. The city was the
religion's youthful obsession, stalking its dreams and desires, to
judge by its recurrence in the hadiths, the sacred utterances attributed to the Prophet. 'Constantinople will be conquered,' reads one.
'Blessed is the conquering commander, and blessed his army.'
Mehmet II, whose Ottoman forebears had repeatedly failed to take
the city – his great-grandfather Bayezid had besieged it for eight
years – meant to be that blessed commander. He reminded his forces,
arrayed outside those formidable walls, that to them fell the honour
of ushering in Judgement itself. For that hour would not come, it was
said, until the city was taken by men proclaiming 'There is no God
but Allah, and Allah is great'; only then would the walls yield and the
Muslim forces flood in.

When the young sultan succeeded his father in 1451, privately
pledging before all else to make Constantinople his own, Mehmet II
clearly recognised that invocations to Allah alone were unlikely to
get him in. Rather than rely on divine intervention, he prepared
thoroughly, firstly by binding rival powers in a series of treaties
which freed him to give the siege his full attention. His next step
was to cut off the city from the Black Sea, traditionally a prime
route for supplies and reinforcements, by constructing in six
months a fortress – Rumeli Hisar – that controlled traffic on the
Bosphorus at its narrowest point. He commissioned a new generation
of siege towers high enough to neutralise the defenders' traditionally
decisive advantage. In a brilliantly effective *coup de théâtre* he
reduced a stand of forest to rollers which his forces slicked in olive
oil before using them to drag their war galleys ashore and uphill,
around the Byzantines' defensive boom, and down to join battle on
the waters of the Golden Horn. He commissioned the world's

greatest cannon, capable of reducing the massive walls with missiles each weighing over half a ton. Then, in case that were not enough, he readied some 80,000 fighting men, perhaps eight times what the defenders could muster. It was clear, as the besieged Byzantines recognised with growing dread, that the Ottomans meant business this time.

Acknowledging those whose ancient example had inspired the sultan, I levered off my boots and followed the pilgrims into a gloomy interior containing the tomb of Kab, one of the Companions. A walnut-wood sarcophagus, draped in shrouds of green laced with gold Kufic script, lay beyond glass where the pilgrims queued to press their palms. These they then transferred to their faces, running their hands from crown to chin and rubbing the grace into their pores as if it were a balm. I left them murmuring their devotions to follow the walls inland.

These walls, with their protruding towers, were immense; from an orderly base of ashlar blocks coursed with bricks they rose with increasing irregularity. The upper tiers, testimony to centuries of pounding, were intensively patched with classical column drums, chunks of Roman architrave and whatever other spolia had been to hand. Along the top, where the battlements had largely collapsed, loose rubble supported a broken rampart of etiolated saplings. I left the cemetery, and where a highway raised on concrete columns ran close I followed the walls across a stretch of open waste ground. Here was a broken campsite. Loosely guyed tents, the fabric stained and faded, stood among discarded food tins, strewn possessions and the ash circles of night fires, and an old man tottered from the rubble of a curtain wall, buttoning himself. Then the raised road bore away, taking the traffic tumult with it, and in a tatty orchard a man pastured his tethered foals, and beyond more tombs of fallen Companions I passed through a gate into the old city.

It was quieter still within the walls, their lee seeming to preserve an earlier time. A narrow lane ran past shabby houses, their timbers patched with the rust rectangles of flattened catering tins. Potted plants pressed beseechingly at dusty windows, and the ears of sleeping dogs twitched, and in the arched vaults at the foot of the walls men tacked together vegetable cartons or turned chair legs on lathes, or sat on low stools, smoking as they wiped the wood dust from their brows. Further up, where the walls stood lately restored – by the city's heritage people rather than those charged with its defence – the first European tourist I had seen for days had got herself into trouble on the battlements. Only after the woman had admired the views and turned to descend did she note that the stairway was without a safety rail, which reduced her to a tearful fit of vertigo. A local mechanic, wiping away the engine oil with a cloth, mounted the stairway and calmly took the woman's hands in his. Then, taking her by the shoulders and turning her back to the drop, he walked her slowly down, offering encouragement at every step in what I took to be poor German, and at the bottom she sighed loudly and gave the man a tentative hug before she walked away, and there was laughter, and the encounter seemed rich with the promise of something I could not define.

Through a half-open door a litter of kittens trailed before a boy herded them back inside with a hiss. From another doorway a shawled woman appeared with a rug which she unfurled with a snap before laying it in the lane. Behind her a tousled girl emerged with a bucket and the two knelt, one at either side of the rug. They worked the hot suds into the weave, their heads nodding at the effort, and the grey water ran off in rivulets which I sidestepped, and the rug revived, shining in the sunlight.

I emerged from these domestic scenes at a choked highway, its four lanes punching a gap in the walls at precisely the point where the Ottomans' great cannon had caused the fatal breach, as if the calculations of medieval bombardiers and twentieth-century city planners had led them to the same conclusions. I tacked between the stationary traffic where drivers broke from leaning on their horns to wave away vendors of water bottles and paper tissues. Where the walls resumed I came to an arched gateway where an inscription told of the Conqueror – Fatih in Turkish – who had passed here on his triumphal entrance into the city.

Nearby, at the spot where the great cannon was said to have been sited, the organisers of the 1953 celebrations had raised an antique Ottoman campaign tent in readiness for the commemorations. After their commencement, marked by the roar of 101 guns which warships moored on the Golden Horn met with a salvo of their own, an invited audience of municipal delegates, foreign consuls and Islamic leaders, as well as representatives of the city's old Rum, Armenian and Jewish communities, gathered at the tent for a speech by the governor of Istanbul. The governor spoke of the 'Turkish embrace of free conscience and religion', citing the sympathies said to have been offered the Greek Patriarch by the Conqueror, a scene featured on one of the commemorative stamps. The governor also cited as evidence another such scene – the Conqueror's magnanimity towards a Byzantine girl said to have presented her welcoming bouquet to the wrong man. Though this mis-delivery of the citizens' traditional gesture of submission was potentially catastrophic, not least in implying that the Conqueror of the city was indistinguishable from the rest, the insult was one Mehmet was said to have had ignored, even acknowledging the recipient to be more deserving of the blooms.

Some might have queried these cameos, knowing this to be the same sultan who just two years earlier had slain his infant half-brother to secure the throne; who was in the habit of having his enemies impaled, of slaughtering or enslaving the citizens of cities which did not surrender to him; and who did away with the architect commissioned to build his Fatih mosque for failing to give it a dome to rival Aya Sofya's. But those sceptics who thought it as likely that Mehmet II had in fact thrown the girl to his soldiers were not about to say so.

Upon the conclusion of the speeches the civic leaders and worthies left the tent to find themselves among milling crowds of men in felt robes, slippers, baggy *şalvar* trousers and high turbans, with scimitars tucked under their sashes. These men were dressed as Janissaries, the elite Ottoman troops whom history credited with leading the decisive assault on the walls; their ceremonial band were to have the honour of heading the quincentenary procession. To the din of kettle drums, bugles and whistles the assembled crowds moved off, halting at the place where Hasan of Ulubat was said to have been overcome, and the band fell silent, the crowd too, in honour of all the Muslims martyred in the siege. The solemn parade continued through crowded streets to the Fatih mosque, burial place of the Conqueror, where it arrived just before noon. In the way of the Democrats, adept at managing events of religious significance, the timing proved excellent. It was down to luck that 29 May 1953 fell on a Friday – the holy day when the angels station themselves at the mosques to register those in attendance – but careful organisation saw to it that the procession's arrival coincided with the start of Friday prayers. A floral crown was laid at the Conqueror's tomb and a *mevlut* – an ode in honour of the Prophet's birthday, traditionally heard at Turkish funerals – was recited.

This was to sacralise the Conquest commemorations, according them an Islamic significance which the secularists viewed with profound disquiet; and so 29 May became another cause over which the two sides braced to do battle. Its opponents resisted attempts to establish the anniversary which they succeeded in suppressing, sometimes for several years in a row. But the impetus was inexorably with the celebrants. The decisive breakthrough occurred in 1994 when the Islam-oriented Welfare Party, victorious in Istanbul's mayoral elections, threw its weight behind the anniversary. That year the pageantry was put on an altogether grander footing; to great fanfare, a squad of Janissaries in false moustaches dragged a boat through crowds of shoppers along Istiklal Caddesi – Independence Street – a convenient approximation of the route thought to have been taken by the Conqueror's war galleys, and down to the shores of the Golden Horn. Crowds packed the Beşiktaş football stadium for the main event, cheering the sultan, his fine white horse, and the heroic Janissaries as they made short work of the city walls, or at least of the painted plywood partitions supposed to replicate them. Among those in attendance was the guest of honour, the lately elected mayor whom the Welfare Party's confident supporters throughout the campaign had touted as 'the new conqueror of Istanbul'. His name was Recep Tayyip Erdoğan.

*

I continued along the walls to a spot I remembered from my teaching years. Here I had often awaited long-distance buses whose passengers leapt aboard as the horn sounded, leaving nothing of themselves but scattered sunflower seed husks, smouldering cigarette butts and fading farewells as the bus bore us into the night. The bus station had disappeared; where it once stood was a large rotunda, set in newly landscaped parklands, a terminus where journeys of another sort entirely now began. I joined the queues at the entrance.

This was the Panorama 1453 Museum which Erdoğan had supported from the project's infancy, shortly after he first became prime minister in 2003. For though he was not so reckless as to neglect the national founder, knowing how his opponents would exploit any such shows of indifference, he nevertheless felt free to align himself with his core support's greater enthusiasm for Istanbul's Ottoman conqueror. Erdoğan saw no reason why those who took pride in 1453, and who wished to celebrate it regularly, should have to wait a year for 29 May to come round again.

At the security check the guard gave the contents of my rucksack – a map, a notebook and my new copy of Nazım's *Human Landscapes From My Country* – a thorough examination before gesturing me through. I followed a corridor as it wound past brass plaques and illuminated display panels, all antique prints and maps of the city, to a spiral staircase. I set off up the dimly lit stairs, a portal into the past, which rifled me back beyond this self-same spot's bus station decades, through the preceding centuries, to set me down on 29 May 1453.

I emerged onto a circular viewing platform beneath a painted firmament foregrounded by the scattered detritus – water barrels and powder kegs, mallets, weapon crates, cannonballs – of siege. The roars of the attackers and the cries of the dying, the clatter of weaponry and the crack of the cannon rang out. Beneath a blue sky scored by arrows and flaming missiles, ranks of Ottoman soldiers broke against the city walls. Infantrymen raised their round bossed shields at the Byzantines' arrows, and red standards streamed from the lances of horsemen as they charged gaps in the defensive stakes or poured into the sweat-hazed breaches where the fighting was thickest. Artillery men set torches to the fuses of their falconets while the fallen, supported beneath the armpits and the knees, were carried from the fray to waiting carts. Pigtailed Ottoman warriors scaled ladders at the crumbling walls where the Byzantines' standard, the double-headed eagle, hung defiant from the high ramparts. Defenders stood in silhouette, awaiting the attackers with rocks, arrows and pails of molten wax. Within the walls I saw the domes of the city's basilicas where the citizens sought sanctuary among their treasured icons, praying for protection.

These prayers were in vain, as the defenders knew well, for they too had observed what I now saw as I circled the viewing platform; beyond the Ottomans' tented camps the innumerable ranks of reserves, with their pikes, their double-headed axes and their bows at the ready, rested and resolute. At the Panorama Museum the battle, though it still raged, was already won. The museum celebrated the victory not only of the Ottomans over the Byzantines in 1453, but of the supporters over the detractors of 29 May in the time of Erdoğan. Here was a conquest the president's people were now free to welcome not every 500 years, not every year but every day.

*

The museum was no place, of course, for those who considered 29 May a battle lost. Chief among these were the so-called Rum people, descendants of the Byzantines, whose older families claimed heroic forebears among the city's staunchest defenders during the siege of 1453. Some of the Rum – Turkish for Roman – even traced their lineages as far back as Agamemnon's fabled victories at Troy, which were said to mark the advent of the Hellenic presence in the region.

For all their regret, the survival of Istanbul's Greek-speaking, Orthodox Christian communities into the 1950s, when they numbered about 100,000, did indicate the comparative leniency with which the Ottomans had treated the city's residents in 1453. Following the standard slaughter, rape and enslavement, the lot of all citizens who defied the Ottomans, the Conqueror rapidly established autonomous arrangements for the city's remnant resident populations. He allowed the maintenance of the office of the Patriarchate, the spiritual leadership of the Rum communities, and guaranteed freedom of worship. Although he converted many of the great churches into mosques, he left others to continue as before, only insisting that the bells be silenced and replaced with timber clappers. He let the Rum convene their own courts, and guaranteed their trading interests. He exempted them from military service, in the Ottomans' view a holy calling which only true believers could undertake, leaving the Rum free to concentrate on commerce. They retrenched in city districts like Samatya, Fener, the Princes' Islands in the Sea of Marmara, and in Pera on the north shore of the Golden Horn, duly prospering in the Ottomans' famously cosmopolitan and multicultural society.

For centuries the Ottomans' relationship with the Rum and other minorities such as the Jews, the Armenians and the Catholics remained largely untroubled. Only as the empire's decline gathered pace did systemic signs of discord appear. By the nineteenth century the Ottomans were shedding territories on all sides as subject peoples aspired to national self-determination; and the independence from Ottoman rule of Greece in 1839 further encouraged the idea that the resurgent Hellenes might reclaim lands that were theirs by long usage, most of all their great ancient capital on the Bosphorus. The idea resonated in the city; when the First World War ended with the defeat of the Ottomans and Istanbul's occupation by Greek and other Allied forces, some Rum made no attempt to disguise their delight. They not only gave a rapturous welcome to the Allied fleet but paraded portraits of favourite leaders, especially Eleftherios Venizelos and David Lloyd George, and raised awnings in the Greek national colours outside their hotels and bars. Some even went around knocking fezes from the heads of the humiliated Muslims.

In the course of the ensuing War of Independence centuries of harmonious co-existence between Turks and the Rum counted for nothing as the opposing armies butchered the populations that each claimed to represent. In the Aegean region, especially around Adnan Menderes's home city of Aydın, the carnage was so brutal that the local Rum people, fearing reprisals from the advancing Turkish nationalists, fled in their hundreds of thousands to Greece in the final months of 1922. By the time of the nationalists' victory, the sectarian hatreds were so virulent that total physical separation of the opposing communities appeared the only way to prevent further massacres. At the Treaty of Lausanne in 1923 the Turkish delegation, led by Ismet İnönü, pressed for the wholesale expulsion from the new nation of the Rum people, holding them collectively culpable for the traitorous support some had lent the invading Greek armies. The terms of the treaty confirmed as permanent the departure of those who had already fled. They also mandated the compulsory deportation to Greece, with no more than the little they could carry, of Anatolia's remaining Rum populations, but with a couple of exceptions, notably the Rum community of Istanbul.

This exemption, which the Greek delegation and their British allies held out for at Lausanne, was largely predicated on historic sentiment; but the Turks – aware that their own insistence on the Rums' expulsion would have spelled the effective end of the Greek Orthodox Patriarchate, an institution their adversaries considered of such symbolic significance that they might have gone to war over it – finally conceded the point.

But grudgingly. Many Turks nursed vivid memories of Rum disloyalty, which only spurred their resentment of the disproportionate prosperity that these *gavur* (infidel) people, historically the city's commercial class, continued to enjoy. These grievances only worsened with the young Republic's determination to bolster an exclusively Turkish identity, further stoking anti-minority sentiment which gave many of Istanbul's Rum cause to regret that they had not also left. The situation deteriorated with the Second World War and the introduction of the infamously heavy-handed Capital Tax, a scheme designed to recover to the cash-strapped treasury the ill-gotten gains of wartime profiteers, wholesalers and import-export dealers but which had a devastatingly disproportionate impact upon the minorities. By 29 May 1953, those Rum who felt it in their interests to attend the Conquest celebrations had reason to question the governor's talk of the 'Turkish embrace of free conscience and religion' – from their own experience under the Turks if not that of their Byzantine forebears.

*

One man was not at the quincentenary celebrations.

Prime Minister Menderes had stayed away to spare sensitivities, it was said, in Greece where the newspapers had denounced the Conquest commemorations as a triumphalist provocation unworthy of a NATO ally. Adnan Bey was warier still of accusations that the Islamic revival under his watch amounted to a betrayal of Atatürk's vision. It was time to row back on reaction, publicly distancing himself from one conqueror to affirm his commitment to the other.

Adnan Bey's government had been quick to demonstrate its loyalty to Atatürk following the attacks on the statues, making any defamation of the great man's memory a crime; it was now time to dispel whatever doubts remained by putting the government's energies behind the question of Atatürk's final committal. The interminable delays to the completion of the Ankara mausoleum – Anıtkabir – put Adnan Bey at an advantage over the Republicans, self-styled guardians of Atatürk, who had demonstrated a marked lack of urgency in relation to the matter. For over a decade Ismet Pasa's people had lodged the leader's remains at Ankara's Ethnography Museum. The building was imposing enough, with spacious interiors and sweeping views over the city, but this repository of Sufi artefacts, carpet looms, traditional kitchenware and crumbling mannequins hardly commended it as a national shrine, even of a man who cared so little for shrines. The Republicans' best efforts at the Ethnography Museum – the centrepiece sarcophagus of white marble and the perpetual guard of honour – could not disguise the fact that Atatürk lay not at rest but in storage. The Democrats changed all that by pushing on with the completion of the great hilltop mausoleum and arranging for the transfer of the remains there in 1953, and on the only date in contention – 10 November.

That morning crowds gathered along Ankara's boulevards as a stream of official vehicles delivered ministers, aides, high-ranking army officers, diplomats and foreign dignitaries, all in full ceremonial dress or military uniform, to the Ethnography Museum. In their braid and medals, their top hats and cockades they mingled on the terrace as mandarins escorted the chief mourners – Turkey's leaders, in morning dress, and Atatürk's one surviving sibling Makbule – into the museum. As Makbule Hanım approached the swagged catafalque to rest her palm upon the flag-draped mahogany coffin, Ismet Paşa caught the eye of President Bayar.

'You got it done,' said the former president to the current one, extending a conciliatory hand to his oldest rival. Now was no time for their many differences.

'Oh, the credit goes to our perpetually busy prime minister,' replied Bayar briskly, gesturing to the dapper and diminutive figure at his shoulder. Adnan Bey acknowledged the compliment with a slight inclination of the head.

'Well, it certainly needed doing,' said Adnan Bey, cupping a hand to his hair in his habitual manner. 'After all these years.'

Ismet Paşa, briefly checked, seemed unsure of his reply. 'The endless problems with the contractors,' he eventually murmured. 'The war years. The budget cuts.'

'Cuts which did not, if I recall, confine the presidential train to the sidings,' replied President Bayar.

'But—'

'In my day,' Bayar snorted, 'we didn't keep close comrades waiting. Buried them as soon—'

'Gentlemen,' interrupted Adnan Bey, stifling a smirk. 'The time is almost upon us.' Moving between Turkey's two great surviving statesmen, he planted a palm in the small of each of their backs and steered them out into the cold morning where the cortege was preparing.

At five minutes past nine, as the nation stopped, so the gathering fell silent. For five minutes only a line of ragged birds in the grey city sky disturbed the stillness. Then ten cadets bore the coffin from the museum to a waiting gun carriage drawn by forty comrades. An honour guard of lieutenants fell in before the carriage while behind it the main cortege formed: twelve generals, then an admiral carrying a velvet cushion topped by a single decoration, the leader's War of Independence medal, and the chief mourners. The procession moved off, winding through the city to Anıtkabir, a hilltop terrace planted with trees donated by many nations. It drew up before the mausoleum, austere and magnificent, where President Bayar spoke of Atatürk's immortal vision before the founder's remains were transferred to a marble hall of honour. They were interred in a vault carved from a single piece of granite to mingle with earth brought, in keeping with tradition, from every Turkish province.

The following spring the country went to the polls again. The May 1954 elections saw the Democrats returned with an even bigger majority, taking 490 out of an increased total of 535 seats. By accommodating the two conquerors' constituencies, appealing to those who would hear the Arabic *ezan* without unduly alienating those who would rather cheer for Miss Turkey, it seemed that Adnan Bey had maintained his balancing act.

CHAPTER FIVE

6 September 1955

Riots devastate Istanbul

In the summer of 1954, shortly after the Democrats' emphatic return to power, Adnan Bey summoned Ahmed Emin Yalman.

'The elections have clearly revealed how much the citizens like the road I have taken,' announced the prime minister in lofty tones. 'So far I have attached value to consultations with you journalists. Metaphorically speaking, I used to seek your advice on whether to use aspirin or Optalidon as a cure for nerves. Now the people's lively confidence makes it obvious that there is no further need for such consultations. I am going to have the final word and use aspirin or Optalidon as I please.'

It was an abrupt way to call time on an old friend and supporter, especially one lately riddled with bullets. But in recent months Yalman's newspaper had been increasingly ambivalent towards, even critical of, a government better at managing symbols, it seemed, than figures. *Vatan* had been forthright in its coverage of the first signs of economic turbulence – rising inflation, the widening balance of payments deficit, shortages in the shops – and in forecasting a poor harvest, the first in years. Other outspoken associates, not only in the press but the universities, the judiciary and elsewhere, also discovered they were to be distanced from the prime minister, who even abandoned the 'counsel with his colleagues and with the parliamentary following on which his position depends', as one diplomat noted.

In dispensing so precipitately with his court, Adnan Bey caused people to wonder what had become of the committed democrat

– now so arrogant and cutting towards even constructive criticisms of his policies. One commentator ascribed it to the national trait 'in Turkey and in the oriental countries in general, to present as intolerant, even cruel, when criticised'. Such an 'authoritarian tendency and intolerance of criticism', others surmised, had combined with latent complexities in Adnan Bey's personality which the stresses of leadership had laid bare – and to dramatic effect; a prodigiously gifted man, stalked since his traumatic childhood by impulses, enthusiasms, infatuations, obsessions and especially insecurities, whose skin had never hardened into the hide which other politicians developed to protect themselves from the slights and slurs of daily life in a democracy. It was only to be expected that a man so avid for approval, so reliant on the roar of the rally, should have proved allergic to criticism, even to the consultative process, and increasingly disinclined to put up with either. It appeared that the scale of his victory in the 1954 elections had finally convinced Adnan Bey that he was now free to make up his own mind. He would run the government – '*his* government, in a very real sense', as a British diplomat emphasised – by himself, and with a degree of personal control which bordered on the obsessive. 'If the Hilton Hotel needs foreign exchange to buy toilet paper,' as one Western resident was to tell *Time* Magazine, 'Menderes probably has to approve it.'

Not that Adnan Bey entirely dispensed with advice. Apart from continuing to consult with President Bayar, he also kept Fatin Rüştü Zorlu and Hasan Polatkan close – the same three men, it happened, who were seen to be inspecting the mosque model in the photograph which had first brought Adnan Bey to my attention. For much of the 1950s he retained Zorlu and Polatkan as his foreign and finance ministers. He no doubt trusted these men and valued their counsel, the combative Zorlu's especially.

But the other factor was their portfolios' increasing relevance to what was fast becoming his administration's most pressing concern: foreign financing.

*

I had arranged to meet somebody at the Hilton.

Through the Pera district I walked down Independence Street, a broad boulevard lined with English-language bookshops, contemporary art galleries, vegan cafes, art-house cinemas, consulates and churches. Music pulsed from the chain stores where girls tilted heads, dangling contending crop tops before reflected torsos. *Fin-de-siècle* filigree portals gave onto glass-roofed arcades lined with fruit and fish stalls, and *meyhane* taverns whose impeccably dressed tables – starched white damasks, shining cutlery and condiment sets – did not disguise these haunts' raffish, even ruinous, promise. Low wicker stools and *nargile* smoking pipes clustered outside teahouses, and the neon signs which hung along the most alluringly unsavoury of the side alleys were inoperative, like the recuperating habitués of the nightclubs the signs advertised. Beyond one door a tattooist, heavily pierced, worked in a pool of citric light, his staccato jabs transmitting a perpetual tremor through his hunched form. Couples sauntered past, arms around waists, his fingers invisible to the knuckles down the back of her belted jeans. Long-haired boys stood in circles of trampled cigarette butts, their Styrofoam cups baited with a few coins, strumming Nirvana tracks and Anatolian folk songs.

Pera, from the Greek word for beyond, describes the district's historic location outside the walls of the imperial city. Since 1273, when the Byzantines made a gift of it to the Republic of Genoa, Pera had been a distinct city, an independent walled trading colony which drew merchant settlers from all over Italy and beyond. When, 180 years later, Mehmet II's forces ignored it in concentrating their assault on the adjacent imperial city, Pera's citizens opted for skilful equivocation. They offered what support they could to their besieged co-religionists across the Golden Horn without appearing so partisan as to incite Ottoman action against them. Come 29 May 1453, however, Pera's authorities wasted no time in throwing open the gates to the Conqueror's armies, thus saving their city from the sack taking place across the water. Pera's surrender, though late, was grudgingly accepted; the sultan ordered the destruction of the defensive walls but otherwise spared the city. As Pera had been a centre for minorities under the Byzantines, so it continued under the Ottomans, notably for the displaced Rum populations.

Of these minorities the only remaining signs were historic, most visibly the names of the belle-époque apartment buildings along Le Grand Rue de Pera, as the last generations of Ottomans knew Independence Street: Lukzemberg, Ravouna and the Botter Apartments, the last named for the Dutch tailor to Sultan Abdul Hamid II. The masonry bore occasional inscriptions – to 'Yenidunia et Kyriakides, Architectes', and to 'Michelini, Entrepreneur' – which reflected these old communities' cosmopolitanism. Where plastic shopfronts had been ripped away in readiness for new tenants – sellers of accessories, smartphones, suitcases, artisan coffee, kebabs, sunglasses and the rest – I glimpsed Greek script in faded cartouches, ghosts of the Rum businesses which had occupied these premises until the 1950s.

At the approach to the Hilton security men passed extendable mirrors beneath arriving taxis. I stepped through a scanning machine into a Corbusian vision of 1950s modernity. In place of walls, glass expanses looked out over the Bosphorus, framing the half-built domes and minarets of Erdoğan's hilltop mega-mosque at Çamlıca. With time to spare, I wandered the lounge, taking in the photographs: founder Conrad Hilton posing proudly beside an architect's model of the hotel, only the second he was to build outside the Americas; Celal Bayar enjoying his hundredth birthday party at the hotel, and Ismet Paşa his eighty-fifth; and Adnan Bey, dapper in dinner jacket and bow tie, at the hotel which he intended as a shining symbol of the modern prosperity he would bestow upon the country.

The Istanbul Hilton opened in June 1955, a startling block of concrete and glass which drew comparisons with the new UN Building in New York. The hotel, built with American aid, was the biggest in the Near East and the only five-star establishment in the city. The government even issued a postage stamp in commemoration of the event, hoping the hotel's opening would announce the long-eclipsed city's return to international prominence, kick-start a much-needed tourism industry, and confirm Turkey's place in the family of

Western nations, which its membership of NATO and its dispatch of forces to bolster the anti-communist coalition in Korea had already signalled.

For the grand opening Hilton spared no expense, chartering two Pan Am airliners nicknamed the Carpets – Flying and Magic – which it filled with over a hundred 'celebrities from the American and European world of movies, radio, television, press, national magazines, news magazines, news wire and picture services, and feature syndicates', and some 1,200 items of luggage. On their arrival at Istanbul these guests were greeted by a 'solid wall of humanity that reached from the steps of the plane to the terminal building'. In scenes of near hysteria film stars including Irene Dunne, Merle Oberon, Ann Miller and 1930s Hollywood legend and Olympic figure-skating champion Sonja Henie breezed down the path that the police had forced through the crush. In their wake came Broadway stars, cover girls, society columnists and 'Cisco Kid' star Leo Carrillo, who drew a roar of approval as he raised his trademark sombrero to the crowds.

At 'Conrad's Seraglio', as the hotel was nicknamed, the new arrivals exclaimed at the views beyond the plate-glass expanses. They oohed over the cabanas, the clubs and the sky garden, and aahed over the mini-mall, the skating rink and the rooftop dancing lounge. In their air-conditioned rooms they admired the wall-to-wall carpets hand-woven in the Konya region, the three-channel radios, the on-tap iced water, the Bauhaus-style lighting, and the teakwood balconies with grand views over Asia.

The celebrations lasted for five days, with the guests enjoying boat trips up the Bosphorus, a garden party at Beylerbeyi Palace and a gala dinner at the Caribe-Hilton buffet, its centrepiece an ice sculpture of Istanbul's signature Blue Mosque. In his after-dinner speech Conrad Hilton rhapsodised over 'the magic of this famed city of antiquity' and commended Turkey's transformative leadership for making the hotel possible. Hilton expressed pride in adding Istanbul to his family of hotels which he described as 'friendly centers where men of many nations and of goodwill may speak the language of peace'. How fortunate it was for the Western world, Hilton continued, 'that the new republic chose to continue one element of the foreign policy of the sultans – a deep and very sound mistrust of its great northern neighbour'. By symbolising 'friendship between nations, which is an alien word in the vocabulary of the Iron Curtain', his hotels represented 'a challenge – not to the peoples who have so cordially welcomed us into their midst – but to the way of life preached by the communist world'.

The city's emergence from the shadow of decrepitude cast by the Iron Curtain lent Istanbul a fresh allure which the Menderes administration determined to exploit. With the opening of the hotel, Istanbul moved to establish itself as an international conference destination, rapidly attracting august organisations like the International Monetary Fund and the International Committee of Corporate Law, and events as diverse as the International Road Congress and the Conference on Byzantine Studies. That September, it prepared to host the twenty-fourth annual conference of the International Criminal Police Commission, or Interpol.

*

With the simultaneous entry into the NATO alliance of Turkey and Greece in 1952, and the subsequent flurry of state visits between Ankara and Athens, including the very first to Turkey by a Greek monarch, Istanbul's Rum people had reason to feel a welcome degree of security. But trouble loomed on the horizon – if, to be literal, only on those exceptionally clear days when Cyprus could be made out from the nearest stretches of Turkey's Mediterranean coast.

The island had been an Ottoman possession for centuries before it was leased to the British, who annexed the island in 1914, but the population had been largely Greek for millennia. As the British began to shed their imperial assets after the Second World War, so the Greek Cypriots under the rousing leadership of Archbishop Makarios began to agitate for *enosis*, or union with Greece.

Enosis enjoyed clear majority support among the islanders. The Greek Cypriots' wish to determine their future had already given rise to symbolic acts of disobedience, with youths marking Queen Elizabeth II's coronation – just four days after Istanbul's quincentenary conquest commemorations – by tearing down the Union Jack outside official island buildings. Under EOKA, a newly formed paramilitary organisation, the militants' stance hardened into hostility. Armed resistance began in April 1955, with attacks on British police stations, courthouses, homes and radio stations across the island. As the British scrambled to convene tripartite talks in London that August, the Greek government reconfirmed their formal backing for Greek Cypriot claims for self-determination.

All of which was to ignore the 100,000 Turkish Cypriots, roughly one-fifth of the island's population, who had no wish to be governed by the historic enemy, not least because the Greeks' treatment of their own minorities, notably the Muslim Turks of western Thrace, gave the Turkish Cypriots no cause for confidence. The Ankara government took sides accordingly, confirming its support for the Turkish Cypriots. At a dinner in Istanbul for Foreign Minister Zorlu's delegation on the eve of its departure for the London talks, Prime Minister Menderes asserted that Turkey would accept no outcomes other than the status quo or reversion of the island to Turkey. He questioned the Greek government's craven pandering to Archbishop Makarios whom he dismissed as 'a provincial cleric'.

In Istanbul's Rum neighbourhoods these developments caused a mounting sense of alarm which only deepened when word went out that EOKA meant to mark the opening of the conference by slaughtering Turkish Cypriots. These rumours, though baseless, were vigorously stoked by Istanbul's press, with one paper warning that there were 'plenty of Greeks in Istanbul' – closely equivalent in number, conveniently enough, to the Turks on Cyprus – should any such slaughter take place. Other papers cited historic instances of treachery by the Rum communities, demanded proof of their loyalty to the Turkish state, and accused the Patriarch of collecting donations for the *enosis* campaign. Reports from London of Zorlu's uncompromising opening conference statement – that unless Greece modified its position, Turkey was ready to reconsider its commitments under the Treaty of Lausanne, which was tantamount to threatening the country's remaining Rum population with expulsion – only added to the tensions. On 4 September Greek newspapers were burned in Taksim Square and some 20,000 banners emblazoned with the slogan 'Cyprus is Turkish' were distributed. It was in this febrile atmosphere, as Foreign Minister Zorlu advised his government that only a demonstration of Turkish intent might save the London talks from stalemate, that the British writer Ian Fleming flew into Istanbul Airport where he was driven to his suite at the newly opened Hilton Hotel.

Fleming – delighted to discover that the Association of Former Eunuchs, the membership down to twelve, had lately celebrated its annual reunion in the city – was in Istanbul to attend the Interpol conference. It was to be a packed programme; presentations on drug smuggling, bank robbery, psychological profiling, fingerprint forging, counterfeit cheques and the exemplary friendliness of the London 'Bobby' promised to satisfy the imagination even of James Bond's inventor. But Fleming was distracted from the moment on the second day when word reached him via the police chiefs among the delegates – the first, inevitably, to hear of such things – that a bomb had exploded the previous night in the Greek city of Salonica. The attackers had targeted the compound of Salonica's Turkish Consulate, birthplace of Mustafa Kemal Atatürk.

News of the attack was first reported on Turkish radio's lunchtime news and confirmed in the afternoon editions of some Istanbul newspapers, which cast it as a hideous affront to Atatürk's honour. Though the damage would turn out to be slight, and to little more than a few windows, the effect of the bomb was to prove fatally incendiary. Through the afternoon large crowds of young men began to congregate in Taksim Square, chanting 'Cyprus is Turkish'. As darkness fell these men, now armed with staves, mallets and crowbars, broke off into groups clustered beneath Turkish flags and headed for Independence Street and the surrounding areas, vowing vengeance. They set about the plate windows of patisseries, tailors' shops, haberdashers, hardware stores, delicatessens, shoe shops and pharmacies. They broke through corrugated-metal shutters and ransacked the interiors. Soon the streets lay deep in shards of glass, trampled bolts of cloth, suits and shoes, broken crockery sets, cake stands, toys, chandeliers, fish tanks, rugs, washing machines, pianos and mannequins. Congealed cream cakes and cheeses, the contents of broken beer barrels, fish trays, pickle jars and bottles of olive oil, and thick smuts from burning buildings cast a sour smell over the city.

Following his journalistic nose, Fleming left the Hilton to venture 'into the city, where mobs went howling through the streets, each under its streaming red flag with the white star and sickle moon'. 'In every noisome alley and smart boulevard,' he wrote, 'hatred erupted and ran through the streets like lava.' Districts like Samatya, Fener and even the usually somnolent Princes' Islands, all known for their minority populations, descended into violence. Gangs ran amok, overturning vehicles and bellowing out chants which threatened 'Death to the infidels'. They attacked Rum schools and newspaper offices, and Greek airlines' offices. They ransacked the churches along Independence Street, overturned crosses and statues in the cemeteries, broke open vaults and scattered the bones. A priest was set upon and circumcised. Women were raped. It was as if Pera were being subjected to the sack it had sidestepped in 1453.

Amidst the destruction one thing was spared: the portraits of Atatürk, common to most premises, were retrieved by the rioters from smashed shops and carried before them. They bore these looted icons aloft, among the Turkish flags carried by their companions, as if to permit the great man an elevated view of the vengeance they had visited upon those they held responsible for Salonica, careless of the fact that these Rum had loyally hung Atatürk's portrait on their own walls.

*

Witnesses to the destruction which engulfed Istanbul on the night of 6 September 1955 described a carnival atmosphere, with women and even children joining in the mayhem which the city's law enforcers showed little interest in preventing. Crowds gathered to cheer as buildings were torched and as trolleys, tables and washing machines were heaved out of upper-floor windows.

Michael Stewart, chargé d'affaires at the British Embassy, reported that neither 'the police nor the garrison troops, who were out in some force by 8.30, made any real attempt to restrain the rioters'. 'Indeed,' he added, 'the police in the Pera district, with the exception of four mounted officers who rode aimlessly up and down the main street, armed with hunting whips, which they were careful not to use, seemed to have generally disappeared from the scene by nine o'clock.' The troops, who 'paraded up and down the main street in trucks to the accompaniment of the applause of those who could take time off from the more engrossing occupation of pillage, were useless'.

Some considered it curious that the security presence outside particular buildings, notably the Greek Consulate-General, the Patriarchate and the Hilton Hotel, was contrastingly high, with military detachments reported to have taken up position even before the trouble began. And the rioters did not appear to behave in typically arbitrary fashion. Observers wondered how so many of them had acquired hammers and crowbars, not to mention specialist equipment such as bolt cutters and acetylene torches, and how it was that taxis and minibuses were readily on hand to ferry them to the trouble points proliferating across the city. The events appeared orchestrated, with some men seen to identify premises by referring to lists of shops earmarked for ransack, whose forced doorways were subsequently found to have been marked with a cross, often made with a sooty finger.

Adnan Bey was not to hear of the troubles until later that evening. He and the president were on the night train to Ankara. As the train left Haydarpaşa Station on the Asian shores of the Bosphorus, trundling through the city's eastern suburbs and down to the Sea of Marmara, they dined together before retiring to a private compartment where they continued their discussions over coffee. The two leaders spoke of matters arising from the day's official engagements, and of the London conference on Cyprus, a most difficult affair according to Zorlu, whose recent dispatches had repeatedly urged some gesture of Turkish determination if the proceedings were to have a more favourable outcome. They spoke of their hopes for a better harvest, and for the International Monetary Fund's confer- ence, scheduled to open in Istanbul the following day, with Polatkan entertaining former heads of state, economists, bankers, finance ministers and other key delegates at the Hilton.

The train passed through a series of poorly lit ports along the Sea of Marmara, the moon showing through the gathering clouds to illu- minate patches of low swell beyond the shore. At about ten o'clock it slowed suddenly to an unscheduled halt alongside the platform at Sapanca. After a few minutes the restless Adnan Bey rose to his feet, crushing out a cigarette, as an aide appeared at the door of the compartment.

'Let me look into the delay, gentlemen,' said the aide as he disap- peared down the corridor. From the window Adnan Bey scanned the platform where he spotted a man slumped in a chair beneath an overhanging mulberry tree, a railway cap pulled down over his eyes.

'Without wishing to disturb,' Adnan Bey enquired, exaggerated in his courtesy, 'but I wonder if the platform attendant might be good enough to advise as to when we can expect to continue? We happen to have business in the capital.' At the sound of the voice in the night, authoritative and cultivated, the attendant stirred, scatter- ing the cats that had gathered at his feet. Brushing himself down and straightening his cap, he hurried towards the train, starting as he recognised the prime minister at the window.

'Ah, Adnan Bey, begging your patience. Let me make enquiries right away,' he said, bowing before he scuttled down the platform. Adnan Bey returned to his seat where he lit another cigarette.

'You appear anxious to be home,' said the president.

Adnan Bey shrugged. 'I have seen too little of the family,' he said.

'Indeed. As some have seen fit to observe. I had it in mind to suggest you might spend rather more time at home.'

'Would that I could, my esteemed President,' said Adnan Bey. 'But as first minister these are responsibilities I'm obliged to bear. Besides, my energies—'

'Oh, I have no doubt as to your energies,' the president interrupted. 'I'd only counsel that you might expend them more judiciously.'

'Oh, Berin Hanim knows that the needs of the nation must come first.'

'Forget the needs of the nation, Prime Minister. I'm counselling you to pay your wife closer attention than you have of late. Do you imagine that these things go unnoticed?' Adnan Bey, not one to be lectured on his indiscretions, even by the president, drew deep on his cigarette as hurrying footsteps sounded along the corridor. The aide appeared in the doorway, the local chief of police at his shoulder.

'Adnan Bey, President,' said the aide struggling for breath. 'It seems disturbances are taking place in Istanbul.'

'Across Istanbul,' the police chief added apologetically. 'Pera and Nişantaşı, Eyüp and Balat, Samatya and the islands, Bakırköy and Yenikapı . . .'

'I take it I may have confidence in the authorities? That they are in control of the situation?' asked Adnan Bey. The police chief hesitated.

'Not according to my colleagues in the city, Adnan Bey. There has been widespread destruction of property, often belonging to members of minority communities, and many buildings are on fire. Reports are of casualties.'

'Casualties?'

'Yes, sir,' said the aide. 'The governor judges it essential that you both return immediately to the city.'

'One of my cars is ready to drive you back,' added the police officer.

'Thank you, gentlemen,' said the president. 'Perhaps you might leave us for a minute while we gather our belongings. We'll join you at the front of the station.' The president waited for the aide and police chief to withdraw before removing his steel-rimmed reading

glasses, as he might have done in his younger years when readying
himself for a brawl.

'So you saw to it that Zorlu got his demonstration, it seems,' he
said in even but glacial tones.

'You yourself saw his telegram from London,' explained Adnan
Bey. 'That we back his tough talk at the conference with something
to show the Greeks that we are serious about Cyprus.'

'Limited street protests, then – a few hotheads letting off steam
over that business yesterday in Salonica. Wave a few Turkish flags,
burn a few Greek ones, smash the odd window, agreed. But casualties? Buildings on fire? What arrangements were made?'

'A limited show . . .'

'A limited show? But not so limited as to exclude burning buildings? Casualties?'

'Nothing was said of casualties.'

The police car was waiting outside the station, the passenger
doors open, its lights flashing. They sped back to the city where the
first signs of trouble showed at Pendik; smashed shopfronts, overturned vehicles and the smell of smoke. As a mob spilled out of an
alley into the street, brandishing crowbars and yelling 'First your
houses, then your lives,' the driver swerved, accelerating away.

'Well,' said the president, 'it looks like you've a full-blown pogrom
on your hands. My advice? Blame it on the commies.'

Shortly after midnight the government placed Istanbul under
martial law. By the early hours the military had brought the riots
under control. Daylight revealed Sherman tanks patrolling the
streets of a burned and broken city. Over breakfast at the Caribe-
Hilton buffet the Interpol delegates learned that the lunch the city's
beleaguered chief of police had arranged for them was cancelled as
the restaurant had been razed. 'It was,' an American correspondent
wrote, 'as if every third shop on Madison Avenue and half of those
on the Avenue of the Americas had been ripped apart and their goods
strewn on the streets.' That evening saw the delegates confined at the
Hilton where they and their Turkish hosts mingled with the newly

arrived bankers from the International Monetary Fund. The two congresses, Fleming reported, 'lugubriously danced at the centre of the curfew'. There ensued a flurry of cancellations, especially among the delegates for the Conference on Byzantine Studies, the Greeks heading home on the advice of their government which considered 'its alliance with Turkey de facto in a state of suspension'.

In the aftermath of the riots the authorities rounded up a number of leftists, the army in Istanbul padlocked all trades-union premises, and in the National Assembly the prime minister gave a speech blaming the disturbances on the communists. Few believed him, not least because his regular boasts that barely a Red remained at large appeared to contradict any such possibility. The newspapers expressed the general view that a demonstration 'in favour of Turk-ish claims on Cyprus' – secretly stoked by the government, even to the point of issuing local police and military units with instructions not to intervene – had got completely out of hand; the authorities were even said to have been behind the Salonica bomb. The desecra-tion – 'of a type more proper to the Middle Ages', as one witness put it – was to have devastating consequences for the city and its people. For the terrorised and mutilated victims of the riots as well as for the wider Rum community whose members from that night lost any faith that they had a future in their ancestral city; over the following decades they would leave in their tens of thousands until only a handful remained. For Graeco-Turkish relations and all those who since the War of Independence had worked for reconciliation. For Conrad Hilton and his 'fabulous modern hotel', that shining symbol of Turkey's place among the modern Western nations, now under martial law in a smashed and smouldering city. And for Adnan Menderes, whose secret manoeuvrings had so tragically misfired, plunging the city into an explosion of violent sectarianism. It was a gross miscalculation at what would prove the midpoint of his rule, and the first intimation of its end.

*

I left the Hilton for nearby Taksim Square, the traditional venue for the city's political gatherings, demonstrations and May Day meetings. On the northern edge of the square I came to a small park, Gezi, where an old man sat beneath the plane trees, reading a broadsheet which he held so close to his failing eyes that it might have been a riot shield. On another bench lay a worn young man. Alive to the hazards of rough sleeping, he had slipped an arm through the straps of his rucksack, securing them in the crook of his tightly closed elbow before surrendering to sleep; as for his laceless shoes, evidently a less coveted target, these were neatly stowed beneath the bench. People exercised their dogs.

Three years earlier, when I happened to be in Istanbul on a travel assignment, crowds of dog walkers, environmentalists and other park partisans had gathered in this very spot. They had determined upon a peaceful occupation of this tatty but cherished space which Erdoğan, without regard for the park's legally protected status, had vowed to develop; he meant to turn Gezi into a shopping complex, but one which in its symbolically charged design honoured the Ottoman barracks which had once stood on the site. It was 29 May 2013, the 560th anniversary of the Conquest, an especially big day for Erdoğan who spent it opening various development and infrastructure projects. He began by laying the foundation stone at the site of the Third Bosphorus Bridge, then opened Istanbul's new centre for archery, an activity which enjoyed Erdoğan's support, largely because Mehmet the Conqueror's forces were said to have excelled at it. At the ceremony Erdoğan reprised the Conqueror's commitment to defend the beliefs and freedoms of the residents of the city. 'In our civilisation,' Erdoğan declared, 'conquest is not just about taking countries and cities; it is also about the conquering of hearts.'

Not that any such conquering extended to the hearts of the Gezi lot; that rabble were not about to stand in Erdoğan's way. The police waited until dawn the following day to charge the park's occupiers. They set off tear gas, torched tents and kicked out at the emerging protesters, catching one of them with a brutal blow to the testicles. Phone footage of the violence spread rapidly, drawing in

sympathisers. By the time I happened upon Gezi that afternoon –
researching a story, ironically, about Istanbul's open spaces – the
park was frantic with activity. Placards had been hung from the plane
trees, pledging to protect them, and environmentalists were assembling tents and tables, and organising protest petitions. The protesters
had been joined by activists of every stripe united in their opposition
to a regime they condemned as authoritarian, divisive, corrupt and
venal. Anti-capitalists were busy painting cartoons of Erdoğan with
dollar signs for eyes, and leftist slogans proclaimed that 'Taksim is
Red and Will Stay Red!' Other protesters were daubing messages –
'We are Taksim's Sentries; We can Stop this Project' and 'Live Like
a Tree, Single and Free, and Like a Forest, in Brotherhood' – on bed
sheets which could have done with a wash, though the signs of soil-
ing were at least evidence of how rapidly the defensive effort had
mobilised. In a commune atmosphere students sat on the grass, in
earnest conversations which the signs hanging from the branches
described as forums. Vendors sold corn cobs and bottles of water and
beer. Defence committees distributed fliers which advised on protective strategies against pepper spray and tear gas. Film crews wandered
the encampment, watching for newsworthy developments, while the
police took up position beyond the partitions erected by the park's
would-be developers. In the shadow of the riot vehicles and water
cannons they awaited further orders.

    In a series of dawn raids the police baton-charged the Gezi
protesters and doused them with pepper spray. These crude deter-
rents only caused the protests to spread across Istanbul, then the
country, where neighbourhoods soon rang with the clatter of sauce-
pans, the traditional soundtrack of civil discontent.

    Turkey descended into mayhem; but where an old man now read
and a young one slept, an enchanted calm had prevailed. Behind
barricades of burned-out police buses a crowd of idealists, activists
and citizens made their stand. Nationalists, communists and Kurds
even put aside their enmities and broke bread together, the heroes
on their respective banners – Atatürk, Nazım and Abdullah Öcalan,
the Kurdish leader imprisoned on the island of Imralı in the Sea of

Marmara – united in common cause. Fans of the city's three big football clubs, otherwise sworn to mutual and perpetual contempt, manned the barricades in T-shirts which read 'Istanbul United'. LGBT activists, housewives and bankers all lent a hand, installing a library stacked with protest volumes, a kitchen and a first-aid centre. They raised a stage and a mosque, and put on yoga sessions, Quran readings and piano recitals. Vendors did a brisk trade in swimming goggles and surgical masks, which were said to offer protection, of sorts, against pepper spray or tear gas.

It was reported that across the country some 11,000 people were treated for exposure to tear gas over the following fortnight. Additional injuries, eighty or so according to estimates, were inflicted by the tear-gas canisters as they rained down on the battle grounds. Protesters took to protecting themselves with hard hats which soon proved popular not only for their practical value but for their innate personality; they proliferated, often in fairground pinks and yellows which did much to establish them as cherished symbols of defiance. They became the national headgear of Gezi, the natural complement of the goggles and the surgical masks, the whole get-up suggestive of some dystopia-themed fancy-dress party; there was joy in this make-shift rig, even if defending the territory in it was like facing down machine guns with pitchforks. That this was all they had – the hats, the masks and their homespun courage – made the protesters magnificent. And that these outfits so contrasted with those of their persecutors – military-issue body armour, boots, shields, helmets, visors, batons, munitions and gas masks – exposed the riot police to derision.

After a few weeks the police resolved to end the Gezi insurrection. One night in June they stormed the park, trampling the tents and stalls, and scattering the protesters who fled for the safety of nearby hotels whose staff were known to be sympathetic. Among these was the Hilton where several witnesses were to capture the ensuing scenes on their phones. The footage opens as the police, all in black but for their futuristic white riot helmets, burst into the hotel foyer like a sci-fi extermination squad. With their batons drawn they appear ready to rumble, intent on dishing it out, when something stops them in their tracks. It's as if a spell has been cast, the pervasive refinement of the surroundings – the shiny glass and the impeccably presented staff, the vases of lilies, the vitrine displays of silk ties, fountain pens and monogrammed cufflinks, the perfumed guests, the cultivated foreign utterances, the nuts in silver bowls, the late-night notes of the piano and the ping of the elevator – reining in the police. These men know, even in their base adrenalised state, that the random violence which they have committed so freely on the streets has no place here.

It seems that the hotel's civilising ambience has saved the day. But protesters and police remain in close proximity, the mood ugly as the two sides eyeball each other, and only a series of timely managerial interventions keeps the violence at bay. As for a peaceful resolution, it's clear that the police should leave, and in better order than they arrived, if ever the protesters are to feel confident that it's safe for them also to go. The problem for the police, now that brutalising the protesters no longer seems an option, is finding some means to demonstrate their authority which will allow them to leave with their honour intact. An arrest or two would suffice, but no protester is about to submit to arbitrary detention. It's some time before one of the officers calls his men close to share with them his plan.

When the police break from their huddle, like players with secret field instructions, it's to mingle among the protesters whom they set about relieving of their hard hats. The move is unaccountable, wrongfooting protesters who find themselves deprived of their hard hats before they have had time to react. Others, though, have fastened their chin straps tight by the time the police reach them; though they do not resist, they refuse to assist with the confiscation of their property. The police are drawn into close-up encounters with the protesters – lawyers among them – who observe that no law forbids the wearing of hard hats. Is it only the police, says one, who get to protect themselves? Ah, to make the fight fairer, another suggests sarcastically. Or is it, says somebody, that the police prefer the pink hats to their regulation-issue white ones?

The police complete their job. Beneath tottering stacks of pink
and yellow hard hats they troop out of the foyer to a rising murmur
of contempt. Some of the officers turn to confront the laughter at
their backs before, thinking better of it, they file into the night. The
violence has been stemmed, but in the summer of 2013 it seems
there are battles ahead.

CHAPTER SIX

21 September 1956

A newspaper boy is tried for shouting a headline

Nazım's kaleidoscopic *Human Landscapes From My Country* opens in Istanbul's Haydarpaşa Station. An assorted cast of politicians, students, officials, drifters, businessmen – and prisoners – gather beneath the fairy-tale turrets, steep dormered roofs and decorative porticos of this historic terminus on the Asian shores of the Bosphorus.

It is a spring day in 1941, the year Nazım had in fact begun work on his great prose poem when he was three years into the absurd and unconscionable sentence that would confine him to Bursa prison until 1950. Nazım's defiant spirit and the solace he found in his art, turning the harshest experiences to account, is eloquently expressed in the pride of place he gives in the opening scenes of his sprawling masterpiece to a lowly group of prisoners. For their criminal taste in literature, which Nazım wholeheartedly shared, these 'politicals' are being dispatched to jails in the Anatolian interior. Among those awaiting the Ankara train is dockyard worker Fuat, imprisoned at nineteen 'for reading a book with two friends', and writer Halil, who has learned from experience how best to turn the pages, despite the handcuffs, of the books he devours even as his captors shuttle him between prisons. Incarceration is a predicament these erudite prisoners treat with the same airy disdain of their confrere creator, joking and laughing as they mount the station steps at the point of their guards' bayonets.

Seventy-five years later, on a spring morning of my own, I was also taking the train to Ankara – and my destination was a prison. Like the prisoners, my own journey should have begun at Haydarpaşa. But that Rhineland-style schloss, the kaiser's gift to the sultan, had closed for restoration; boarding was instead to take place at Pendik, a suburb on the Asian side, where the high-speed Ankara line currently terminated.

Getting to Pendik was a haul – only relieved by the satisfying irony that the newly constructed metro station where I began my journey east was located directly beneath Sirkeci, the decrepit terminus where the fabled Orient Express to Venice and Paris had once begun journeys west; an apt reflection, perhaps, of the about-turn lately performed by a Turkish leadership apparently uninterested in maintaining good relations with the Europeans. Marmaray, the line this new underground station served, ran through a tunnel beneath the Bosphorus and out past a string of brand-new stations. I travelled east as far as the incomplete line allowed before a series of shiny escalators bore me back to the daylight. I followed Adnan Menderes Boulevard – not the first time I had noticed streets named after the man – to Pendik Station where passengers were heaving suitcases through the airport-style security checks.

My carriage was unremittingly modern, with numbered blue-plush seats whose occupants were busy locating sockets for laptops and phone chargers. There were announcements in English and a refreshments trolley stacked with film-wrapped teabags and disposable plastic cups. The train pulled out on schedule, with neither the statutory clank nor the valedictory whistle that this storied route – from the sultans' waterside metropolis to the Republicans' steppe bastion – so merited. TV screens preferred to dwell on the miracle that was Turkey's transformed rail network and of the man credited with the high-speed trains, the new metro lines and the rest. Barely had our journey begun before another of Erdoğan's vaunted achievements – Turkey's biggest suspension bridge, due to open any day – loomed beyond the windows at Gebze.

For my part, I preferred Nazım's personable prisoners to Erdoğan's vanity projects, losing myself instead in the period sights the characters in *Human Landscapes* had glimpsed through the barred windows of the guard's van on that fictional day in 1941: a woman in a yellow dress hanging out washing beneath a pistachio tree; folk streaming down to the beach beneath broad straw hats; an aged black eunuch, relic of an ousted world, taking the air on the station bench at Göztepe; and a group of girls on the way home from school hugging books to their chests. Nazım scattered his imaginary worlds with books just as they littered his life, glorying in them for the beliefs they freely expressed. It heartened me that I had thought to bring my copy of his book along; and that the book should now be replicating the exact journey of the characters within its pages, following Fuat, Halil and their companions down the tracks to the capital and to the same prison awaiting them there.

Beyond Sapanca I lifted my gaze to the window as our train left the water's edge and began labouring towards the plateau. At Arifiye rivers swirled coffee-brown in the breaks between the bank-side alders. On the high flat lands tiled roofs showed beneath the distant fuzz of poplars, the sunlight catching on the metalled minaret cones, and long furrows tailed tractors beneath gusted clouds of dust. Factories and depots stood in broken barbed-wire hems, their high gates topped with red initials in antiquated fonts, while in the corner of the TV screen a speedometer pushed past 200 kilometres per hour. As the train accelerated so the jolts grew fainter, finally vanishing altogether, and beyond the window a young boy beside a row of spinach had barely raised his head to us before he was wrenched away, he, hoe and horizons, and in the toss of its tail a chestnut horse had blurred and was gone, and then we were slowing for the city of Eskişehir.

We made Ankara – almost 500 kilometres away – in under four hours. As I stepped onto the platform I was reminded of Adnan Bey's triumphal return after the Gatwick incident, and the celebratory carnage which greeted him – then of the recent slaughter which

had occurred here. On 10 October 2015 hundreds of demonstrators
– trade unionists, left-wing activists, pro-Kurdish groups, members
of peace organisations and students – gathered outside the station to
condemn the hostilities the government had lately renewed with the
Kurds, a conflict which by all accounts had reduced urban areas of
cities like Diyarbakır to rubble and caused gross suffering to resident populations in the process. The atmosphere was insistent but
good-natured, the demonstrators holding hands as they chanted,
when two suicide bombers blew over a hundred of them into
memory. Six months on only a few desiccated stems remained of the
vast bank of garlands which had accumulated in the days following
Turkey's deadliest terror attack. A display emblazoned with doves
and photographs of the dead appealed for Endurance, Peace and
Democracy.

*

After the 1954 harvest failed, so it did the following year. A succession of droughts saw Turkey go from the world's fourth largest
exporter of grain to a net importer. The inflow of aid also dwindled
as US and European donors increasingly lost patience with Adnan
Bey's headline plan to get there fast, his full-tilt construction of
roads, dams, cement factories, refineries, pipelines, power stations,
processing plants, silos and ports punching an ever-widening hole in
the country's reserves.

Finance Minister Polatkan resorted to printing money. The subsequent inflationary surge, which caused prices to rise by 35 per cent
in six months, led consumers to hoard what goods they could lay
their hands on. The government imposed rationing on such basics as
sugar, salt and cigarettes. The embattled Polatkan attempted to resist
the downward pressure on the Turkish lira by setting the national
currency at 2.8 to the American dollar at a time when the greenback
fetched fully fourteen lira on the black market. American wholesale buyers responded by declining to bid on Turkey's tobacco crop.
The country's other export commodities – wheat, cotton, raisins,

hazelnuts, copper, chrome, antimony, figs, chestnuts, mohair, medic-
inal opium and rose oil – were also priced out of overseas markets,
which led reserves to fall yet further.

The lack of foreign currency throttled imports; those without
dollars struggled to get hold of tools, soap, pots and pans, razor
blades, needles, bath plugs, picture hooks and horseshoe nails. There
were shortages of petrol and tyres; and though the country had
plenty of new roads, the lucky few with the wherewithal to travel
them passed the time counting the scores of broken-down buses and
trucks that they encountered. The situation was as dire in the fields
where the lack of spare parts caused 'an unduly high casualty rate
among farm machinery'. Production facilities wound down, and
when the unequal struggle to procure the necessary raw materials
caused Istanbul's light-bulb factory to cease production in 1955, a
darkness overwhelmed the country that did not lift with the dawn.
Shortages even of coffee, 'as tragic for the Turks as no tea would be
for the British', offered a damning illustration of economic failure.

In the villages, where tea from the Black Sea was generally
preferred, not least because it was cheap and free from coffee's taint
of metropolitan refinement, it did not matter so much. The villagers,
synched with the seasons and more used to making do than city folk,
could get by without light bulbs. With generous wheat payments
further easing the pain, the affection for Adnan Bey remained as
warm as ever.

But in the towns and cities, where inflation gnawed at static state
salaries, life grew harder by the day. Newspapers like *Vatan* no
longer covered the dedication ceremonies for Mr Menderes's new
dams, factories and ports with the same enthusiasm. Instead, they
began carrying photographs of the sugar queues. They wrote of the
weeks people must wait while cargoes of coffee crossed the seas from
Brazil or Colombia; people, they added, who could hardly be blamed
for calling their country Yokistan – the Land Where Nothing is
Available.

*

Ankara sprawled to a horizon of arid brown hills. From the station it was a short walk to the old town which clung to dusty slopes beneath the castle. In Youth Park the cafes stood empty, and ducks stirred the murky shallows of the pedalo ponds. On Republic Street clots of grey-clad citizens were gathered at bus stops, their eyes narrowed against the sun, its glare fierce at these altitudes. I walked up to Nation Square where a statue of Atatürk, in military garb, appeared on horseback amidst citizens and soldiers in heroic poses, oblivious to the weight of the Soviet-supplied howitzer shells hoisted on their shoulders, and to the pigeon shit in which they were splattered. I watched families arrange themselves to be photographed before this national monument to the independence struggle, wondering what they knew of the square's less palatable associations. There was no display board to inform them, for example, that here Atıf Hoca had been hanged in 1926 for writing his pamphlet in protest at Atatürk's reforms.

But at the nearby Ulucanlar prison, where the doomed cleric was held prior to his execution, these facts were fully acknowledged; walking to the prison, along the broken pavements of the dusty tree-less lanes beneath the citadel, was to trace Atıf Hoca's last journey in reverse. When Ulucanlar closed in 2006, the inmates rehoused at a new facility outside the city, alternative proposals for the building included its conversion to a shoemakers' bazaar. But the local author-ity opted to keep Ulucanlar intact. When the building reopened in 2011, it was as a museum memorial to the many inmates real and fictional – Atıf Hoca, but also the criminalised bookworms in Nazım's *Human Landscapes*, plus Nazım himself and a litany of film-makers, journalists and editors – whose only crime had been to create, consume or circulate the written word.

Beyond the ticket booth metal doors once locked had been left open, pointedly, in perpetuity. I stepped into a narrow alley where the porcelain-coloured walls rose to a strip of blue sky. This outer corridor led via another metal door to a walled lane – called, yet again, Adnan Menderes Boulevard. I advanced into a concrete warren of maze complexity, all high-security walls and watchtowers, which eventually

brought me to the wards and exercise yards. These yards were feature-
less but for the photographs of prominent inmates displayed on the
walls. Here was Nazım, his guarded smile set in the sepia of a 1930s
summer day, here prominent 1970s inmates including the film-maker
Yilmaz Güney and the student activist Deniz Gezmiş.

A corridor hung with harsh lights was lined by the solitary cells;
through the door grilles I saw bare bed frames where pallid mannequins languished in poses of poetic despair. A soundtrack of groans,
sighs and screams accompanied the wide-eyed stares and the
disordered hair, the kicked-off shoes and the clenched cigarettes.
One of the wards was called the 'Hilton', the Istanbul hotel having
quickly established itself as a national byword for luxury; the nick-
name was an ironic reference to the modest extra space on offer in
the ward, and no doubt to the comparative civility and erudition of
the prominent politicals for whom it was reserved. On the concrete
floor were metal-framed bunk beds with neatly folded blankets, and
stands which displayed inmates' biographies. The photographs
showed studious men, mostly in glasses, in collars and ties, their
minds awash with opinions the authorities considered dangerous.
The captions revealed that many of these journalists, editors, propri-
etors and writers had served their time here during the late 1950s.
The freedoms Adnan Bey had so fervently championed when he first
came to power, and which the like of Ahmed Emin Yalman took to
signal a new democratic age, had not survived the decade.

*

In the course of turning Ulucanlar into a museum, the curators came
across three identical timbers, roughly twice a man's height, in the
prison attics. It turned out that these were gallows, of the distinctive
tripod design traditionally favoured in Turkey. Over the decades
eighteen men had been hanged from these wigwam-shaped timbers,
either in the prison yard or in the public setting of nearby Nation
Square. Among them were Atıf Hoca and also Berin Menderes's
relative – whose grim fate, after being falsely accused of conspiring

to assassinate Atatürk, would spur Berin Hanim's vain attempts to keep her own husband from politics.

Ottoman executioners of old were an imaginative lot, their competencies varying from the silken bowstring – the mode of bloodless dispatch reserved for royal pretenders – to the weighted sacks in which they stitched disfavoured concubines before dumping them into the Bosphorus. But by the nineteenth century such graphically creative practices had long ceased; and in 1858 further reforms saw the Ottomans adopt the French penal code. By mandating the mode of execution generally favoured across western Europe – hanging – the empire dissociated itself from barbaric Arabian practices like beheading and stoning, as well as from the firing squad, that Slavic preference which the Ottomans appeared to find singularly distasteful.

Barely had the Ottoman authorities followed the European lead, however, than reformers in the West began introducing further procedural amendments. To ensure against death by asphyxiation, the agonisingly slow end which victims of hanging commonly suffered, the 'long drop' was introduced by means of a trap door. A length of fall, based upon the condemned prisoner's body weight, was calculated to break the neck without decapitating the man – which it invariably was – and affording him the comfort of a quick and essentially dignified end.

In Ottoman Turkey, where an entrenched traditionalism constantly resisted over-identification with European liberalism, these developments were never adopted. Until capital punishment was finally outlawed in 2004, the gallows and stool were retained, sometimes with farcically grisly results. When in 1909 Sultan Abdul Hamid II's hated enforcer, Twisted Beard Pasha, stepped off the stool in Istanbul's Eminönü Square, the fall failed to see him off; the combined weight of two attendants, directed 'to swing on his legs for several minutes', was required before 'the once-dreaded head lay harmless in the noose'. This left humane executioners, or those who aspired to competence, to develop more efficient ways of

dispatch. One was to hitch the noose at an angle, close to the collar-
bone on one side and tight by the ear on the other, so that even a
short fall should serve to jerk the neck laterally and so snap the
crucial vertebrae – which, if it gave Berin Menderes any solace, had
reportedly been effective in seeing off her relative.

Rather than appoint state executioners, as the Europeans did,
the Turks also persisted with another tradition: hiring gypsies to
do the work. It was an old custom, its origins lost, which reflected
an established contempt for gypsies whom Ottoman society
despised and mistrusted. The tradition also served to humiliate
the condemned, the high-born especially, by entrusting their
dispatch to those they so viscerally disdained. A defining measure
of a man's self-respect, of his calibre and courage, was to dismiss
his gypsy executioner's offer of an olive and glass of water, traditional signs of peace, before kicking away the stool himself.
Nazım, who lived under the perpetual threat of the gallows, hoped
to find such courage in himself: 'Death – a body swinging from a
rope,' he wrote in November 1933. 'My heart can't accept such a
death. But you can bet if some poor gypsy's hairy black spidery
hand slips a noose around my neck, they'll look in vain for fear in
Nazım's blue eyes!'

At Ulucanlar the gallows, complete with noose and stool, still
stood in one of the prison yards beneath a poplar tree. Around the
tripod a padlocked cage had been constructed to convey the
museum's support for Turkey's abolition of capital punishment. I
might have taken this imaginative installation as heartening evidence
that the country had put the past behind it, but only until I thought
of all the journalists and writers currently held on charges of terror-
ism and treason in Erdoğan's Turkey, and in the psychologically
brutal solitary confinement which was increasingly the norm under
Turkey's penal system. The tragedy of this remarkable museum,
having been brave enough to confront a past it at least thought done,
was that it in fact told of a present which with every day turned still
darker.

*

In 1956 the government of Adnan Menderes – who no longer cared to
hear what people were saying about him; not now that the journalists
had stopped asking grateful villagers gathered around newly installed
water fountains and turned instead to people in the queues for sugar
or petrol or by cleaned-out shelves of the coffee shops – tightened the
press laws. These new restrictions added to the ones the Democrats
had first introduced two years earlier, and to general dismay. The
1954 legislation threatened those responsible for publishing news
deemed false, or liable to impair the political or financial integrity of
the state, with prison sentences of up to three years. It afforded exceptional protection, furthermore, to the very people who had passed the
new laws, stipulating that anyone found guilty of invading the private
life or insulting the honour of deputies or government officials would
not only face imprisonment but be denied, preposterously, the right
to prove the substance of what they had written.

    In the hands of prosecutors and judges indifferent to due process,
especially if it interfered with their toadying, these laws led many

pressmen to be charged with insulting leading figures in government. Among the many who served time in Ulucanlar's 'Hilton' prison ward in the late 1950s was eighty-year-old Hüseyin Cahit Yalçın, one of Turkey's most distinguished voices, whose alleged insult of Adnan Menderes earned him a sentence of twenty-six months and twenty days.

The consequences of the 1956 laws proved surreal, with a newspaper boy arrested in Ankara's Nation Square for shouting a headline – 'Finance Minister Resigns!' – deemed offensive to the Democrat Party. In a landmark case the author of a work of fiction, *The Puppets*, and the editor responsible for the novel's serialisation were convicted on charges of causing offence to the Democrat Party. Even jokes were deemed a crime, as a magazine editor learned to his cost after being fined and jailed for publishing one which told of a visit to a Turkish news-stand.

'A copy of *Freedom*, please,' says the man.

'We don't have *Freedom*,' retorts the vendor.

'Then I'll have *Life*.'

'We don't have that either.'

'As I should have guessed,' sighs the man. 'For there can be no life where there is no freedom.'

For his part, Adnan Bey increasingly wondered what use critical journalists were to him; what use dissenting party colleagues, carping academics and a disruptive opposition were, for that matter. It was his pleasure, serving the people; his problem was with all those, in press and parliament, who liked to doubt, even deride, his efforts. The requirement to consult on every project, to compromise on every plan served only to slow him down. He was better off relying on his own energies, ideas and organisational abilities to run the country, as the people had tasked him to do.

It seemed that democracy disagreed with Adnan Bey, which appeared to negate him as a democrat. Unless, that is, he could find a way of disagreeing with democracy's definition – by making it mean something else. He must revise the word's import – by stripping it back to first principles; that the people, as he reminded crowds at his rallies, were the only power in the land. It was they who had

voted him into office; and it was under their mandate – what Adnan
Bey took to calling *Milli Irade* or the National Will – that he would
rule. The intelligentsia, the journalists and professors especially,
might not like the loss of the influence they had enjoyed under the
single-party state. But the truth was they now had no greater say
than goatherds or porters. For this was a democracy in which it was
Adnan Bey's sworn duty to attend to the wishes of the masses – those
who had elected him – rather than, as he disdainfully put it, to 'the
shouts and criticism of a handful of intellectuals'.

Milli Irade played so well at the rallies that Adnan Bey made the
persuasive phrase his own. In fact, it implied a drastic reduction of
civil freedoms, which not only saw consultative arrangements abandoned but the democratic process limited to the ballot box, as the
British ambassador noted. Turkey, said the ambassador, seemed to
suffer from its 'own brand of semantic confusion over the use of the
word *democracy*'. Many people, he observed, found it 'more or less
normal that the political power won at the polls should be used to
deny to others the exercise of democratic rights other than those of
voting in elections every few years'.

The international press turned on the man it had lately lionised.
Mr Menderes, the *New York Times* observed, had apparently developed the 'conviction that he can plot Turkey's future with the
certainty of a blueprint and it follows that whoever opposes him is a
traitor'. It concluded that 'the democratic principles espoused after
1946 were nothing but a thin veneer'.

All of which made sense of the name they had given the prison's
main thoroughfare, no less ironically meant than the 'Hilton' ward;
rather than remember Adnan Menderes for the injustices he was to
suffer, like so many of the country's boulevards did, this one in fact
called him to account, the jailer of journalists, for the serial injustices
he himself had dished out.

*

I left the prison for the castle and headed into the oldest part of the
city. I followed crooked lanes which I had walked back in my time

living here, the cobbles at their shiniest where the slope steepened, and passed timbered houses hung with rusted downpipes and stove flues; the upper-story window *kafes*, the lattice-wood shutters which had preserved Ottoman women from the gaze of the street, were now in their final decay. The *ezan* sounded, deepening my nostalgia for these neighbourhoods, and at the brick minaret of the thirteenth-century Aslanhane mosque I halted to watch the old men gather at the entrance. I wondered if these were the rheumatoid, rackety ghosts of the young men who had once welcomed me here, and for a moment thought of slipping off my own shoes to join them in that warm, walnut-wooded interior. But I pushed on, passing through the outer gates of the castle where Roman statues were crudely tiered into the Ottoman fortifications. Beyond the inner bailey I climbed to the high battlements where I found myself alone. Beneath a sky fading to cobalt I sat and looked out over the city, now home to several million people.

I wondered at the place which not a century before had been 'a town still chiefly composed of mud'. In 1922, months after the victory of Mustafa Kemal's armies in the War of Independence, the English correspondent Grace Ellison visited to discover dirt streets and a few hole-ridden filthy inns. According to Ellison, not quite sure whether she should be horrified or impressed, there were just two pianos in the town, one of them in Mustafa Kemal's residence, and the French Embassy was housed on a floor of the old station building. Yet it was on this expanse of steppe, far from the waterfront palaces of the traitorous sultans and beyond the reach, as Ellison put it, 'of possible interference from dreadnoughts', where Mustafa Kemal had centred the new nation.

As I watched, the lights went on across districts that Ellison had known as orchards; in homes and hotels, kebab houses and shopping malls, in the opera house and the ministries, the station, stadia and the parks. Across the thickening stipple, threaded by lines of head-lit traffic, I tried to make out the neighbourhood where I had lived when I first came to Turkey in the autumn of 1984.

CHAPTER SEVEN

27 October 1957

Adnan Bey calls early elections

Turkey had suffered a coup, its third, shortly before I first set foot in the country. At the time I knew nothing of much, certainly not of coups, only that Ankara looked unimprovably like the sort of place where one might happen. A comfortable upbringing in southern England had not prepared me for this austere steppe city. Sagging tiers of sandbags still lined streets which bore the impress of tank tracks. Crumbling and blistered apartment blocks wore the livery beiges, buffs and greens of the correctional institute, the rust-streaked balconies hung with cracked plastic signs advertising the services of lawyers, dentists and accountants, where German umlauts and French cedillas swarmed among diacritical marks of an altogether alien cast.

The school, where I was to teach English to mature students, put me up on Meşrutiyet Caddesi – Constitution Street. My top-floor apartment looked out over Ankara's gimcrack roofscapes, a vista of sagging brown tiles, stained chimney stacks and TV aerials frequented by stumbling crows, the whole dominated by the mysterious construction project taking place on the nearby Kocatepe hill. The city's few trees, planted along streets that aspired to pass for boulevards, were spindly on account of the effort the roots had put into forcing the concrete slabs; experience soon taught me the same respect I noted among the residents for these wildly canted pavements.

Imagine my delight, then, to discover that any correspondence between the shabby city and its citizens did not exist. My students, laden with gifts, turned out to hold even rookie teachers in high regard. Lawyers, dentists and accountants, housewives and administrators, secretaries, officials, university students and army officers, they also appeared determined to correct any impression their scuffed and soiled city might have given. With a fervour that transcended their limited English, they extolled Ankara for its sacred significance as Atatürk's operational headquarters in the War of Independence, as capital of his new nation and as his final resting place, splendidly impervious to any idea that a city's comforts, sights or facilities should also count for something. Ankara's lack of sophistication appeared only to have deepened their attachment. They considered it miraculous, no less so than Atatürk's military feats, that the great leader's engineers and architects should have conjured the new capital from a setting denied all the advantages so patently enjoyed by the old one. Though the diplomats were known to grumble, these students saw the capital's relocation – the fabled shores of the Bosphorus for a malarial marsh sunk in sere steppe at the foot of an Anatolian citadel – as cause for celebration. Ankara was where the nation had started anew; the capital stood for self-respect, a renunciation of Ottoman decadence for an upright and honest Anatolian vigour, which made these Turks proud of the city and of their place in it.

In their ambition to make something of themselves my students recognised English as a key attainment which they were determined to acquire, and to my own lasting gratitude; for their inexhaustible enthusiasm to learn, which made teaching them such a pleasure, also inspired the curiosity I had long sought in myself. Into the breaks between lessons, over glasses of sugared black tea and rough Turkish cigarettes, I not only fielded their questions but shoehorned in plenty of my own. So this was Atatürk, the man on the walls and the banknotes, and whose mausoleum – as the students repeatedly urged – I must visit? What else did they advise me to see? What of all these dates which the streets took as names? And what could they tell me of the building site which I could see, and hardly fail to hear, from my apartment window?

As autumn turned to winter, bringing chill north winds from Crimea, I turned up my collar to walk the city, and so my own attachment to the place deepened. I explored the old town and delighted in the gloaming views from the castle battlements. I discovered the mosques, tentatively at first, as if I should expect intolerance there. But at the Aslanhane mosque, where I often lingered to admire the thirteenth-century timber interiors and the exquisite azure tilework, the neighbourhood's worshippers – none of whom were in a position to finance English lessons – would silently clasp my hand in eloquent expressions of brotherhood. In the evenings I sat and read while the arc lights beyond my window illuminated the cranes, the jack hammers and concrete mixers at work on Kocatepe hill. As the first snows fell, the flakes mixing with the coal smuts to form brindled drifts along the windowsills, I began making a few inroads into the formidably difficult language and the giddying history. To the consternation of my students, I took to visiting the neighbouring cities on the central steppe – Kayseri, Afyon and Konya – which they deplored as benighted, backward and religious, their own dream itineraries rarely extending beyond Istanbul's more chic quarters or summer resorts like Bodrum and Antalya. Their bemusement at my enthusiasm for the old town's mosques further signalled the divergence in our interests. As I began to ask the students what I judged more interesting questions, so their readiness to answer appeared to wane, as if those questions must have taxed their English if not their knowledge. In time I realised that the students preferred not to answer when I asked, for example, what business a colonel in full military uniform – khaki green, with yellow braid – had running an English language school; and why their capital, with only neighbourhood mosques like Aslanhane, had nothing to compare with the great domes of Istanbul.

Working all this out, along with the hydra of questions that every answer spawned, has occupied me ever since.

*

A story told of a diplomat, usually identified as British or French, who attended an official reception shortly after being posted to Ankara during the Second World War. According to this tale, which we may best understand as a peevish swipe at the arrogant disinterest which Turks alleged against the major European powers, the diplomat asked the prime minister about the pointy things that he had observed all over Istanbul but which did not seem to exist in the capital.

'Those pointy things,' replied the prime minister, 'mark our places of prayer. Our mosques. This being our new capital, we are yet to build them here.'

It was a gracious and patient answer, and more diplomatic than the question, but disingenuous. To judge by the abundant construction – of stations and stadia, ministries and offices, universities, lycées, opera house and the rest – which had taken place since the 1920s, when German and Austrian architects were first commissioned to plan Ankara's new city, the Turks had had every opportunity to endow the capital with mosques by the 1940s. The truth was that Atatürk's devotees took active pride in the city's lack of mosques; Ankara's was a skyline without minarets – the only world capital, according to Ahmed Emin Yalman, without a major place of worship. They condemned every mosque as a breeding ground for provincial fatalism and inertia – every minaret, as the phrase went, 'a tombstone underneath which there lies a Turkish village'. The capital's citizens, their minds as modern as the city rising around them, had no need for mosques. As for those mosques in the old town, home to stubborn pockets of reaction, it was assumed that if the nation's progress towards rational enlightenment did not do for their congregations, or if decrepitude did not cause the mosques' tired foundations to give way, then the natural course of events would soon enough see off their ageing congregants.

But not even Atatürk, it seemed, could cure his people of Islam. Within years of his death tentative voices were raised in support of a landmark mosque for the capital. To this end a foundation was established, though not until the 1950s did it attract substantial support. The central hilltop at Kocatepe, which overlooked the capital's ministries, was identified as a site and acquired in 1956. Prime Minister Menderes lent his support, presenting the foundation with the proceeds from the sale of a string of English thoroughbred horses. The prime minister also gave his backing to the national competition which the foundation announced in 1957, inviting architects to submit designs for the mosque.

It proved an explosively divisive scheme, the more so because the mosque's hilltop location expressly challenged Atatürk's mausoleum for domination of the capital's skyline. The Kemalists were outraged by a proposal they considered nothing less than blasphemous; the sultans might have raised their mosques on the hills of Istanbul, but in the secular capital, the heights were reserved for a purer purpose. Ankara's hills were for heroes, a title no Democrat deserved, least of all Menderes whose private life, increasingly the subject of lurid conjecture, hardly qualified him as a champion of Islam. To his adversaries the prime minister's high-profile support for a landmark mosque in the capital could only be a desperate attempt to bolster his popularity – the state of the economy being such, they pointed out, that mosques was the only card Adnan Bey had left to play.

By the autumn of 1957 the country's finances were in tatters, as the international media described in terms that would have meant imprisonment for their Turkish counterparts. With Zorlu's and Polatkan's missions to secure new loans ending in failure, *Time* Magazine likened the Menderes government – 'backed up against a wall, fighting off creditors one by one' – to 'a horse-opera hero picking off the members of an Indian war party'. Its policies, said to have caused 'economists of international repute to raise their hands in horror', were compared to a 'bus confronted with a swollen ford of uncertain depth', the driver convinced that 'the best thing to do is put his foot on the accelerator and keep going at all costs'. No less an authority than *The Economist* described Turkey as 'an economist's nightmare'.

With no sign in sight of an upturn, the government called early elections for 27 October 1957. It adopted a campaign strategy which appeared to vindicate opposition suspicions, shamelessly presenting the Democrats as the party of Allah. Any pretence of a commitment to secularism was abandoned as Democrat politicians went out of their way to be photographed at Friday prayers, brazenly shoehorning themselves into sacrifice shots. They openly consorted with sheikhs, those outcasts of former regimes, who reciprocated by lending their official backing to Adnan Bey's campaign, with one describing a dream in which the Prophet had given the prime minister the seal of state by way of confirming his fitness to continue running the country. Other holy men warned their congregations that any vote cast for the opposition was effectively a vote against Islam itself. Democrat politicians decried the irreligious opposition for the calamitous moral decline which had attended their years in power.

In its close identification with Islam, the governing party abandoned any proportion, its electoral pamphlets warning in apocalyptic terms of the consequences of a win for the Republicans. The villagers, they said, could expect their houses to be raided and the Democrat faithful – the veterans of 14 May 1950 – taken out and hanged. Allah Himself would be proscribed, with those who persisted in worshipping Him shot in the back of the head. Moreover, the peasants would be mercilessly tricked, with prices quadrupling even as the government beggared farmers by paying rock-bottom prices for their wheat. The courts would be shut down and replaced with revolutionary tribunals. The pamphlets went so far as to predict that a Republican victory would result in a mule giving birth to twins, a sure sign of the impending End, so that the people in their regret would remember Bayar and Menderes as saints.

As for life under Menderes, the campaign literature promised, the devout could look forward to an Islamic paradise on Earth. Istanbul would be established as a place of Islamic pilgrimage second only to Mecca, and the schools for Quran students would be transformed. The Democrats reminded voters of the many mosques – 15,000, it was claimed – that Adnan Bey's administration had built or restored,

including the great Süleymaniye in Istanbul, and the generous donations that the prime minister had provided out of his own pocket.
They would build mosques, the Democrats vowed, as they had built
factories – until a minaret was seen to stand beside every chimney.

The opposition, incensed, accused Menderes of abandoning the
nation to the forces of reaction. Dispatches from the hinterland
painted dire scenes of illegal turbans openly worn, of polygamous
marriages sealed and of the *yobaz*, 'the bearded fanatic of the Anatolian villages', once more 'muttering his Arabic prayers, sunk in
ignorance and prey to superstition'. Opposition newspapers, once
given to featuring Miss Turkey contestants, now carried photographs
of covered women, the so-called 'crows' or 'cockroaches', whose
infestations were said to have spread to every neighbourhood. The
nation's very future was at stake. In *Vatan* Ahmed Emin Yalman, now
vehement in his condemnation of the party he had once done so
much to help, denounced Turkey's headlong return to Ottoman
obscurantism; he framed the upcoming elections as a national struggle for freedom and independence no less momentous than Gallipoli
or the War of Independence.

*

The controversy surrounding the Kocatepe mosque raged for
decades, construction work on the project only beginning in the
1980s – when I witnessed from my apartment the building of what, I
duly learned, was then the biggest mosque in Turkey. I did not get
around to visiting it until 2016 when I crossed Constitution Street
one morning, wondering what I would find there of Aslanhane's
warmth, beauty and brotherhood.

A steep road not meant for walking led past buildings of indeter-
minate function, some stranded in various stages of non-completion,
the protective plastic films flapping ragged from the aluminium
window frames. Where the road forked, one half plunging into an
underpass, I slipped between lines of traffic to reach the top of the
hill where the mosque stood amidst parked cars.

From these drear landscapes the mosque's immense grey dome rose above a cascade of secondary domes and semi-domes, a confection of bubbles pegged by the minaret at each corner. On a site which not a century before had been steppe they had replicated a 400-year-old Ottoman imperial mosque – the minarets' triple balconies, the arches and the marble patterning especially recalling the Şehzade in Istanbul – but in a city of so little consequence to the Ottomans that it was otherwise largely devoid of their architectural heritage. If the effect was baffling then the intention was bluntly obvious; to glorify the Ottomans at their sixteenth-century apogee, then to eclipse them by exceeding the dimensions of even the Ottomans' greatest monuments. They had built Kocatepe to be bigger than the biggest of the imperial mosques, size having mattered in the 1980s – as it mattered still; the mosque had since been overtaken by yet vaster examples, most recently the mega-mosque Erdoğan was inflicting upon the former football grounds and picnic areas of Istanbul's Çamlıca Hill.

Kocatepe stood out, literally; a vast concrete base served, in the way of a soap box, to elevate the mosque high onto the skyline while also making basement space for facilities visitors might find useful. I was drawn through automatic doors into a discount supermarket but only to stay long enough to watch some plastic-wrapped vegetables, a pack of antiseptic wipes, some biscuits, a packet of aspirin and a sink plunger – an eloquently dispiriting insight into one shopper's life – go through the tills. I popped my head into a cafe and made desultory forays down corridors which led to clerical offices, toilets and locked doors. Signs pointed to an auditorium. Lifts descended to an underground car park. In my aimless wanderings I ran into a security man who appeared highly discomfited by my presence; hands paddling like ducks' feet, he ushered me out of the doors.

Over this assortment of prosaic functions a mosque said to accommodate 26,000 people squatted; the adjacent plaza had space for 75,000 or so souls. That morning, I found myself alone outside the mosque. Inside there were just three people. One lay sprawled in sleep and another stared at a phone screen while his father stood beneath the dome, palms outstretched. I found myself unmoved; in an attempt to sense more than the building's size, an attribute apt to induce astonishment rather than awe, I stretched out a palm of my own to touch one of the four great supporting columns – cut ashlar, with its agreeable granular feel in the Ottoman originals, but made here from smooth reinforced concrete.

I withdrew my hand as if scalded; that the mosque's builders had exceeded the Ottomans' architectural achievements by using materials to which their forebears had not had access was enough to disqualify Kocatepe, draining it of achievement and grace. Being big for big's sake, an idea of monumental vacancy, exposed the dome's vast extent as an empty boast, industrialising a space which could achieve a transcendence in the original mosques it so slavishly copied. Kocatepe, the first of a nationwide rash of pseudo-Ottoman mosques, appeared to me fake, inarticulate, unimaginative, regressive and suggestive of something still grosser: that it existed not to serve a religious community, like Aslanhane, but to host shows of strength by way of bolstering a political constituency. It had been raised not to the glory of God but so that regimes and their leaders might tighten their grip on power.

Adnan Bey had not lived to see the completion of this mosque, only the models which the competing architects had submitted for consideration in 1957. So I found myself back at the moment portrayed in the photograph which had first piqued my interest in the man – the prime minister presenting one such model to President Bayar, Foreign Minister Fatin Rüştü Zorlu and Finance Minister Hasan Polatkan; men fated to be remembered for having more in common than an interest, however cynically contrived, in mosques.

*

I was leaving Kocatepe when Metin texted with news from Istanbul: there had been a shooting outside the Court of Justice. The target was a distinguished journalist, Can Dündar, who was at the court to hear the judgement in the case the state had brought against him and a colleague, Erdem Gül, on charges of knowingly assisting a terrorist organisation, of espionage and disclosing state secrets. The gunman repeatedly cried 'Traitor!' before taking aim at Dündar and firing several shots. He missed his target but winged a nearby journalist before being overcome by Dündar's wife and members of his defence team.

Dündar's alleged crime was to have published, as editor-in-chief of the venerable left-leaning opposition newspaper *Cumhuriyet* (Republic), front-page articles and photographs which revealed that the state security service had been smuggling arms to jihadist groups in Syria. Turkish border guards had stopped three trucks purportedly delivering humanitarian supplies in which caches of missiles, crates of ammunition and mortar rounds were found concealed. This was not the first time, one of the drivers admitted, that they had carried such cargoes.

These drivers were duly investigated, but it would be the diligent border guards who were removed from their posts. And though *Cumhuriyet* had by common consent done precisely its job, landing a notable scoop in exposing illegal state practice to public scrutiny, President Erdoğan chose to condemn the newspaper's actions as treacherous. The president's involvement turned personal when he filed a lawsuit – to add to the 2,000 or so allegations of insult which the courts were already processing on his behalf – and vowed that those responsible for running the story would pay heavily for it. Some people, among them the more biddable figures in Turkey's fast-failing judicial system, and Dündar's would-be assassin, appeared to take the president's words as their cue.

Later that year Dündar and Gül were arrested and committed to pre-trial detention. They spent ninety-two days in solitary confinement at Silivri prison near Istanbul where scores of other journalists were also being held. The two men, charged with a range of offences including espionage, learned that the prosecution intended to seek life sentences. In a compelling defence Dündar observed that any spy who ran a story in a national newspaper rather than deliver its contents to a foreign paymaster was not worthy of the title. The court appeared to concede this point, acquitting the defendants on the espionage charge. It did, however, find the two men guilty of disclosing secret documents and sentenced Dündar to five years and ten months in prison.

On hearing the verdict Dündar spoke of having experienced two assassination attempts in two hours, one with a gun, the other judicial. 'The incident we originally covered was the crime,' he insisted. 'Not our coverage.' Dündar fled abroad before his sentence began.

Dündar's would-be assassin went on to receive a sentence of ten months.

*

From Kocatepe I made my way to the mosque's secular skyline rival. As I approached Atatürk's hilltop mausoleum, past the security details and the honour guard of carved Hittite-style lions flanking the paved avenue which led to the vast forecourt, I remembered the visit I had made, on the urging of my students, in the 1980s. On that occasion I had climbed the broad flights to the eternal leader's place of rest where guards stood to attention before a colonnade of square pillars. I was admiring the walls' heroic bas-reliefs and the leader's inscribed exhortations to the nation's defence – 'O Turkish children of the future, save the Republic! The power resides in the noble blood that runs in your veins' – all in the silence this hallowed place demanded when an army officer younger than myself bellowed at me to remove my hands from my pockets. Silence did not suffice, it seemed; my apparent indifference to authority, a look I had determinedly cultivated all through my school years, evaporated in the instant it took me to realise that almost fifty years after the leader's death this remained a place of exceptional sanctity – whose sentinels now had my chastened attention.

For Turks there was no higher calling than that of the soldier, and no greater warrior than the Gazi, as they termed their great martial leader. The least lack of respect was nothing less, evidently, than a grievous affront to the man's memory and to his officers, as much guardians of Atatürk's vision as of the territories he and his revered

comrades had wrestled from the enemy, winning them for the homeland. In their comportment army officers demanded the highest
standards of themselves and in return expected to enjoy exceptional
prestige, with even political leaders obliged to defer to them. It was
a status they took for granted.

But things changed after the Democrats came to power in 1950.
The ruling party's imperative, in accordance with democratic
process, was to maintain the loyalty of the constituencies which had
put them there. The Democrats' posture – one arm around the
shoulder of the pious peasant, the other of the newly affluent businessman – had the effect, if not the intention, of excluding others
from their embrace. And as inflation bit into static salaries army
officers felt especially neglected, even humiliated; restaurateurs took
to dismissing them as 'lemonaders' for their tendency to wave away
the spirits menu, obliging them to wait while waiters served tables
whose occupants looked likely to order more expansively. Rather
than show army officers around airier apartments, reckoning the
rent to be beyond them, landlords directed them to dark basements
widely disdained as 'staff-officer flats'. Storekeepers ignored them.
A girl whose head would once have been turned by a young officer
now heard, even heeded, her mother's warning talk of 'shiny uniforms
but empty pockets'. Tales were told of officers forced to moonlight as
bus drivers to feed their families and of retired generals taking on
translation work to boost their meagre pensions. A colonel's wife was
obliged to take a position as a governess, only to suffer the mortifica-
tion of running into foreign friends at her employers' home.

Officers might have felt able to endure their straitened circumstances if the Democrats' espousal of wealth as a hallowed objective
– one of Menderes's headline vows was to make a millionaire in every
neighbourhood – had not dishonoured the essential asceticism at the
core of the Kemalist creed. What the Democrats acclaimed as prosperity, the army officers decried as luxury; the very decadence which
had so tainted the Ottomans. One officer, on leave in Izmır, spoke for
others when he found himself 'at a restaurant filled with well-heeled
politicians and businessmen who received adulation and respect

while we were ignored. I looked at my friend and told him that things could not go on like this. Corruption and materialism seemed to dominate everything. It was not that we needed money, for officers had always been ill-paid. But we had had honour and respect in the past. Now these were gone. I asked my friend what we were waiting for and he nodded significantly.'

I was pondering those significant nods as I broke away from the throng bound for Atatürk's mausoleum and made for the opposite end of the plaza. Here a sarcophagus of polished red marble, angular and austere, stood in cloistered shade. It was discreet and modest, deliberately dwarfed by that of the great leader, but the fact that it was the only other tomb in the sacred precinct conferred a unique honour upon its occupant, Ismet Paşa, who was laid to rest here in 1973. In describing Ismet Paşa as his trusty successor, the ailing Atatürk had hailed him as the man capable of solving all problems. The compliment, often cited by Ismet Paşa's supporters, recognised his illustrious achievements as soldier and statesman, but especially as a strategist. He had a flair for combat but also for guile, proving himself a formidable opponent on the battlefield and at the conference table. He was correspondingly good at chess which visiting leaders and other dignitaries often acknowledged by presenting him with sets of chess pieces (the one from Stalin pitting heroic workers against capitalist dogs).

The Democrats had reason, then, to remain wary of their old adversary. When dealing with Ismet Paşa, Adnan Bey liked to say, even Allah would need to have his wits about Him. Despite reducing his party to a handful of seats, the Democrats never let up on Ismet Paşa, not only banning his statues and removing his image but discrediting him at every opportunity. The jingle 'Geldi Ismet, Kesildi Kismet' – 'With Ismet, Your Luck Ran Out' – saddled him with all the failings of the single-party state. In the 1957 election campaign Democrat newspapers carried photographs of Ismet Paşa above captions which read 'God protect us from his grudge and anger', 'İnönü is disseminating poisonous gossip' and 'He has left the nation in ruins'.

Such attacks failed to prevent Ismet Paşa's Republicans from making big gains in the 1957 elections, not only taking the capital but unseating several ministers as the opposition's seat tally went from 31 to 178. Ismet Paşa's supporters began to believe he might yet be the man to solve all their problems while his opponents, Adnan Bey especially, were obliged to acknowledge that the old general was not done yet.

CHAPTER EIGHT

14 July 1958

A coup takes place in Iraq

Ankara's former National Assembly building on Republic Street
dated from 1923 when the street, 'wide enough for three or
four carts to pass', was known only as 'the principal road from the
station' – and for the excellent reason that Turkey was not yet a
republic; the shock proclamation would not be made until 29
October that year. The building's late-Ottoman features – the Moorish arched windows and vaulted balconies, the decorative trims of
turquoise tiling, the projecting eaves and the star motifs on the
wooden ceilings – appeared designed to reassure the traditionalists,
eloquently acknowledging the accommodations Mustafa Kemal was
obliged to make at the beginning of his rule. It would be some years
before he could impose his Westernising agenda in full – which the
capital's uncompromisingly modern architecture was to reflect from
the 1930s.

The building, where the National Assembly met until 1960, has
served as a museum in recent decades. On visiting, I found the
administrative and ministerial offices given over to display vitrines
where visitors stooped to read of Atatürk's reforms and achievements and inspect sundry outfits belonging to the Gazi and the
personal effects of statesmen like Ismet Paşa, another of his chess
sets included. Off the other side of the polished parquet corridor,
where uniformed museum officials patrolled in boots sturdier than
the custody of a museum appeared to warrant, or the parquet floors
to withstand, I pushed through doors into the chamber of the

National Assembly. In that imposing hall, hung with chandeliers and draped with star and crescent flags, there were no such displays; though the chamber no longer smelt as it had during the Assembly's fraught decades in service, the cologne and pomade, the tobacco and sweat having given way to wax polish, it was otherwise easy to believe that Turkey's parliament had not relocated but merely gone into recess.

At the head of the hall red-carpeted steps rose to a high pulpit surrounded by battlements of intricately carved panelling. A lectern looked out over rows of benches backed with black leather, the wooden desktops as suggestive of traditional schooling as the lectern was of religious instruction. In the early decades of the Republic MPs convened not to dispute or interrupt but to attend to the words of the leader, most memorably over six days in November 1927 when Mustafa Kemal subjected his audience to a thirty-six-hour account of the young nation's history and achievements.

In the circumstances it was not surprising that the Assembly's architects should have designed a space akin to a lecture hall, even a place of worship, rather than a debating chamber. No attempt was made to concede, let alone facilitate, the robust realities of democratic dialogue by adopting the configuration favoured in the parliamentary chambers in Britain and other Western nations, where governing party and opposition confronted each other across the floor. For in 1920s Turkey political dissent equated 'with disloyalty in the minds of both rulers, and ruled', and institutionalised opposition was considered an alien and unwelcome innovation.

Such attitudes underwent a rapid transformation after the Second World War. Just as the introduction of democracy gave citizens new ideas, often exaggerated, of their rights – 'Peasants who had never before dreamed of going over the head of the village head-man', *Time* reported, 'now stomp into governors' offices with complaints, happily buttonhole parliamentary deputies on the street' – so it radically recast the roles of politicians. Their new parliamentary responsibility, rather than endorse interminable speeches with occasional nods of assent, was to stress-test the fitness of the government's policies and personalities at every turn. Dissent, debate, discussion and even derision, far from evidencing treacherous intent, were now understood as obligatory attributes essential to the effective function of the multi-party system. The politicians soon acquired these new skills and proved adept at deploying them – but in an Assembly designed for pre-democratic times, where the floor they should have had to cross to get at each other's throats – two swords' lengths, famously, at London's House of Commons – was absent. In light of the new system's latent combustibility this failure to adapt the Assembly's layout was to have consequences.

In the immediate aftermath of the 1950 elections, however, it seemed that lasting political harmony might be achievable. Thanks to the statesmanlike influence of Ismet Paşa, the Republicans proved themselves good losers, despite an unfamiliarity with the experience, when they relinquished power to the Democrats with dignity and grace. It was a remarkable surrender, described by one commentator as 'the greatest revolution in the history of Turkey, accomplished without bloodshed . . . and leaving no further obstacle to progress'. Some optimists took the frictionless handover to signal the parties' commitment to lasting respect and cooperation in their dealings with each other, and to the benefit of a grateful nation.

These hopes were to be dashed; what the parliamentary press corps had taken for mutual deference was exposed as the silence of duellists focused on familiarising themselves with the workings of their newly issued weapons. They were to get there soon enough. The Democrats were first to break the peace, narrowing eyes at the opposition's apparent goodwill which they took to mask Republican fears that those newly in possession of the keys to government would duly find the ones to the filing cabinet marked Confidential. A 'witch-hunt' ensued as the Democrats turned up allegations of multiple irregularities which they levelled at leading Republicans, claiming they had been substantially overpaid for land appropriated for ongoing construction projects like Atatürk's mausoleum, or had engineered land acquisitions at a steal. The Democrats, in keeping with the newly transparent age, saw to it that parliamentary proceedings were relayed by loudspeakers outside the Assembly building where the crowds were left to conclude, to the governing party's satisfaction, that the 'former rulers were little better than gangsters'.

Any lingering hopes of detente were banished when the Republicans hit back, dismissing the Democrats as 'mere seekers after office, have-nots striving to become haves'. In no time the Assembly exchanges had turned strident, acrimonious and finally virulent, with the two leaders often concentrating their fire on each other. Prime Minister Menderes, with no record of office to defend, was unconstrained in savaging the former government of Ismet Inönü's Republicans. In a speech made only days after taking office he described the legacy his government had inherited as embarrassing; the Republicans' interventionist, monopolistic and bureaucratic policies had paralysed the state and failed the people.

He was subsequently to accuse them of a pro-communist agenda 'as disgusting as the broadcasts of Moscow'; of keeping the Democrats from power in 1946 by electoral fraud; and of presiding over the country's descent into godless immorality. The leader of the opposition, the prime minister alleged, appeared to be suffering from some kind of disease caused by his fall from power, and from which he seemed incapable of recovering.

Ismet Paşa, though heavily outnumbered in the Assembly, was a veteran of considerably worse scrapes. The leader of the opposition, who knew a thing or two about the art of the counter-attack, bided his time before finally unleashing one which was to last, with pauses for breath, for the rest of the decade. In the course of the Democrats' years in office Ismet Paşa was to accuse them of using the Americans' money not to solve the country's economic problems but to deprive the people of their freedoms; of conniving in a slide into Islamic reaction which amounted to a betrayal of the great Atatürk's vision; of rank ineptitude when it came to economic planning; of cheating, put bluntly, given the underhand methods they had used to win the 1957 elections; and of being led by a dictator with no idea of what democracy actually meant, despite his party's name, and who was whispered to be 'a psychopathic case, suffering from identifiable symptoms of paranoia'.

In these skirmishes the opposition had a particularly damaging weapon, especially when Ismet Paşa wielded it, which was to remind Republicans, to their evident glee, that the closest Adnan Bey had ever got to an actual battlefield was the political rallies he took such pleasure in attending. This charged observation not only fixed the prime minister firmly in its cross hairs but reminded the government's ministers and MPs of a key difference between the parties: the Democrats tended to be younger and came from the rising classes of provincial professionals and business people – lawyers, doctors, gentleman farmers, entrepreneurs – unlike the mostly older Republicans whose establishment ranks included a high proportion of retired, and often decorated, soldiers.

In the defining respect of military mettle, the cap feather which Turkish males coveted above all others, Adnan Bey had an especially poor hand, having succumbed to the physical weaknesses which had dogged his childhood just as he might have proved himself. All appeared well when, in his last year at school, he was conscripted and sent to train as an officer in Istanbul, emerging as a second lieutenant. In the summer of 1917 he boarded a train at Haydarpaşa, along with hundreds of conscripts, bound for the Syrian front. The young Adnan had not left Anatolia when he went down with a bout of malaria and was unceremoniously offloaded at a country halt near Adana. In hospital his weight dropped to forty kilos before he began to recover. He spent the rest of the war in administrative posts, mostly in Izmir. He never saw action in Syria where an officer called Ismet, as Adnan Bey's political adversaries were to take every opportunity to remind him, had already attained the rank of general.

Adnan Bey fared no better in the War of Independence; this time a liver infection prevented him from participating in the rout of the Greeks in the autumn of 1922. When he did return to service it was not as a front-line soldier but as a translator attached to the information office which the Turks established after their reoccupation of Izmir. All of which meant any military comparison with Ismet Inönü

the rubbish . . . we must display our mosques, fountains and other treasures by making them visible from the great streets we will build so they gleam like gemstones. The traffic must flow like water.' They would build an opera house on Taksim Square. There would be a subway under the Golden Horn and a bridge over the Bosphorus. Adnan Bey outlined plans for a first-class airport link, the construction of multi-lane boulevards and new littoral roads, enlarged squares and the demolition of shanty neighbourhoods to improve views of the imperial mosques and other landmarks.

By the summer of 1957 whole quarters of Istanbul had been reduced to building sites as 'forests of unsightly shacks were swept away'. The streets shook with blasts of dynamite and the din of bulldozers as they rooted 'through Istanbul's cluttered slums and crowded business sections'. Along the Golden Horn entire settlements were cleared while the shops and houses which surrounded the squares at Eminönü, Karaköy, Aksaray and elsewhere were destroyed to make room for wider streets. 'Bedrooms and bathrooms,' reported *Time* Magazine, 'peek nakedly from the fronts of half-demolished houses.' The impression was of such devastation that one American tourist even expressed astonishment at the extent of the bombing evidently suffered by the city during the Second World War.

Adnan Bey, who tended to fall prey to his every enthusiasm, became so absorbed in the redevelopment of Istanbul that he decided to take personal charge of the project. The 'Architect of Istanbul', as he was dubbed, began to spend lengthy periods in the city. He took possession of the entire first floor of the Park, a landmark hotel near Taksim, and commandeered an office in the city's municipality building whose officials could expect to be summoned at any hour. Those who knew the prime minister from his farming days, up before dawn to ride the fields, were not surprised to learn that he kept the same hours in Istanbul. The city's early risers – the bakers and sellers of *simit* rolls, fishermen, ferrymen and muezzins, as well as the barflies, prostitutes and playboys on their unsteady way to bed – spoke of stumbling into hastily convened assemblies of blear-eyed aides, surveyors and officials. Often unshaven, still shrugging their way into suit jackets, clutching folders of plans and projections, these men strove to keep pace with the prime minister who was out in front discussing lines of sight with architects, compulsory expropriations with the mayor, the day's demolition schedule with foremen, and street routes with surveyors. The project obsessed the prime minister at all hours, even when he was on official business abroad, and to its minutest details. On a trip to Baghdad, it was reported, Menderes jumped out of bed in the middle of the night to send a cable announcing, 'Have decided to tear down house opposite the Spice Bazaar. Proceed with expropriation.'

While there was no denying Adnan Bey's dynamism, others observed that it was not for the prime minister to spend so much time in Istanbul; not when Ankara was the seat of his government and of the National Assembly – as well as the home, they pointedly reminded him, of his own family. It was improper, this infatuation with Istanbul, its underhand purpose to distract people from the country's political and economic woes. It was as if the prime minister, who despaired of sorting the shortages, the soaring cost of living, the foreign currency crisis and the deepening political enmities, had effectively abandoned governance for knocking down buildings, having discovered that this better reflected his foreman competencies.

'Oh, they accused him of all sorts of things,' said Ahmet as the ferry approached the Eminönü quayside. 'Like demolishing our precious architectural heritage – "Menderazing", they called it. Like expropriating private properties without due process. Like forcing out tenants without notice. Like dreaming up the entire development scheme to mask personal reasons for wishing to spend so much time in the city. But it was Adnan Bey who made the city work at last. We admired him enormously for his hard graft and vision.'

'Then we moved to the States in the 1960s,' said Ayşe. 'But rather than forget Adnan Bey we decided to call our firstborn son after him. Not that the kid cares for the name – he says it makes him sound like a terrorist – but it's our way of honouring the man.'

*

Metin had put me in touch with an organisation called Academics for Peace, some of whose members agreed to meet me the evening I got back to Istanbul. We gathered in a top-floor *meyhane* off Independence Street, a partisan place hung with portraits of Atatürk and İnönü. Over meze plates – mashed aubergine, pickled samphire, slabs of salty white cheese, olives, garlicky yoghurt and anchovies – and too many glasses of rakı, the talk turned impious.

'Say what you like,' said somebody, cutting through the barrage of wholehearted abuse, 'but you must agree Erdoğan's a great lover of democracy.'

'He's what?' we spluttered.

'Well,' he replied, 'he's certainly fucked it hard enough.'

'More rakı!' somebody shouted amidst the general laughter.

Academics for Peace was founded to promote peacemaking initiatives in Turkey, especially among the country's increasingly alienated, in some cases violently hostile, Kurdish population. All the group's efforts at reconciliation were undone when the Kurdish conflict, which had been in abeyance for decades, suddenly resumed in September 2015. Members were appalled when the Turkish forces took the battle to the streets and alleys of Cizre, Silopi, Diyarbakır's Sur township and other densely populated urban areas of the country's Kurdish south-east, turning heavy weapons designed for use in the field on civilian neighbourhoods, reducing them to rubble. Survivors of the explosions, the tear gas and gunfire were subjected to curfews, some lasting twelve days and nights, during which they were denied food, essential supplies and medical help. The failure of water and electricity supplies only added to the misery in areas where civilian vehicles, even ambulances and hearses, were refused access.

By January 2016 the academics' despair over the resumption of hostilities had turned to outrage. The organisation convened a press conference to issue a statement signed by more than 1,100 members, condemning the state for crimes in the south-east. The signatories refused to be party to what they called a criminally 'deliberate and planned massacre'. They demanded an immediate end to state violence, compensation for victims and access for international observers. Among them was Gül, a research assistant in Marmara University's Economics Department, whom I sat beside in the *meyhane*.

'I didn't think twice before signing it,' said Gül. 'I was as angered as everybody else by events in the south-east.'

For his part, President Erdoğan was incensed at being called to account in so public a manner, denoucing the signatories as traitors whom he vowed to punish. Within days officials in the security forces and the national education council, and numerous university rectors, had leapt to the president's bidding without pausing to consider their obligations under the constitution, not least its guarantees of free expression. The judiciary initiated proceedings against the academics on charges of spreading terrorist propaganda, and ordered leading signatories rounded up.

'It turned vicious overnight,' Gül remembered. 'Especially at universities where the state had extensive influence. At Marmara, where the rector threw us to the wolves, signatories had their doors marked in red. Religious and right-wing students were encouraged to write that they didn't want to be taught by terrorists and to call for their teachers to be fired. Pictures labelling us terrorists circulated on social media. The universities opened disciplinary investigations into our activities. Signatories experienced everything from sudden and drastic cuts in research funding, suspensions and dismissals to the confiscation of passports. I learned I had lost my job; when I went in to clear my desk, I found that somebody had already done it for me. All my possessions had been thrown into boxes and dumped in a storeroom.'

Gül filled her glass, blinking back tears. 'So they've turned me into a non-person who's banned from working anywhere in the state sector. I'm no longer free to travel abroad. And simply for calling our government to account for the real crime of waging a brutal war against its own people.'

Only later, when I reflected on my time with these brave and unbowed people, did I locate the echo I'd heard in the joke about

Erdoğan's love of democracy; back in the 1950s the distinguished academic Bernard Lewis had overheard the same joke while sitting in the faculty lounge at Ankara's School of Political Science – only it was about Adnan Menderes.

*

On the morning of 14 July 1958 Adnan Bey, in a break from the usual round of demolition inspections, was at Istanbul's airport. The prime minister, who cherished an enthusiastic welcome as much as anybody, was there to provide one for his Iraqi counterpart. The veteran statesman Nuri As Said was due that morning from Baghdad, along with King Faisal II and other leading members of the Iraqi royal family.

Under Adnan Bey and As Said, a high-ranking Ottoman officer from Iraq's days as an imperial province, the two countries' anticommunist and pro-Western stances had increasingly aligned. A mutual fear of Soviet encroachment, intensified by Colonel Nasser's overthrow of Egypt's Anglophile monarchy in 1952 and a red-tinged 1954 coup in Syria, led to a series of high-level visits between the neighbours. The result, the Turco-Iraqi Pact of 1954, was renamed the Baghdad Pact upon the inclusion of Pakistan and Iran; the pact's leaders were to meet that day in Istanbul.

Adnan Bey pulled at his cuffs, patted his hair and straightened his sunglasses before casting an eye over the arrangements – the flags of the pact's nations flying from the airport building, the ceremonial guard, the band, the red carpet beneath a sun canopy – and not for the first time. He checked his watch. The flight was late. This was not unusual – summer sandstorms commonly caused problems at Baghdad's airport, as autumn stork infestations did at Istanbul's – though the airport authorities' unaccountable inability to reach their counterparts in Baghdad was a cause for concern. Given the show that the Turks had arranged – Adnan Bey's heavyweight welcoming committee included President Bayar, the president of Pakistan and the shah of Iran – the delay was unfortunate, especially in the wilting heat, which had driven the visiting dignitaries to take cover in the airport building.

'You should join them until we have more news, Adnan Bey,' suggested an aide, having received word that even the Iraqi ambassador in Ankara had had no success in raising Baghdad.

It transpired that before dawn rebel detachments of the Iraqi army had seized Baghdad's radio station to proclaim the fall of the imperialists. Then they attacked the Al Rehab Palace where the royal family awoke to the sound of artillery shells pounding the palace roof. The royal guards, loyal to the last, vowed to resist but the crown prince refused to order Iraqis to fire upon their compatriots. He bade the guards surrender before dispatching a servant to fly a white flag from what remained of the palace roof.

The members of the royal family, resigned to the fall of the dynasty, hoped at least to escape with their lives. They recalled how Egypt's deposed King Farouk had been permitted to leave on his royal yacht – and with a twenty-one-gun salute to see him on his way. Even so, a number of the royal household were seen to be clutching copies of the Quran as they emerged into the Al Rehab's courtyard to face the rebel officers. The officers told them to face the wall before disposing of the Iraqi royal family – as the Bolsheviks had done in Russia forty years earlier – in a hail of bullets. Another detachment made for the prime minister's residence to discover that Nuri As Said, alerted by the gunfire, had already fled.

When news of the coup reached Istanbul's airport, where no flight would be arriving from Baghdad, the military guard was stood down, the red carpet was rolled up and the pact's surviving leaders were left to ponder the fate of their Iraqi friends and what it might mean for the rest of them.

*

'By 1958 the country was in such a state,' recalled Ülkü, a retired teacher I visited in her Istanbul apartment, 'that we just had to do something.'

Raging inflation, Ülkü told me, had crippled her husband Demir's salary. Finance Minister Polatkan's decision to drastically devalue the lira, causing the price of imported goods to rocket, only made matters worse.

'We were living in Malatya where Demir had a teaching post. We were having to get by on his salary – it seemed to shrink every day – as I was still training to be a teacher. Once we'd paid the rent we barely had enough for fruit and vegetables, cheese and bread. We had a young child, whom we could ill afford to clothe, and couldn't even think of stumping up for train fares to visit our families back in western Turkey.

'Idealists, Atatürk's children to the core, we were not only bitter at what the Democrats had done to our incomes but livid at the other injustices their hateful regime was committing, not least the imprisonments, the newspaper closures and the widespread repression. With our teacher friends we began to make a plan; we decided to send a telegram.

'In many ways it was Demir's idea – he was some twenty years older than me – but we were all right behind it, myself included. I insisted that the telegram should be in my name as we could not risk the family's breadwinner getting into trouble. Some friends advised me against putting myself in harm's way, but I wasn't having it.

'One evening, in our kitchen, we all settled on the wording of the telegram which I took down to the post office in Malatya the next morning. I remember the young officer's audible gasp as he read the telegram; I remember him rereading it, and the long look he gave me before he disappeared to seek advice in a back office. He reappeared, cleared his throat and suggested I rewrite the telegram, perhaps to make it a little milder in tone. Though I was still in my teens, I looked him in the eye and said: "You'll send it, please, exactly as it is."'

So it was that a young woman instructed a telegram officer to dispatch her message to the prime minister. 'Dear Mr Menderes,' it read, 'After the latest series of price rises, can we humbly ask you to make an exception when it comes to the price of shroud material so that we can at least afford to die?'

'That afternoon something strange happened,' Ülkü recalled. 'There was a knock at the apartment door. It was a postman asking me if I had sent a telegram that morning. On being asked why he needed to know, the postman replied that the people at the post office had mistakenly overcharged me for the telegram, by twenty-five kuruş, and were anxious to make good the mistake. Heartened by the post office's honesty, I made a point of showing the coins to Demir when he returned that evening. But Demir only snorted. "Don't you believe it," he said. "It's their way of checking where you live."'

In Malatya, Ismet Paşa's parliamentary seat, there was considerable support for the Republicans. Ülkü's telegram was the talk of the town. The greengrocer made a point of checking over the apples and apricots in the young woman's bag before adding a few free ones. 'You're the one who sent the telegram to Menderes, sister,' he said approvingly. 'I'm not having you leaving my shop with bruised fruit.'

A few months later, Ülkü learned that she was to be investigated for her telegram. Demir had been right about the postman. The investigating officers, who charged Demir with responsibility for the actions of his young wife, removed him from his teaching post. In 1959 the family were ordered from their home and reassigned to another town.

*

Iraq's fallen prime minister took refuge in a friend's house on the far bank of the Tigris. Fearful that they would soon track him down there, he made arrangements the following day to be transferred to a more secure hideout, disguising himself beneath a woman's ankle-length *abaya* for the journey. When the car ran into traffic in Baghdad's al-Battawin quarter, As Said decided to make a run for it only for somebody to raise the alarm after spotting expensive men's shoes beneath his *abaya*; the fugitive was apprehended, exposed, shot and buried in the cemetery at Bab al Muazzam.

But mere murder was not about to satisfy the Baghdad mob. For years Iraqis had suffered the repressive rule of a man they despised as a stooge of British imperialism; a man, moreover, who had allied his people not with their Arab brothers but with Turks, 'their hereditary oppressors and enemies', as well as with foreign Pathans and Persians. They dug up As Said, tied his freshly buried corpse to a car bumper and dragged it through the streets. What remained was then burned and mutilated before being repeatedly run over by Baghdad's municipal buses until it was said to resemble *bastourma* – Iraqi pastrami.

It was a time of coups. All over south-east Asia, Latin America and the Middle East discredited monarchies and fledgling democracies were toppled by ruthless army officers with dynastic ambitions and a penchant for designer sunglasses and open-top jeeps. Of the many leaders deposed since the Democrats' rise to power, none had come to as grisly an end as Nuri As Said. The barbaric murder of a man he had come to respect and like appalled Adnan Bey. The events in the neighbouring country no doubt also made him wonder what they might mean for himself, not least when opposition leaders invited him to do so.

For Ismet Paşa's Republicans, buoyed to belligerence by their showing in the previous year's elections, the Iraq coup could not have been more timely; it equipped them with a psychological weapon, the spectre of assassination, to deploy against their vulnerable target. As a fear of assassination had unsettled previous leaders, in some cases to the point of paranoia – in 1903 Sultan Abdul Hamid II required the empire's newspapers to report that the king and queen of Serbia, shot by army officers at Belgrade's Royal Palace, had in fact died there of indigestion, simultaneously – so it was sure to play on Adnan Bey's frayed nerves. With Ismet Paşa to the fore, his remarks 'full of renewed dark references to Nuri Said', the Republicans drew comparisons 'between the methods of Nuri Said and of the present Turkish prime minister . . . warning the latter that he had better mend his ways before it was too late'. Opposition press cartoons served as reminders of the fate that befell dictators by depicting As Said alongside Caesar, Hitler, Mussolini, Juan Perón of Argentina, overthrown in September 1955, and President Batista of

Cuba, who was to flee the country before Fidel Castro's advancing forces in the early hours of New Year's Day 1959.

Not that such heavy-handed prompts were necessary; how could it not occur to the hypersensitive Adnan Bey that the dread fate of As Said – his immediate counterpart, after all, in a closely allied neighbour state – might have implications for him? The pills helped, of course, as did the reassurance he took from reminding himself, regularly, of the pointed differences in the two men's situations. While As Said had served an autocratic and widely despised monarchy Adnan Bey led a democracy whose citizens had elected him on three consecutive occasions. While Iraqis held As Said to account for Britain's exploitation of the country's resources, notably oil, most Turks welcomed ties with America which had brought material benefits and national security without threatening the nation's independence. These were key differences, but Adnan Bey's greatest insurance was that Turkey's armed forces, unlike the rabble detachments of less disciplined nations, were bound by Atatürk's absolute insistence that the military was to keep out of national politics.

In establishing the Republic, Atatürk had staked his authority on the principle that soldiers were to have no part in running the nation. The War of Independence had barely been won when the new leader asserted that Turkey's true liberation lay ahead, in civic achievement, and that the army was beholden without qualification to parliament. There was to be no role whatsoever in government for army officers, who were required to divest themselves of military office before embarking upon political careers. Officers and soldiers, including cadets and civilians engaged in military service, were not even allowed to vote. The message was indisputable: any military challenge to civilian supremacy was an unconscionable affront to the express orders of the great leader.

Given Atatürk's unconditional proscription of any kind of military intervention, Adnan Bey might have dismissed the opposition's insinuations without another thought. But at a party rally in the autumn of 1958 he gave the impression of being thoroughly rattled. In his speech he incessantly castigated the Republicans for carrying 'their boldness to such an extent as repeatedly to publish in their newspapers photographs of politicians killed in neighbouring countries and insolently to write allusive threatening remarks as captions . . . these people cite Iraq as an example and persistently incite the nation as if saying: "Is there not a villain or leader who will kill these people?" By publishing in their papers week after week the pictures of those killed in a neighbouring country they want to incite a desperado to act in this country . . . we will show them what it means to carry boldness and insolence to the extent of leading to provocation for rebellion.'

The prime minister concluded with a threat of his own, reminding the Republicans of the fate which befell those who had plotted against a former leader of Turkey, Mustafa Kemal Atatürk.

'Let them remember,' he said, 'that those who dared to do so died on the gallows and derive a lesson.'

*

Even as the debts mounted – Zorlu and Polatkan relentlessly tapping the US, the Europeans, the International Monetary Fund and others for yet more loans – the infrastructure works continued. The ports and grain elevators, the textile mills and dams. The coal-washing facilities and power plants. The factories, sugar refineries and cold-storage depots. The new roads, like the asphalted highway between Izmır and the city of Denizli – where cars could do 'sixty or seventy miles an hour in safety and comfort' – and which Adnan Bey travelled one day in the autumn of 1958, but not at that speed as his motorcade was stopped 'no fewer than 25 times' by villagers and peasants determined to honour their man. They crowded around the prime minister's car as the statutory ram, its horns tied with ribbons, was led out to be sacrificed. On each occasion the tireless Adnan Bey climbed from the car to shake hands, often walking 'to look at a new

school, mosque, factory or anything new which the villagers wished
to show him'. As they stooped to kiss his hand he replied only that
they deserved all this and more; for he knew of the privations they
had suffered under the single-party state. It demonstrated, as one
commentator noted, how great was Adnan Bey's understanding of
the Turkish peasant.

As great, the commentator cautioned, as 'his understanding of
the Turkish officer was small'.

CHAPTER NINE

28 April 1960

Students die in Istanbul protests

By the early months of 1959, when Adnan Bey walked all but untouched out of the Gatwick woods to revive the flagging Democrats, the Republicans were themselves back to fighting fitness. They felt ready to match the ruling party punch for punch, stunt for stunt, which was what they thought of the prime minister's Ankara charade; as Menderes had done, so Ismet Paşa would now take to the train to show that he too could pull a crowd.

But a crowd without the sacrifices and the superstition – patriotism rather than piety being the opposition's preferred suit. The Republicans accordingly played to the strengths of their venerated leader by arranging a train tour which was, as *The Times* put it, 'clearly evocative of the ghosts of his former military triumphs'. They even billed the tour, which was to take in the fabled battle-fields, billets and landmarks of the War of Independence, the 'Spring Offensive'. It was a stirring title but, given the outright hostility which now existed between government and opposition, whose politicians and supporters were at each other's throats, a provocative one; the Democrats took it as a literal call to arms. At the western Anatolian town of Uşak, where Ismet Paşa had famously received the surrender of several Greek generals in 1922, a mob of government partisans armed with clubs was dispatched to see off the Republican retinue with a fighting show of their own. On leaving the train the visitors were pelted with rocks, one of which struck Ismet Paşa, who duly sounded the retreat.

Not that a glancing blow was about to see off the veteran
campaigner. The following spring, when the national politics had
turned yet more venomous, it was arranged for Ismet Paşa to take to
the train again, this time for the city of Kayseri in central Turkey.
On the morning of the visit Ismet Paşa received a telegram inform-
ing him that the danger of political violence obliged Kayseri's
governor to cancel all rallies – including the one planned that day by
the opposition leader. Ismet Paşa telegrammed the reply that he saw
no constitutional reason why he should not visit Kayseri, whether as
party leader, MP or as law-abiding citizen, given that no state of
emergency had been declared. He and his retinue of MPs and journalists accordingly set out from Ankara as planned.

This time the reception proved more welcoming. The crowds
which gathered along the line showered the train not with stones but
spring flowers and cries of encouragement; even in the countryside,
which the prime minister liked to think of as his exclusive territory,
it seemed that the opposition leader's illustrious achievements could
still stir powerfully positive sentiments. All went to plan until the
train came to a sudden stop at Himmetdede, a country halt on
the wide steppe, where the government had dispatched troop units
to ensure that Ismet Paşa did not reach Kayseri.

The governor of Kayseri, who appreciated that any confrontation
with the great man was unlikely to be in his interests, cited a full
diary in dispatching his deputy to deal with the problem. That
hapless official duly made his way to Himmetdede and took up position on the platform, shifting from one foot to the other, as the train
drew up. The deputy governor, a colonel at his shoulder, boarded the
train and made for the opposition leader's compartment, carrying a
letter from the governor which informed Ismet Paşa that he would
not be permitted to continue; that the train would not leave until he
had disembarked; and that a car was at his disposal to return him to
Ankara.

This time, however, there was to be no retreat; without opening it
Ismet Paşa tore up the governor's letter and let the pieces flutter to
his feet. He was entirely within his rights to visit Kayseri, he informed

the deputy governor, denouncing the curbs on his freedom of movement as 'a completely illegal and unconstitutional act'. The deputy
governor, who had no more experience of outright defiance than he
had of dealing with anybody of Ismet Paşa's calibre, scurried from
the compartment to report back to his superiors. In a series of
increasingly fraught telephone calls to Ankara the governor's office
advised the national authorities of the situation and requested further
instructions.

Passengers, whom the motion of the train had rocked to sleep,
now began to stir. They blinked, levelling puzzled frowns at fellow
passengers who motioned beyond the faded curtains to the cordon
of soldiers standing to attention in the bright April light. 'The Paşa's
on the train,' somebody murmured. 'And they want him off. Something to do with a ban on political meetings. Not that he's shifting.
Seems, even at his age, that he's got one more stand in him.'

'That's the Paşa,' somebody chuckled approvingly. 'Seems we
might be here for a while, then.'

'Got to hand it to him, eh?'

The opposition leader and his retinue were pondering their
next move when a knock sounded at the door of their compartment. In came an elderly man with a stick. 'My sincerest respects,
Paşa, I was with you at the front in March '21,' he said. 'Shrapnel
did for me, but I was back in the ranks by '22. Saw the Greeks into
the sea at Izmır,' he said, patting his leg, then the medal pinned to
his chest. 'As I dare say you'll see off this lot,' he added. A woman
followed the old man into the compartment, steering a boy by the
shoulders.

'Flowers, my Paşa,' she said, touching the old general's hand to
her forehead before kissing it in the traditional gesture of reverence.
'Lost my father at Sakarya. They never found him. So I honour him
in the places they say he loved – in our garden, and down by the mill
– where I've laid enough blooms for him over the years, so these ones
are for you. What's left of him is his grandson,' she said, tugging at
her son's chin before pushing him forward. 'A fine soldier in the
making.'

In their wake other admirers followed into the compartment. 'In
the Gazi's glorious name you have our total support, Paşa,' a doctor
exclaimed. 'Kayseri can wait, and so can we; if they prevent you from
continuing, then it's here we all stay.' A train guard entered with a
tray, bowing low as he set a glass of tea before Ismet Paşa. As news of
the stand-off spread, more local people came to the station to pay
their respects. The elderly and infirm, having received assurances
that no ticket was necessary for simply boarding the train – which
was not, moreover, about to carry them away – stepped up after
pushing off broken shoes which they left in neat pairs along the platform. Others gathered at the window, touching their foreheads to the
great man.

When a group of young army officers appeared the civilians were
quick to fall back, clearing a passage which the officers, caps under
their arms, followed into Ismet Paşa's presence. One stepped forward.

'Our orders, Paşa, are to prevent you passing,' he said. 'Of all you
will understand that it is our sworn duty to obey, whatever our orders
require, whatever the cost, even if it means our lives. Not that our lives
mean anything to us, though our honour is all, and no order more
deeply dishonours us than this one, Paşa.' As he stepped back with a
solemn nod the other officers joined him in replacing their caps,
straightening and saluting before backing out of the compartment.

At the door the deputy governor appeared again, looking flus-
tered. 'I really must insist,' he said, 'and for the last time that Ismet
Paşa leave the train. On Ankara's orders.'

'Ismet Paşa will do no such thing,' one of his party replied evenly.
'Not of his own will, at least. If the authorities insist, they can always
order his forcible removal, though I'm not sure I'd advise that.
Personally.' A concluding shrug suggested that it was for the deputy
governor to judge whether any officer would obey orders to man-
handle the septuagenarian – not only a former president but one of
the army's own, and the most exalted of them all at that. In retreating
to the platform, the deputy governor appeared to concede that no
such order was advisable.

The stand-off continued for three hours. The frustrations had given way to late-afternoon languor, the passengers dozing or gathering in knots along the platform to smoke and drink tea delivered on pewter trays from the Himmetdede teahouse, when their desultory exchanges were interrupted by a shout; it was the guard beckoning the passengers back to their carriages with the news that the train staff had been given permission to continue. Cheers rang out as the whistle sounded and the troops stepped back from the tracks as the wheels began to turn. The train gathered speed, and with a departing salute the officers and soldiers snapped to attention as Ismet Paşa's carriage passed.

So Ismet Paşa made it through, adding Kayseri to his long list of triumphs, as his more exuberant supporters in the press put it. The government was incensed, seeing the incident as an intolerable challenge to its authority. The radio raged against the deliberate provocations of the opposition, dismissing its behaviour at Kayseri as no better than that of Balkan brigands. The government condemned Ismet Paşa, spluttering dark warnings that it could not remain indifferent to such divisive strategies. It vowed that there would be consequences.

As to Kayseri, and what the incident revealed of the army's sympathies, the radio was silent. Certainly, no mention was made of the three senior officers who resigned their commissions after Himmetdede, denouncing their orders as incompatible with the freedoms of movement guaranteed citizens under the constitution. The resignations were a further cause of satisfaction for Ismet Paşa, who contented himself that though he had got stones where Adnan Bey got sacrifices, he had also got salutes. And salutes, as events were to prove, would decide matters.

*

During my visit to Ankara I had been to see Baysan, an elegant woman in her mid-seventies who lived in Çankaya, a district of

well-to-do residences and embassies on the heights above the
Kocatepe mosque. In August 1959, when she was a seventeen-year-
old schoolgirl, Baysan had been among the crowd which gathered at
Istanbul airport to greet the famous English couple who had rescued
Adnan Bey from the plane wreck.

'I think I was taken along to meet the Baileys because of my
English,' explained Baysan, offering me a seat before taking her place
beside a table topped with family photographs in frames and albums,
and a box of paper tissues. 'We had an excellent English teacher;
being made to learn jingles like "Come Down to Kew in Lilac Times"
seemed to help.'

Baysan's father, Kemal Aygün, had been made Istanbul's mayor
in 1958. 'Dad was closely involved in organising the Baileys' visit,'
she explained. 'As it was the school holidays, I ended up spending a
lot of time with them. They were guests at our summer house where
we went swimming together. We were all to become lifelong friends.'

Baysan had other reasons to remember the summer of 1959; she
had just become engaged to a young politician, a rising star in
the Democrat Party. 'Our family was close to many of the leading
Democrats,' she explained. 'My mother was a cousin of Refik
Koraltan, leader of the Assembly and one of the party's four found-
ers, and since school days Dad had counted Hasan Polatkan as a
close friend. Dad had always meant to steer clear of party politics,
fearing where it could take him, but the leadership of Istanbul's
Democrats was foisted upon him when they made him mayor. That
was when they moved us into the fancy apartment on Teşvikiye
Street, one of the best addresses in Istanbul. The apartment became
one of Adnan Bey's favoured meeting places – he had always
admired Mum's cooking. At the time Adnan Bey was often in Istanbul on the project, overseeing the city's big remake. He was forever
phoning Dad in the early hours, dragging him out to walk the roads
he wanted widened or rerouted, or to inspect buildings he planned
to have demolished, and to discuss the necessary permissions and
paperwork.' Baysan showed me a photograph of a dinner her father
had hosted in honour of the 'Architect of Istanbul'. In the

photograph the two men, smiling broadly, shake hands as Istanbul's mayor presents the prime minister with a gold trowel in recognition of his work.

Another photograph was of an occasion at the Aygün apartment on Teşvikiye Street. '24 May 1959,' Baysan recalled fondly. 'We were celebrating my engagement. We had asked Adnan Bey to honour us in the Turkish way by putting gold rings on our fingers.' In her dress Baysan appears radiant if a little overawed by the high-ranking officials and ministers gathered around her; her father, of course, but also Istanbul's governor as well as the interior minister, the leader of the Assembly and Adnan Bey himself. Everybody leans into the lens, anxious to be included in this celebratory gathering of the ruling clique, oblivious to the least sense of impending calamity.

For hours Baysan reminisced. The sun had worked its way to the horizon, Baysan through the box of tissues, by the time I left.

*

Once a grand expanse, Beyazit Square has become a scruffy waste-land in recent decades, the crumbling concrete set with the pawprints of stray dogs. The square abuts the main entrance to Istanbul University and also the city's newspaper library, housed in an old mosque complex, where I made my way one morning.

The broadsheets from the period, preserved from the mayfly existence which should have been their lot, came in leather bindings so heavy as to bend my back as I carted them to a reading desk. The volumes gave off puffs of dust, the spines shedding perished parings of leather, as I set them down beneath the vaulted and domed ceilings of the mosque's former *kervansaray*, or pilgrims' hostel. After more than fifty years the pages were fragile, and the poorly printed photographs had the textured translucence of pressed flowers.

I was at the library to research Said Nursi, a holy man whose emergence from obscurity in late 1959 had further stoked tensions in Turkey. Nursi might have disappeared decades earlier, the proscriptions of the single-party state doing for him as they had for so many other sheikhs, dervishes, divines, wandering preachers and other peddlers of Ottoman superstition. But the Wonder of the Age, as Nursi's followers knew him, had endured as an outspoken opponent of what he called the state's aggressive atheism, openly defiant of the dress laws – only with his head, he famously declared, would his trademark turban come off – as well as the ban on the Arabic *ezan*. His chief offence, for which he was repeatedly imprisoned or placed under house arrest in the Anatolian back country during the 1930s and 40s, was his writings. The voluminous *Epistles of Light*, which the state banned as subversive, nevertheless proved an inspiration to Nursi's growing band of followers, who took to copying out the forbidden texts by hand, and often in the proscribed Ottoman script; it was a measure of their devotion, and of Nursi's remarkable influence, that over half a million handwritten copies were said to be in circulation by the time the Democrat government finally permitted the *Epistles*' publication in 1956.

In lifting restrictions on the *Epistles*, a fusion of faith and science which aspired to reconcile the Quran with the technical age, the

Democrats displayed a marked leniency towards Said Nursi, whom they had initially cleared of criminal charges in the general amnesty of 1950. These moves, which commended them to Said Nursi and his followers, at once horrified secularists who charged the Democrats with aiding and abetting a religious reactionary – a malign and persuasive force whose extensive influence only demonstrated the country's extreme vulnerability to social regression, even to full-blown theocracy.

If anything comforted the guardians of Atatürk's vision, however, it was that the ageing mystic largely confined himself to the provinces for much of the 1950s. They allowed themselves to hope that there he would stay until the day of his death, this spectre from the Ottoman recesses, his disruptive aura degrading along with his earthly remains, and about as rapidly. But in December 1959, perhaps sensing his time to be short, Nursi was seized by a restlessness which the gathering clamour of his followers only deepened. Despite failing health, he summoned his energies to address his devotees in cities like Konya, Ankara and Istanbul where he travelled in the 1953 Chevrolet which his supporters had given him. But the authorities, which remained guarded against the least manifestations of public religion, had not forgotten Nursi whose Chevrolet had barely taken to the road before a security vehicle was on its tail; opposition journalists, advised that this dire threat to the secular state was on the move again, scrambled to cram into cars which fell in with the convoy. Upon arriving at his hotel, this fragile figure in robes and turban emerged beneath his trademark black parasol which a disciple carried to shelter the holy man from the photographs he disallowed for religious reasons. Journalists followed Nursi into the foyer, pestering him for the comments he was too exhausted to give and the photographs he refused to permit; they even bribed hotel staff for access to the balcony of the holy man's hotel room in the hope of sneaking an illicit shot of him at prayer.

The newspapers dismissed Said Nursi as a pretend Prophet, a manipulative religious retrograde whom the government had wilfully encouraged, his outfits 'more backward than those of the sheikhs of

Yemen'. He was the inspiration for the cartoons of stereotypical reactionaries which I came across in the newspapers, all baggy trousers and long beards, cloaked in the cobwebs of benighted ignorance. One article reported that students from Istanbul University sent the old man a selection of Texan-style brimmed hats with commands that he wear them in place of his confounded turban. To them Said Nursi was nothing but a *yobaz*, a fanatical preacher of the sort who stalked the villages – 'the great dead weight which is dragging Turkey back out of Europe'. And Menderes? His accursed apologist.

Nobody was more exercised by Said Nursi's return to public prominence than Ismet Paşa, who suspected the government of co-opting Nursi in their political designs. He was not about to forget the crucial support Nursi had given Adnan Bey in the lead-up to the 1954 elections when he described the prime minister as a 'champion of religion'. During a visit Nursi made in early 1960 to the capital – where his very presence struck Ismet Paşa as a grievous provocation – the opposition leader rounded on Adnan Bey in the Assembly. 'You are trying to bring back Islamic law, to revive reaction,' he cried. 'And that is why you let Nursi travel around.'

Adnan Bey reminded the opposition leader that freedom to travel was guaranteed by the constitution; that this was an old man, worthy of every sympathy, who had been inexcusably mistreated by the Paşa's single-party state; and a man who, despite every provocation, had remained avowedly non-violent. 'Why is the Paşa so frightened of religion and religious people?' he asked. 'Does he not know that he too will die? What harm has come to him from this man? What does he want from a holy man who spent his entire life in the cause of religion? Why does he take pleasure from this man's torment, and love to see him suffer difficulties?'

Those difficulties were about to end. In March 1960 Said Nursi was felled by a bout of pneumonia – an illness which appeared only to exacerbate his restlessness. Before succumbing to delirium he let his closest disciples understand that he must visit Urfa, a holy city in south-eastern Turkey, and that there was no time to lose. Obedient to their stricken master's every instruction, they drove through the night. By the time they reached Urfa, Said Nursi was so weak that his followers had to carry him up the stairs to his hotel room. The Urfa authorities, loath to have the controversial charismatic on their patch, ordered that Nursi return home immediately, only for a doctor to announce that the severity of the patient's fever rendered him unfit for travel. Two days later Said Nursi died in his Urfa hotel room; as he was laid to rest in the holy precinct opposite the cave which Muslims revere as the birthplace of the Prophet Abraham, Said Nursi's secular enemies might have assumed that their troubles with him were finally over.

*

In his third-floor Moscow apartment the poet Nazım, tiring of the receptions in his honour and the visits to workers' and artists' collectives, yearned for all he had left behind; a wife, a young son, friends and family, and the homeland where it remained his dearest wish to be buried. He wrote of love, and grief, and all he most missed about Istanbul; a favourite cafe in Beyazit, dusk over the city, a kiss snatched in a garden of jonquils in Kadıköy or evening promenades during Ramadan.

He also bemoaned the plight of his beloved country, which he described as 'fighting for its life under the heel of a gang of thugs'. The focus of his rage was the man who had signed his release papers in 1950, and whom he might once have commended for his efforts to improve the lives of ordinary Turks. But for depriving the country of freedom, for turning it into what he called an American dependency and for sending young Turkish soldiers 'to murder their brothers' in Korea, Nazım could never forgive Adnan Menderes.

The exiled poet devoted his remaining energies to waging war on the prime minister, calling the day of Adnan Bey's conception the saddest in Turkey's history. He likened him to a wild pig loose in Turkey's fields, a fire raging through its towns. In one poem he wrote as a young soldier who had lost his life in Korea, and whose vengeful ghost vowed perpetual pursuit of the man who had sent him there.

Nazım branded Adnan Bey pompous, venal and mean-eyed, his
clammy hands forever stroking his brilliantined hair or pawing
his mistresses' breasts – when they were not patting his fat wallet. In
another poem he predicted the prime minister's comeuppance,
describing his maltreatment of the opposition and of journalists as a
cartoon folly akin to 'cutting the branch on which you're sitting'. In
'Fear' Nazım evoked Menderes as sunken-cheeked and sleep-
deprived; haunted by the spirits of those he had sent to their deaths,
persecuted or failed; and consumed by what Nazım considered the
ultimate dread – of having sold out his country to the Americans.

The Turkish authorities, though they had banned Nazım's works,
had less success blocking his radio broadcasts, latterly from a station
in Leipzig, as the poet intensified his attacks on the lackey regime.
He denounced Menderes for his lies, compared him to a mad sultan
who threw coins into a pond to feed fish, and condemned the petrol
shortages and the inflation. Insistently, he called for the overthrow of
the 'little dictator'.

*

Within Turkey, where the few newspapers still loyal to the Menderes
government showed the prime minister snipping ribbons, admiring
mosques, picnicking with cotton workers and attending dinners in
his honour, a subtler dissent operated. The strategy of the opposition newspapers, as I saw for myself at the library, was to get round
the restrictions on what they could write by publishing photographs
of the nation's ills, leaving readers to conclude that the prime minister was to blame for them: the long queues for petrol, the oil tankers
at anchor in the Bosphorus, their owners awaiting exceptional
payment guarantees from the cash-starved regime before agreeing to
unload; veiled women and bearded Islamic reactionaries; a bandaged
Ismet Paşa after being struck by the stone at Uşak, or resolutely
waiting out the stand-off at Himmetdede; and persecuted journalists, among them Ahmed Emin Yalman, imprisoned at Üsküdar,
Istanbul on 7 March 1960.

Months earlier, at a time 'of trial and tribulation during which more newspapers were closed down and journalists imprisoned than any other', the old and ailing publisher had been found guilty of 'belittling' the government of Adnan Menderes by publishing allegations against the prime minister, chiefly that he had used American aid funds not for the country's benefit but to bolster his own popularity. The court imposed heavy fines upon *Vatan*, which it also closed for a month, and sentenced Yalman to sixteen months in prison, signalling its contempt for him when it shortened the sentence, but by a mere fortnight, in recognition of Yalman's advanced age and poor health.

Time was the prime minister would have applauded Yalman's conviction that any country should be able to 'criticise itself freely, because that is the most reliable promise of a better future'; time was the Menderes administration had appeared to offer every prospect of that better future. But those days appeared impossibly distant. It was as if Adnan Bey and his judiciary, blind to the irony that the newspaper they now criminalised and the proprietor they now imprisoned were the ones Adnan Bey had once used to put press freedoms at the centre of the Democrats' bid for power, had forgotten such times ever existed; had forgotten how he had once lambasted authoritarian regimes, insisting that 'governments that do their work well should have no reason to be afraid of freedom of the press'. As it was, the prime minister's wilful disregard for the freedoms he had once embraced with such fervour, back when Adnan Bey was the country's brightest hope, only made his former friend more determined to defend them.

In scenes described as 'grotesque, almost farcical, as if the Editor of *The Times* were standing at the threshold of Wormwood Scrubs', Yalman presented himself at the prison gates, laden with the bedding Turkish prisoners were traditionally required to provide for themselves as well as a stack of books, where he addressed a crowd of supporters.

'I have been a journalist for fifty-three years,' he said as well-wishers pressed bouquets upon him. 'I have spent all those years with the belief and longing for freedom . . . Although my will is strong, if my body cannot stand the strain of prison at the age of seventy-two, I will consider death in this way a service to my country.' An article in *Vatan* expressed Yalman's carefully worded conviction was that 'a normal regime of freedom and justice' would soon come to Turkey.

*

In the days after the celebrated stand-off at Himmetdede, which took place just a week after the death at Urfa of Said Nursi, Ismet Paşa did a lot of thinking. Even more than usual. Ismet Paşa liked to think. He was said to do a lot of his best thinking at dinner parties, even official functions, excusing himself from conversation to retreat into whatever thoughts – a knotty political issue, perhaps, or an especially intricate chess move – preoccupied him. He cited his poor hearing which he blamed on the battering his eardrums had received from artillery barrages during the War of Independence, an ailment which had especially troubled him while at Lausanne where, as the chief Turkish treaty negotiator, he simply failed to hear any proposal which did not meet his approval until those across the table just as simply tired of repeating it.

Although he had made much of not hearing people, Ismet Paşa knew that the time had come for others to hear him. He was, after all, Atatürk's successor – the man to solve all problems. The leader of the opposition's word carried weight. As matters appeared to be coming to a head, to judge by the events at Himmetdede, ever more people wished to know what that word was. What was to be done, in short, about the problem of Adnan Bey and his Democrats whose cynical piety, reckless tolerance of Said Nursi, blatant appropriation of the national radio, draconian press laws, resort to violence at Uşak and elsewhere, and unconstitutional restrictions on Ismet Paşa's own rights to travel, not to mention their gross economic ineptitude, could no longer be tolerated?

Ismet Paşa, said to be possessed of a head containing forty foxes whose tails never touched – crafty, in other words – had never been one to act on impulse. He liked to consider every move from every angle, which in this case must take him back to his democratic credentials. Ismet Paşa took pride in counting himself a democrat; Turkey's first democrat, in fact, the man who had done away with Turkey's single-party state in 1946. He was credited with casting his party's overwhelming defeat in the 1950 elections as nothing less than the greatest of his victories. For these reasons he had rebuffed out of hand the high-ranking generals who discreetly offered more than once, the first time just days after his ousting in May 1950, to intervene on his behalf.

What he had not done was report any of these approaches to the authorities. Just as he had no plans to report the intervention he lately understood some officers to be planning. He had infinite respect for Atatürk's sacred tenet that the army refrain from involving itself in civil affairs; every last soldier did. But since Himmetdede, where Adnan Bey had been the one to defy Atatürk's order, all that had changed; now that the government had moved to involve the army in civil affairs, officers saw no reason why they should not now involve themselves. Given the state of the country, Ismet Paşa sympathised, though he was not about to say so. But he was bound to say what he could. Within the rules. When the chance arose.

That chance occurred on 18 April 1960 when the government acted upon the threats it had been making against the opposition since Kayseri. At the Assembly its MPs voted into existence a commission charged with investigating the 'destructive and illegal' activities of the Republican Party and its supporters in the press. This commission, composed entirely of partisan Democrat MPs, was granted 'extraordinary executive and judicial powers' which it promptly used to ban all political demonstrations and prohibit the publication of any information relating to the commission, to its work or activities. When his time came, the opposition leader rose in the Assembly to condemn the measures as unconstitutional, as he had also condemned the attempts to stop him reaching Kayseri, before making the following observation. He was still saying it – 'If a government ignores human rights and establishes a repressive regime, a rising may occur' – when outraged Democrat MPs began raining their briefcases down on him.

On 27 April the government conferred additional powers upon the commission, which Ismet Paşa took as the cue to go further himself. These new powers allowed the commission to search premises, seize property and documents, and order arrests and prison sentences of up to three years for those who resisted its work. It could close newspapers and even political parties. In fact, it could 'do just about anything it – or Mr Menderes – wants to do, including abolishing the Republican People's Party, the original political organisation of Kemal Atatürk', as the *New York Times* put it. 'History,' Ismet Paşa reminded the Assembly, 'shows that no dictatorship which relies on force can last.' To illustrate the point, he cited the coup which had occurred only the day before in South Korea. Democrat MPs, recalling the dark insinuations Ismet Paşa had taken to making after Iraq, were incensed. As the chamber descended into mayhem, the speaker charged Ismet Paşa with incitement and ordered his expulsion. Later that day the commission acted on its powers to suppress the opposition leader's comments, but not before a newspaper had included them in a rushed-out edition, copies of which duly found their way to opposition strongholds such as Istanbul University.

*

On 28 April 1960 Ali Fuad Başgil crossed Beyazit Square and passed through the nineteenth-century entrance of Istanbul University, an extravagant confection of marble columns, capitols, Moorish arches, recessed panels of gilded calligraphy and crenelated gatehouses, to prepare for his eleven o'clock lecture. To Başgil, the students gathered in the university grounds that morning appeared especially animated, a state of affairs which the professor of constitutional law put down to youthful high spirits as he mounted the stairs to his office. And he thought nothing of the noises he heard there, dismissing them as typical student rumpus, until the commotion reached such a pitch that he left to investigate. Professor Başgil, advised that a colleague had just cancelled the lecture he was to give on the constitution – on the grounds that the government had just violated it – was shocked to find thousands of students milling in the grand hall and along the surrounding galleries and corridors amidst shouts of 'Down with the government!', 'Menderes resign!' and other intemperate slogans. In the melee he caught sight of policemen attempting to clear the building with their batons. On being driven back, the police lobbed tear-gas canisters into the hall, causing the professor to retreat to his office as choking students dashed for the open air. They gathered around the statue of Atatürk in the university grounds to catch their breath, their eyes streaming, before resuming their chants as the police took up positions.

Through the morning the walled grounds, elegant lawns dotted with stands of pines and plane trees, were reduced to a battlefield as the protesters tore up clods of earth and stone kerbs to drive back a troop of mounted police. The police responded by driving their jeeps among the demonstrators, knocking several to the ground. The Physiology Department was requisitioned as a makeshift first-aid centre where students, professors and university staff, asphyxiated and battered, were treated. When university rector Sıddık Sami Onar upbraided the police officers, asking what right they had to enter the university without express permission, he was himself knocked to the ground, his glasses broken, and suffered a minor wound to the head. Bandaged up, more extensively than might have been necessary, the rector addressed the students, imploring them to disperse. They duly did so, only to regroup outside the main gate where the protests had spread to Beyazit Square. The students, incensed at the injuries to the rector, screamed anti-government abuse as the police repelled them with tear gas and baton charges. As the students responded with a fusillade of stones and broken paving slabs, the firing began.

Professor Başgil was consulting with other staff members when the faculty secretary told him there was somebody on the telephone; it was a junior minister, one of the professor's former law students, with an urgent request from Adnan Bey that he come to Ankara at his earliest convenience. As Başgil was one of the few associates whom Adnan Bey continued to regard as a reliable ally, the professor promised to try, despite the trouble he might have getting to Haydar-paşa. He managed to catch his train to Ankara where he learned that the disturbances had spread to the capital's university, especially to the faculty of Political Science, and that for the first time since the riots of September 1955 both cities had been placed under martial law; he also heard the first rumours of fatalities. The following evening Professor Başgil was summoned to dinner at the presidential residence where he told the assembled leadership – President Bayar, Adnan Bey, Zorlu, Koraltan and other senior government figures – of the events he had witnessed the previous day. Afterwards, over coffee, the prime minister invited the professor to give his frank opinion as to the situation.

'That would take me too long,' said Professor Başgil. 'But let me state my honest opinion that by relying, rightly or wrongly, on the firm support of the great majority of the population, you have neglected the country's most active elements: the universities, writers and journalists, and army officers – in brief the nation's grey matter.'

'You really believe,' replied Adnan Bey, 'that rather than improve the lot, as you will know, of those at the nation's physical and social margins, we would have done better to devote our energies to placating a few university professors and journalists?'

The gathering broke up at half past eleven when the president, who was due to attend the NATO summit scheduled to open in Istanbul the next day, excused himself. On leaving the room, he advised his ministers, some of whom showed signs of wavering, his prime minister even offering to resign, that now was no time for weakness. The government should tough it out, not least to demonstrate resolve to their NATO allies.

By the time Professor Başgil got back to Istanbul there were tanks and troops on the streets, the city was under curfew, and the army had closed the university, along with all places of entertainment. All coverage of the protests was banned, so much so that even the NATO delegates were unceremoniously relieved of their newspapers and journals on arrival at the airport. The bellboys and desk clerks at the Hilton were so anxious to know what was going on in their city that they badgered the international delegates for news of casualties among the protesters. *The Times*, the delegates seemed to recall from their confiscated copies, had reported five dead and forty injured, with other sources suggesting heavier death tolls.

Intent on silencing one voice above all, the government banned all reference in the Turkish press to the opposition leader's comments. But the authorities failed to prevent Ismet Paşa from talking to foreign correspondents whose newspapers continued to reach subscribers in Turkey, especially in the universities, where opposition activists had relevant excerpts translated into Turkish and circulated, often by sympathetic army officers, among the protesters. So Ismet Paşa was able to persist with his line – that 'Turkish citizens will never accept a coercive regime'; that the students killed in the recent protests were to be honoured as 'fighters for Turkish freedom' who 'with their blood have shown the people where their duty lies'; and that 'an oppressive regime can never be sure of the army' – safe in the knowledge that his words were heard.

As for the protesters, they could see for themselves that the army units charged with carrying out the authorities' threat – to resort if necessary to extreme force – appeared unprepared to do so. Even in the height of the jostle troops refrained from using butts or bayonets – only broadsides – to push demonstrators back. Nor did they care to make arrests; demonstrators they did pick up – those, for example, who on 2 May gathered at the pedestal in Taksim Square where Ismet Paşa's proscribed statue was to have stood – were generally encouraged to escape on the way to detention centres or were treated to barracks hospitality, along with a hot meal, before being released with a slap on the back the following morning. The fellow feeling was clearly reciprocal; though the students might denounce the police as murderers, the firebrands among them taking every opportunity to lump into the men in the hated grey uniforms, they invariably broke into applause before giving way to troop detachments. 'We will not fight or resist our army,' one protester acknowledged. 'We do not like the police because they are appointed by Menderes.' Professor Başgil personally witnessed a troop of soldiers bear down on protesters, only for the two sides to dissolve in a round of brotherly embraces and to cries of 'Long live the army! Long live the brave Turkish soldier!'

Celebrations on 14 May, commemorating the tenth anniversary of the elections which had first brought the Democrats to power, were necessarily muted. All the government's efforts were focused on retaining control of the situation, which it attempted to do by countering the opposition leader's insurrectionist utterances with increasingly shrill reminders of Atatürk's absolute proscription of intervention. It had become a national shouting match, with Ismet Paşa on one side and government voices on the other providing the army with conflicting interpretations of its obligations. The government appeared to be losing; the declaration which a stern Fatin Rüştü Zorlu made at a government press conference – 'the Turkish officer is fully aware that the army should not interfere in politics' – could not prevent 1,000 elite cadets from Ankara's military academy joining the protests on 21 May. Unarmed and dressed in light khaki, the cadets marched in good order up Atatürk Boulevard, gathering at a statue of Atatürk to sing patriotic songs, as a crowd of several thousand civilians fell in behind them. Troops and police detachments stood by as locals shouted encouragement from the pavements.

By the time the Assembly met on 25 May the atmosphere in the chamber crackled with resentment and hostility. What ensued, in the words of the *Times* correspondent, was 'one of the most violent scenes in the history of the Turkish parliament'. The trouble began when a leading Republican MP upheld the opposition's right to be heard, despite repeatedly being ruled out of order, by refusing to stop talking. He declared it intolerable that the prime minister's speeches were widely published while the least mention of the opposition leader's responses was banned. The Democrats set about silencing the stubborn deputy by force; within seconds all manner of

missiles – chairs, desk lids, inkpots, ashtrays, briefcases and light
bulbs – were being hurled. The parties retreated to respective sides
of the hall to bombard each other. The fighting raged for fully a
quarter of an hour before order was restored and the injured, some
fifteen MPs, were attended to.

As the session drew to a close it was agreed that the National
Assembly should be adjourned, on account of various religious holidays, for a month. In fact, it would be another eighteen months
before a democratically elected Assembly sat again in Turkey; and in
the new building – the fittings fixed, advisedly enough, to prevent
their use as missiles – which even then was rising from foundations
in the new town near Kocatepe.

*

I was up to my elbows in newspapers, immersed in the events of
1960, when a ping announced a text from Metin. 'Our politics at
work,' he said. 'Take a look!' Phone footage recently taken at the
National Assembly – now housed in the building near Kocatepe –
showed what had happened after pro-Erdoğan deputies proposed an
amendment designed to clear the way for the prosecution of opposition leaders, especially those in the Kurdish party. The proposal had
not gone down well. Fingers were pointed and insults hurled, and
voices erupted in anger. As the statutory jostling began, female MPs
backed hurriedly out of their seats, scooping up phones and pausing
to steer frail colleagues clear by the elbows. 'Friends, friends,' somebody implored, but to no avail, the noise gathering to a crescendo
with the opening flurry of punches. With an ease which suggested
the move was not entirely new to them, overweight men vaulted
desks, scattering documents and coffee cups as they threw themselves into the fray. A man clambered onto a table and began aiming
kicks at the surging melee, pausing only to catch his breath and
straighten his tie. Papers flew. Deep in the scrum a man fought on
with one hand, the other pawing frantically about for his dislodged
wig. Everything that was not screwed down – bags, water glasses,

folders – was hurled. Noses were bloodied, and the shaken and injured were helped away only for fresh MPs to step in, ignoring the appeals for calm.

They were another reminder, these brawling politicians, of the insistent parallels: the same jokes, the same building programmes, the same piety, the same persecution of journalists. Even the same phraseology, *Milli Irade* – the National Will – being a term that the president bandied about these days quite as liberally as his inspiration had done. I wondered where events were heading, and what this might mean for Erdoğan, knowing what it had meant for Adnan Bey.

'Remind me what year we're in!!' I texted back.

*

The wounded were still being treated when Adnan Bey left the Assembly for the airport. He had another round of rallies and openings to attend. Of late the prime minister had been cramming in all the rallies he could; demanding them, to the despair of his aides, at increasingly short notice, even when it meant cancelling long-standing official appointments – in this case, a visit to Greece. In the face of it all – the protests, the calls for his resignation, the slights and slurs, the opposition leader's intolerable provocations, and now these unseemly brawls – rallies were his only comfort. He craved the solace he took from the country crowds and their sacrifices, the bunting and the triumphal arches, the applause at every button he pressed and every ribbon he cut. Rallies being the best restorative he knew, nerve pills aside, there was nothing for it but to up the dose.

The prime minister, with the finance minister among his entourage, flew west in a Viscount to Eskişehir. Local dignitaries, the provincial governor among them, had gathered to meet Adnan Bey at the military airfield where he took some air-force officers to be part of the welcome. Descending the steps, he paused to receive their salute, only for the officers to turn their backs and march away across the apron. It was a mortifying moment which the provincial governor did what he could to assuage, rushing forward with assurances that Adnan Bey could expect the warmest of receptions. Arrangements had been made, despite the short notice, for fleets of lorries to ferry thousands of villagers to the city. Placards had been distributed, shops and houses bedecked with the Star and Crescent. Party officials had installed a podium in front of the municipal building; there was a microphone, and no fewer than four speakers, so that Adnan Bey's message was sure to be heard.

It was the message he had been making for weeks – a condemnation of Ismet Paşa's thinly veiled appeals to insurrection. He had come to power, he reminded the Eskişehir crowds, 'by the National Will. I am prime minister by the National Will. No means other than elections can remove us from power.' He dismissed the protests as the actions of those intent on acquiring 'power not by the route of elections but by force'. 'Our way,' he insisted, 'is that of free elections, the fostering of liberty and democracy . . . what they aim to do is to achieve their ends by compulsion and by abandoning proper political process . . . we will maintain order in all moderation without permitting the least dilution of the principle that the affairs of state can only be steered by elections.'

The message, defiant and spirited, nevertheless seemed to leave the Eskişehir crowds oddly unmoved. It turned out that few of them had been able to hear the speech; three of the speakers had not been working, which embarrassed Democrat officials were quick to blame on opposition saboteurs. The Republicans vehemently denied the charge, no doubt taking private satisfaction that the prime minister now knew – like their own leader – what it was like to be silenced.

The technical failure incensed the fraught and exhausted Adnan Bey, a man who expected above all else to be heard. Without a voice, after all, what was a leader? It was a grim, even disabling feeling, leaving him with the sense that he had experienced a catastrophic loss of control; a feeling with which he was about to become extremely familiar.

The next time Adnan Bey was heard in public would be to speak in his own defence.

CHAPTER TEN

27 May 1960

Coup

On 26 May a group of army officers in Istanbul took a telephone call from Ankara. The caller rang with news of the pension fund; of the 2,740 lira received, he told them, articulating the numbers with care, ten lira had been deducted, which left 2,730 lira. The news was passed onto others with an interest in the matter, men who had more immediate concerns than any deductions from the income they could expect upon retirement, namely the action tabled for the following morning, which had now been brought forward an hour.

So it was that troop detachments and tank units of the 3rd Armoured Brigade deployed across Istanbul at 3 a.m. on 27 May. The night curfew, so strictly enforced that transgressors risked being shot, saw to it that nobody was on the streets to notice. Nor after a month under martial law was any night owl, parting the curtains to the rumble of tank tracks and the thud of boots, likely to have given a second thought to these signs of military activity. That evening Istanbul's military commander, who was in on the action, had thrown a dinner party; as the evening drew to a close those military and civilian supporters of the government whom the commander had seen fit to invite discovered that they were to be prevented from leaving. Instead it was their host who left to dispatch his forces as he saw fit – to the Governorate, the central post office, the railway stations, airport and radio station, all of which were promptly seized on his order. The police headquarters submitted without a fight. 'We took over Istanbul in twenty minutes,' one of the officers was to recall, 'without even firing a single bullet.'

The situation was more challenging in the capital where the martial law commander was known to be a staunch government loyalist. But he was not especially popular with his officers, many of whom had discreetly intimated that the rebels could count on their units' support. The commanders of the 28th Division and the 43rd Regiment, both based in Ankara, refused to join in the action but did give assurances not to intervene on behalf of the regime, which nevertheless left the conspirators short of forces on which to call. The decision was taken to make the cadets of the military academy, lately lionised for their protest march, the heroes of the piece; the capture of the capital would fall to the coming generation of brave young officers whose evident commitment to the cause made up for their lack of combat experience. On the evening of 26 May the cadets received their orders, were issued with arms and advised to get some sleep as they were in for an early start. Shortly before 3 a.m. they rose, dressed and clambered into waiting trucks which dropped them at designated points in the city where they linked up with rebel martial law units. When some cadets opened fire, the jittery ones glimpsing phantom shadows in the moonlight, the only response was from disturbed dogs. With fighter jets flying low over the city, few police units chose to resist as troops secured the radio station, the Prime Ministry, the National Assembly, the post office and other key installations.

The next priority was to round up the leading members of the regime. At the presidential residence in Çankaya the Bayar family and staff were woken by gunfire. From the prime minister's house, also located in the presidential compound, they were joined by a distressed Berin Menderes and her youngest son Aydın. President Bayar dressed, ordered the women and children to stay out of sight, and went downstairs to discover that the phone line had been cut. Spotting approaching tanks through the windows, the president took from a drawer his old service revolver which he levelled at the doors as they flew open. A group of armed officers advanced into the hallway.

'Lay down your weapon and give yourself up,' ordered one of them. 'Or I fire.'

'But I am here by the National Will,' the president replied. 'And only by the National Will do I intend to leave. Ah, my Colonel,' he added, noticing the commander of the Presidential Guard among the intruders. 'And there was I thinking it was your duty to protect us.' The president sighed, lowering the gun before turning it on himself. But the old man's movements were slow enough, perhaps by design, that an officer had time to disarm him before he could pull the trigger. Hearing raised voices and sounds of scuffle, the president's wife and daughter rushed down the stairs only to be restrained by a cordon of soldiers as the captive was led outside to a military ambulance.

In the hours before dawn the capital's residential districts resounded with the clatter of boots on staircases, the hammering of fists on doors and the querulous utterances of the rudely awoken, as squads of soldiers led away ministers, MPs, officials, the martial law commander and other government loyalists. Some had not yet taken to bed; Foreign Minister Zorlu, who saw no reason to dignify whatever the military meant by these actions, made no attempt to flee but coolly rang an army contact with the Ankara address where they would find him before returning to the latter stages of a poker game.

In Teşvikiye, Istanbul, eighteen-year-old Baysan Aygün awoke to the dog barking as the lift stopped at the floor of the family apartment. There was a series of strident raps at the door. Wrapping herself in a dressing gown, she hurried out to find armed soldiers in the hall. An officer was telling her father that he was under arrest and was to come with them. The mayor nodded and briefly excused himself, fiercely upbraiding the soldiers who tried to follow him into the bedroom. A few minutes later he emerged, fully dressed, to kiss his daughters whom he told to study hard. He embraced his wife and urged her not to worry. Then he turned to the officer. 'I am at your disposal,' he said. 'I have a wife, a mother, a sister and two daughters. If anything happens to any of them, I will live to take my revenge.

And should I die, somebody else will avenge me.' Then Baysan's father was gone, the dog barking at the rumble of the departing lift.

In Eskişehir Adnan Bey had retired after attending a dinner given in his honour by the regional Sugar Cooperative. After the debacle over his inaudible speech the previous evening this one had gone off well enough, the toasts accompanied by welcome pledges of loyalty to the government, though the news that a number of law professors were about to release a public protest against Adnan Bey's regime had added to his anxiety. He awoke from a fitful sleep to urgent knocking on the door of his hotel room. He opened it on an aide.

'Well?' Adnan Bey asked.

'The army, Adnan Bey,' the aide spluttered. 'It's the army. It seems they've taken over.'

The prime minister reached for his cigarettes. 'Is Polatkan awake? Get me the finance minister,' he said. He tried the bedside phone, which went unanswered. Scooping up a pill and reaching for a glass of water, he wondered if he should pack or whether there was still somebody to do that for him. He was chasing down the pill when a pale-looking Polatkan appeared at the door.

'The colonels?' asked Adnan Bey. Polatkan shrugged. 'Colonels, generals, majors,' he said.

'I dare say we should leave,' said Adnan Bey. 'Make for some-where.'

'Let me see if any drivers are about,' said Polatkan. 'Maybe try for one of our strongholds. Even the border.'

'I'll dress and meet you downstairs, Hasan Bey. With cigarettes, please, if you happen across any.'

When Adnan Bey joined him in the hotel lobby, Polatkan looked worried.

'Drivers,' he said, gesturing at the jeeps outside the hotel. 'Army, though they seem to be taking my orders.'

'Perhaps they're with us, these,' said Adnan Bey, the idea appear-ing to embolden him. Cupping his hair, he strode up to the soldiers standing by the jeeps. 'Good morning, gentlemen,' he said in his usual courteous tones. 'If it's not too much trouble, we'd like to go to

Kütahya.' The driver looked at his companion who nodded before helping the two men into a jeep. As the jeep pulled away Polatkan looked over his shoulder.

'The other jeeps are following us,' he said. 'As if we're in some kind of convoy?'

'Call it a motorcade,' replied Adnan Bey in a threadbare show of bravado. 'Did you get cigarettes?' As Polatkan shook his head, the soldier leant over from the passenger seat to proffer a pack, raising a hand when Adnan Bey tried to return it, the gift a tacit intimation that the prime minister would need more cigarettes than the single one he had taken. The jeeps left the sleeping city for Kütahya; the town, an hour's drive away, was one of the prime minister's most loyal parliamentary constituences. 'Kütahya,' muttered Adnan Bey as he wrapped his jacket close. 'There'll be friends in Kütahya. And from there, who knows, we might even make it to Aydın.' In the darkness it was possible to believe in a way to safety. Then Polatkan looked up.

'Planes overhead,' he said. 'They've seen our lights.'

The world was stirring, the dawn chasing the jeeps westwards across the steppe. Over the years Adnan Bey had known many dawns, on the farm and in the cities, in rooms far from home, even on previous visits to this very town, this adoring constituency, when they'd come out for him in such numbers with their banners and flags. And now he was back, in a dawn like no other, hunched in the back of a jeep, cold and unwashed, as a farmstead dog lunged on its chain as they passed, its barks rousing the birds from their roost in a stand of poplars which seemed to shake itself free of them. At the outskirts of Kütahya figures stirred in the repair yards and the premises of marble merchants, rubbing their eyes and lighting cigarettes. Smoke rose from teahouse stoves. Boys emerged from the bakeries with trays of *simit* rolls. Then, beyond a bend, there were army vehicles in the road; and in place of the well-wishers with their sacrificial animals, men with guns and a colonel waving the convoy to a halt.

*

When had it begun? With the significant nods of those disaffected army officers at an Izmır restaurant, and other gestures of intent exchanged at mess dinners, on parade grounds, across the tables of ops rooms and bars, which duly turned into action as men saw their own readiness to do something reflected in the eyes of others.

From as early as 1954 the first cliques had begun to appear, though only to themselves. A dozen ardent young officers at the Staff College in Istanbul formed an organisation whose members were bound to strictest secrecy. They were forbidden from committing anything to paper, and to limit what they might reveal under duress – under the medieval methods these arrangements evidently appeared to expect of their interrogators – new recruits were inducted into self-contained cells, their contact restricted to fellow members.

By 1957 the organisation had established covert links with like-minded groups in gunnery schools and military installations in Istanbul and Ankara. As discontent spread through the officer corps, so it acquired definition; groups that had initially found fault with the military leadership now directed their resentment towards the civilian government for wilfully debasing the army's cherished prestige, for allowing their salaries to drop to humiliating levels, and for betraying Atatürk by knocking holes in the institutional defences which the eternal leader had raised against Islamic reaction.

Initially the officers contented themselves with amateurish activities like planting anonymous leaflets – generalised calls to action in the defence of Kemalism – in the desks and drawers of potential confreres. In time, however, a plan began to emerge, but one that would only have a shot at success if these colonels, majors and captains, recognising what rank could do for their ambitions, found themselves some five-star support. They aimed high, only for the generals they approached to rebuff them, ordering that they make no further contact with their people. What these generals did not do was report them, which the officers took as their cue to keep looking. The conspirators' secret trawl paid off in 1958 when they succeeded in netting the commander of land forces, only for the general to rule himself out by dying of a heart attack shortly after consenting to work with them.

In February 1959, at the time of the prime minister's miraculous escape at Gatwick, the officers' luck turned. One of the more active plotters, dispatched to attend NATO exercises in Germany, happened to be assigned to the newly appointed commander of land forces, General Cemal Gürsel, a man known for his bluff and approachable disposition. One day the officer chanced to find himself in the same military vehicle as the general along with, inconveniently enough, two American servicemen. Although the officer judged the Americans unlikely to speak Turkish, he was not about to take any chances, the plotters having lately come perilously close to being exposed. Only after asking the Americans the time in Turkish, which caused neither man to look at his watch, did the officer feel safe in telling Gürsel of the grievances increasingly felt across the officer corps and the determination of some, if it came to it, to do something about it. These revelations did not seem to disturb the general; so attentive did Gürsel prove that the officer felt emboldened to solicit his support. By the end of the exercises in Germany the conspirators had their leader. Cemal Gürsel was soon to prove his value in helping assign rebel officers to posts considered key to any action. These included head of personnel at the General Staff, the directorship of military intelligence as well as the command of the Presidential Guard in Ankara, a highly symbolic detachment whose traditionally fierce loyalty to the presidency might otherwise have threatened any action's outcome.

As to the other hindrance, Atatürk's absolute refusal to countenance intervention, well, with undying respect to the Gazi, this was an obstacle that the more committed conspirators appeared determined to find ways around. Was it not the case, they argued, that Atatürk had himself rebelled in the service of his country? Was not the Turkish Republic itself founded on a coup – of 19 May 1919? What did that sacred date commemorate if not righteous revolt? Was there not a point at which the state of the country not only justified intervention but demanded it as a solemn duty? And if that was not now – when partisans traded daily insults and slights in teahouses and restaurants, setting off scuffles which grew into street fights as they spilled onto the pavements, then pitched battles as rival supporters set about each other in town squares and on construction sites, besting even their brawling representatives in the National Assembly – then when could it ever be?

While the protests, the bruises and beatings, the tear gas and the cordite seemed to presage nothing less than civil war, at least to those who sought pretexts for intervention, events did not finally play into the officers' hands until the spring of 1960, when 'military dissidence spread with explosive speed'. For this it was, remarkably, the government that they had to thank; the rebels could not believe their luck when the Democrats called out the army at Kayseri to stop a man – *the* man – whom officers and troops alike held in highest regard; nor when the government put troops on the streets of the cities to embroil them in a fight not of their making and on the side they did not consider their own. The government had effectively obliged the army to choose – which, taking its lead from the utterances of the revered Ismet Paşa, it had already done, however tacitly, by the time the Ankara cadets joined the student protests. The government's decision to impose martial law in the cities, putting its key institutions at the mercy of army units it continued to trust, despite the contrary indications, seemed like a gross misjudgement. Or even the sign of a leadership so fraught with exhaustion as to be willing its own end.

*

When dawn broke on 27 May 1960 many of the cities' windows and balconies were already draped in celebratory flags. From the early hours the radio had issued announcements of a bloodless takeover of the country by a body calling itself the Committee of National Unity. In sombre tones a colonel urged restraint on citizens, ordering them to remain indoors until 4 p.m., when they were free to run essential errands but not to attend street gatherings, and to be back

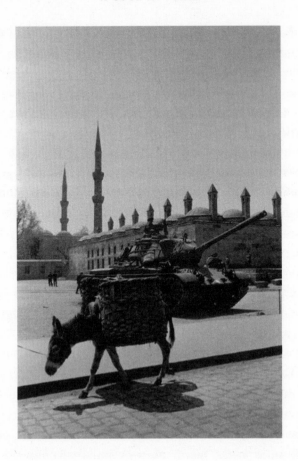

home by 9 p.m. In a country where respect for military discipline ran deep, army orders tended to go unquestioned; and if these were the rules, then the people of Ankara and Istanbul would keep to the curfew – and, if the army insisted, the pavements. The crowds that emerged that first afternoon largely heeded the Committee's instructions, lining the streets and for the most part limiting themselves to polite applause as troop carriers passed, though the more expressive did proffer flowers and sweets, and even break into occasional chants of 'Long live the Turkish army.'

Those who had long disdained the radio as a slavish regime mouthpiece, even forming societies of defiant radio refuseniks, now dusted down their appliances to attend obediently to the

Committee's announcements. These communiqués came thick and fast, first telling of the new man in charge, General Cemal Gürsel. It was said that Gürsel, lately put on extended leave at his home in Izmır by a government doubtful as to his loyalty, was so ready to serve that he had been up since 4 a.m. in full military rig, busying himself with watering the garden while he awaited news of arrangements for him to assume command. Later that morning the officers flew Gürsel to Ankara where he gave a radio statement about the historic task facing the Committee of National Unity. He announced that he had 'taken control of the State and overall command of the Armed Forces', though only to free 'the country from the grasp of ambitious politicians who meant to drag it into misery and crisis'. He denied any intention to become a dictator, insisting his wish was 'to institute democratic order as soon as possible, and to leave the direction of the State to the nation'. Subsequent communiqués reported that leading figures of the former regime had been taken into custody, the president detained at his residence, and Prime Minister Menderes arrested at Kütahya, along with Finance Minister Polatkan, before being flown under guard back to Ankara; the honorable Ismet Inönü and his companions were safe and in good health; the National Assembly had been dissolved; a legal commission headed by Rector Onar of Istanbul University had already begun work on preparing a new constitution; the release of all detained students and academics had been ordered; all closed university faculties and schools were to be reopened, and courses resumed, as soon as possible; all weapons, excepting sabres and swords dating from the First World War, were to be surrendered; and Istanbul's Conquest celebrations, due on 29 May, were cancelled.

It could hardly have gone more smoothly; so much so that some of the officers assumed running the country would prove no less straightforward than taking control. Wiser comrades, ruefully aware that their relevant competencies barely extended beyond the nighttime capture of some buildings and regime figures, in almost all cases freely surrendered, wasted no time in calling in the lawyers.

The airport at Ankara was especially busy on the morning of 27 May; and not long after the buttoned and braided new man arrived to salutes and flashing cameras, and the old one was delivered in a paratroopers' transport which he and his finance minister were obliged to share with a consignment of fuel drums, another flight brought seven Istanbul law professors to Ankara. It was no accident that these professors were all outspoken critics of the regime, their recent comments having provoked the fury and scorn of the prime minister. 'Liberty indeed!' the prime minister had scoffed; these self-proclaimed champions of freedom, were they not the same men who throughout the decades of single-party rule had maintained a craven silence on such matters? Accusing them of abusing their positions, even of inciting the student protests, the prime minister had denounced the professors as nothing less than a profound evil. 'The professors talk about their universities as if they were the Great Wall of China,' he had raged at one of his final rallies. 'Do they think that their professorial gowns will serve as a kind of armour?' The tacit threat – perhaps to the professors' posts or pensions – had turned out to be to their persons when Rector Onar of Istanbul University, a distinguished professor of administrative law, had been knocked to the ground and dealt a black eye, spectacles smashed, while trying to protect his fellow academics and students during the demonstrations.

In the weeks leading up to the coup Rector Onar, whose slight injuries had been displayed to full visibility, like Ismet Paşa's after the incident at Uşak the year before, had emerged as an opposition figurehead; it was he whom the Committee had tasked with hastily assembling the legal delegation which he now led to Ankara. His colleagues passed the flight in fevered speculation; all the rector could tell them – the army officer having been no clearer than the line which carried that morning's early call – was that they were to advise on a new constitution. Such talk was bound to raise legal eyebrows, and even in the tumult of national liberation it was not lost upon some of the professors that no greater violation could be done to a constitution than simply sending out for a new one. It was as if these officers mistook constitutions to wear out much as firing mechanisms did, the old one having suffered such abuse under the former regime as no longer to be fit for purpose.

Whatever their role in all this, the professors' presence in the capital evidently could not wait. Their flight had barely landed before they were ushered down the aircraft steps into the glare of the Anatolian sun where military vehicles stood with doors open and engines idling. The professors were still settling into their seats when the vehicles set off past the tanks and troop carriers at the airport entrance, the soldiers at the roadblocks so caught up in the excitement that they briefly misplaced their customary discipline to urge on the convoy like race-circuit devotees. Horns sounded, scattering roadside flocks of long-tailed sheep, as the vehicles sped across the brown steppe. On their arrival at the capital the professors saw crumbling apartments whose damp-stained exteriors were hung with flags, daubed with pledges of eternal loyalty to Atatürk and demands for Menderes to resign, their residents cramming the balconies while they waited out the curfew. Beyond empty boulevards the vehicles screeched to a halt outside a ministry building where a young officer extended a hand in welcome. He led the way down a long corridor at a parade-ground clip, the portly professors in their rumpled suits panting by the time they reached the briefing room. Officers in crisp khaki uniforms and law colleagues from Ankara University greeted them with hearty handshakes and pats on the back. Congratulations were proffered, along with cigarettes, and light-hearted comments on the previous night – 'Long,' said an officer, 'and memorable, if not for the quality of sleep' – were bandied about before the professors were ushered to seats around a conference table. The laughter subsided as the officers took their places opposite, pushing aside plates of cakes, glasses of tea, scattered telegrams and scribbled drafts of communiqués to make space for their caps. A senior officer, whose stripes marked him out as a general, addressed the table.

'Apologies to our distinguished legal colleagues for disturbing your well-earned sleep,' he said. 'In deference to your onerous professional commitments we would rather have invited you here at your convenience, and with due notice. We hope you will appreciate that the actions we lately undertook rather militated against such courtesies.' The general stifled a yawn, but not before it had told of a long night and of the officers' undertakings on the nation's behalf, which the professors' wholehearted murmurs acknowledged. The general smiled, leaning back in his chair. 'We have done what we did,' he said, 'for the good of the nation, which we hope the people will understand.' His words triggered another round of appreciative utterances which the general curtailed with a raised hand. 'That brings us to the question of what happens next,' he said. 'The question which in fact brings us to you, honoured gentlemen of learning, and you to us. In considering the national interest and the urgent need for stability, it is the Committee's proposal that our esteemed and erudite professors should take the lead in convening an interim council which, time being necessarily short, we would look to see installed by tomorrow. At midday. Now, can we get you some more tea while we leave you to discuss these matters among yourselves and in your own time – if not quite' – the general glanced at his watch – 'at your absolute leisure? More cakes?'

In the silence one of the professors asked if somebody might be good enough to open a window; it had already been a long morning and some of the professors, accustomed to the temperate Bosphorus breezes, were beginning to find the steppe heat uncomfortable. An officer obliged before closing the door behind him as he followed his colleagues from the room.

'Did I hear that right?' a professor eventually whispered.

'An interim council. The general's words.'

'A temporary arrangement, which they wish us to help organise.'

'Organise?' asked somebody. 'God, but don't we have our department secretaries for that?'

'Organise, lead, call it what you will – "taking the lead" was certainly the phrase he used.'

'Lectures are more my thing, to be honest, and attending conferences . . .'

'Giving papers. Getting books written.'

'Hardly taking the lead.'

'The national lead, at that, which is what – unless I'm very much mistaken – he was suggesting.'

'That we, put simply, are the ones to run the country.'

'Starting from tomorrow.'

'At midday.'

'At least after a lie-in, then,' said someone sardonically. 'Did somebody say something about more cakes?'

Later that morning the rector informed the general that the professors must decline the Committee's proposal. They could not take control of the nation, themselves of all people, because the law – which they had sworn to interpret and uphold – did not provide for them to do so. Besides, these ageing academics had neither the training, the temperament nor the stamina to rule. Only those who had overthrown the former regime, whose own army code charged them with protecting and preserving the Republic and the constitution, could take charge.

That said, the professors were more than happy to assist by providing a justification for the previous night's events. They could draw up a legal declaration, the rector explained, a condemnation of the regime's abuses to provide the officers with grounds for their action, even to cast it as a heroic act of national defence. The professors, understanding time to be tight, might even be able to have this report done by the following day; they'd need help – secretaries, typewriters, access to the necessary legal tomes, waste-paper baskets – all of which the Committee officers unhesitatingly offered. In no time the professors were at work, labouring into the night to draft the preliminary report which they set before the Committee the following morning.

The report, which began by insisting that the recent events did not constitute a coup, was all that the officers could have hoped for. It condemned the Democrats for allowing political power to be corrupted by personal and class ambitions. Legality of rule, the report asserted, lay not only in how a government came to power but in its observance of the constitution; by respecting such institutions as the press, the army, the judiciary and the universities – all of which the Democrats had totally failed to do. In the light of these failures, intervention was nothing less than a sacred national duty. A duty which, it pleased the Committee members to discover, the report judged them to have fulfilled with distinction.

*

A few days later the Committee, secure in the support of the cities, gave its blessing to public celebrations of the revolution, a term the officers had been quick to adopt from the law professors. The country was to honour the victims of the fallen regime and recognise the heroes credited with bringing it down; the army, of course, but also the journalists, academics, and especially the students whom admirers preferred to call the Youth, in the heroic phrase favoured by Atatürk. The unrest which had continued up to the coup – the running battles, the clouds of tear gas, the baton charges and the gunfire – gave way to celebratory parades. Ten days after the revolution Istanbul staged a procession of troop carriers, tanks and jeeps which delirious students boarded to strew with flags, laurel branches and flowers. At Beyazit Square, sanctified as the birthplace of the revolution, a dais was raised beneath a giant portrait of Atatürk. Fighter jets flew overhead as the crowds showered generals and university leaders with red and white carnations. A statement read out on behalf of General Gürsel spoke of the Committee's 'closest rapport with the fervour of our Youth whose blood has not been spilt in vain. It falls to us, on behalf of the entire nation and our enlightened Youth, to provide an administration worthy of the nation. Long live Turkish Youth!'

Another parade converged on Taksim Square where army commanders, heads of military colleges and poets praised the achievements of the army and the Youth, with one speaker describing the blood spilt as no less sacred than that lost at Sakarya and Dumlupınar, hallowed battles in the War of Independence. Students waved placards which read 'The army is our religion', and 'What

Youth began the army completed'. They gathered at the plinth where Ismet Paşa's statue was to have stood and which years earlier the former regime had made a point of boarding over. Gleefully exposing the plinth's laudatory inscriptions, they recited their hero's achievements over a celebratory bonfire made from the broken boards. At a ceremony to mark the reopening of the universities the president of the Union of Medical Students urged representations recommending the Turkish army for the Nobel Peace Prize.

In Ankara, where events had caused Atatürk's image to proliferate 'in shop windows, in restaurants, on the front pages of the newspapers', General Gürsel took the salute from the military academy cadets whom he hailed as the 'executing power' of the great action. To cheers of 'Long live Cemal Paşa!' he laid a wreath of carnations at the leader's mausoleum before inscribing a message in the golden book of remembrance. 'Your approval of our actions, in recognising them as consistent with the route that you have chosen,' he wrote, 'is our greatest reward and the cause of exceptional pride.'

Those who queried such presumptions of approval, judging the takeover to be 'in violation of Atatürk's firm principle that the army must not take part in politics', were wise enough to keep their doubts to themselves. For despite radio appeals for 'mutual consideration and respect, regardless of party affiliations', darker feelings had come to surface among the celebrations. With every reference to the former regime the rapturous cheers which greeted the speakers gave way to chants of 'Assassins, assassins, death to the assassins!' 'Those who shouted for Menderes got rich while those who called for liberty became heroes,' the crowds bellowed, waving placards which represented Menderes and Bayar as slavering dogs, their mouths crammed with dollar bills. In Ankara and other cities mobs wrecked Democrat Party offices while breast-beating students pledged their devotion to the revolution by presenting General Gürsel with flags soaked in their own blood. Partisans picketed the homes of detained Democrats, holding placards which accused them of theft and sundry other crimes. Acts of retribution abounded, with the official held responsible for the stoning at Uşak of Ismet Paşa ordered to do public penance by carrying a boulder, emblematic of the missile which had struck the great man, on a circuit of the town. In the view of the *Times* man in Ankara, a reckoning was nigh. 'Terrible feelings of revenge,' he wrote, 'now animate those who accuse Menderes and his followers of innumerable crimes.'

*

Within hours of the coup, the Committee lifted restrictions on all newspapers and publications. A communiqué applauded the imprisoned 'journalists who, without fear, put their pens at the disposal of the development of Turkish democracy', ruling that they be freed forthwith and that all cases against them be dismissed. Among these was Ahmed Emin Yalman. 'I had little inkling this would happen,' said Yalman. 'But I am delighted. This means a new democratic era for Turkey.'

Nor had Ismet Paşa known anything of the takeover, he claimed, when journalists gathered a few days later at his Ankara home to hear of the old soldier's delight at the turn of events. Ismet Paşa further denied any suggestion that his party had colluded with the conspirators, rebutting the specific rumour that the Republicans' involvement extended to providing the army with a list of the individuals they wished to see incarcerated. 'Mine is not a revolutionary party,' he stated. 'But the army action in my opinion was legitimate in the service of the nation. So quickly and clearly did it gain mass approval that one may say the masses themselves participated in the revolution.'

The journalists, less inclined to query the coup than celebrate it, were disposed to take Ismet Paşa's protestations of innocence on trust. To many of them, who for years had been persecuted for telling truths about the Democrats, it seemed no more than a settling of accounts that they should now tell of the 'innumerable crimes' which the Committee levelled against the former regime, even if these could not be completely confirmed or turned out to be exaggerated. Front pages carried colourful 'reports of the corruption of the old regime: of the immense fortunes deposited in foreign banks, the jewels, the yachts, the vast estates'; and of claims that Menderes himself was 'alleged to have transferred currency illegally for the purchase and furnishing of a luxurious villa'.

Other reports told how the thievish regime's disastrous mismanagement of the economy had further drained the national finances, bringing the treasury to its knees. It fell to the army, ever dependable, to do something about it, the officers of the 1st Armoured Brigade stepping up to save the nation from penury, as they had from tyranny, by donating their wedding rings to the treasury. Citizens who followed the officers' example were handed a replacement band, of plain tin, a badge of honour which served to damn yet more deeply the former regime, the more so when journalists were given leave to inspect a box of jewels, estimated to be valued at £12,000, found in the possession of the former foreign minister's wife. The foreign press sounded a note of caution, *The Times* querying the valuation in remarking upon 'the relative modesty of the collection, after the fantastic rumours which have been circulating', but the Turkish newspapers gorged on the story. In the weeks that followed, the least item of jewellery uncovered in the possession of Democrat families was taken to instance the regime's criminal venality, with even halfpenny baubles rousing journalists to new levels of outrage.

Nor, the Committee and its press allies alleged, were the Democrats merely rapacious. In a press conference held at the presidential residence – the Bayar family had since been bundled off to the airport and thence to house arrest at their holiday home near Izmır – General Gürsel denounced the former regime as murderers. He claimed to know that the Democrat leaders had planned the destruction of Ankara's military academy – with its occupants inside – in revenge for the cadets' participation in the demonstrations. 'They were preparing to shoot patriotic youngsters,' declared an enraged Gürsel. 'They decided that 1,500 souls were of no importance.' This was not the only evil scheme that the timely coup had foiled. The Committee claimed to know that the regime had planned to bring serious charges against Republican deputies, university professors and generals, and to expel Ismet Inönü from the country, all moves expressly designed

to provoke further protests which it meant to suppress with ultimate
force. Moreover, the government, intent on putting an end to the
fellow feeling that it so feared between soldiers and students, had
arranged that the killing would be carried out by squads of goons
dressed in army uniforms.

These were lurid allegations, which even the former regime's
most implacable opponents might have thought improbable. Such
was the mood in the cities, however, that few were about to doubt the
word of their hallowed saviours, the Committee, which anyway
claimed to have concrete evidence of iniquities the regime had
already perpetrated upon the country's 'heroic and generous student
Youth'. A communiqué told how the regime had attacked the demonstrators 'with batons and swords, and mercilessly opened fire' on
them, 'with several beaten or grievously injured and a large number
killed'. It further accused the government of 'actions of unimaginable savagery' in hiding and disposing of its victims. 'It seems,' the
communiqué continued, 'the heroes were secretly buried, thrown
down remote wells, and a certain number left in cold-storage depots
or minced up to make animal feed'. These were the foulest of crimes
'perpetrated with a terrifying savagery', which the Committee vowed
to expose at the earliest opportunity. It announced a ceremony of
national remembrance for 10 June, when the martyrs of the revolution would be committed to rest, and the killers brought to justice.

It was therefore a considerable inconvenience, if one which the
press showed little interest in acknowledging, that the military
authorities failed to locate the hidden remains of any such martyrs.
In their search for slaughtered students several graves known to have
been freshly dug in the Istanbul area were exhumed, but to no avail.
The Committee might have put this down to the mincing machines
and the remote wells – evidence, that is, of the former regime's ruth-
lessness in disposing of every last scrap of their victims – if it were
not for the fact that no family members or friends had come forward
to report missing loved ones.

It added up to a grievous lack of victims, and a gaping hole in
any case against the regime. The Committee had made so much of

10 June, however, that it could hardly call the whole thing off. The only option was to go with whatever line-up it could muster, however reduced, and hope that a sufficiently splendid send-off would paper over any cracks. The memorials began on 9 June when two coffins were accompanied through Istanbul by students carrying black-swathed portraits of their fallen heroes. To the chanted whisper of disbelief – 'Can it be, can it be, that one brother kills another?' – the procession passed through Beyazit before coming down to the shore at Sarayburnu. A naval launch in full state regalia transferred the coffins to Haydarpaşa Station where a special train awaited the victims who had given, in the words of one newspaper, 'their lives for liberty and whose reward was to be a final resting place alongside the man who brought freedom to the nation'.

The following afternoon the Istanbul dead were united with the three victims killed in Ankara before the martyrs, five in total, were borne through the capital's hushed streets on flag-draped gun carriages. A cavalry detachment, cadets from the military academy, delegations of university professors and journalists, representatives of the Committee and the Republican People's Party, and an infantry unit bearing hundreds of wreaths formed a grand cortege. The solemn procession made its way to Atatürk's mausoleum where cadets shouldered the coffins which they carried into the inner courtyard. After a minute's silence a student spoke for Youth, a soldier for the army and a young official for the newly constituted authority, each saluting these heroes of liberty who had given their lives for the noblest of causes and to the nation's eternal gratitude.

The speakers avoided any reference to the circumstances of the victims' deaths, and not only because such details had no place in speeches laden with the elevated abstractions of sacrifice. The more pressing reason was that most of these deaths could not be blamed on the regime. One of the victims was a young lieutenant acciden-tally shot on the night of the coup at Istanbul's Central Post Office by one of his own, another a twelve-year-old boy, shot by the army after his father had denied Ankara's curfew to venture out with his son in support of the action. One victim, an Istanbul protester and high-school student, had lost his footing while waving a flag atop a tank and was crushed beneath the tracks; another was an Ankara cadet who had died at his own hand when his Thomson machine gun went off while readying it for action on the night of the coup. That left one victim, a forestry student, who had died from a police bullet during the protests at Beyazit Square on 28 April, as the regime freely admitted, though even this death appeared to have been as the result of an unfortunate ricochet.

There had been no massacre, then, no gruesome disposal of the victims. The deaths had been largely accidental, most of them due not to the regime but to unfortunate failings in the army's own safety practices. Of those gathered to see the martyrs of freedom laid to rest in honoured proximity to the great leader, however, nobody was about to say so, though in the circumstances they might have been excused for ducking as the rifle salute sounded over the graves.

CHAPTER ELEVEN

14 October 1960

The trials begin

On an earlier visit to Turkey I had taken a ferry to the Princes' Islands – an hour's trip from Istanbul. It was a morning in late September, when the summer crowds had evaporated and in the slack air seagulls hung like bedroom mobiles above the ferry station's Moorish arches and tiled facades. Across the water the tops of glass-clad towers poked from the ochre haze that squatted over the metropolis.

The proximity to the city of these islands in the Sea of Marmara had long commended them as convenient places of confinement; the Byzantines banished troublesome members of the ruling family here, as the archipelago's name acknowledged. Prison islands, then – but also favoured refuges for mystics and monks, as well as for Istanbul's prosperous minorities, notably Rum, Armenian and Jewish, who often summered here. The islands' heyday had been in the last decades of the nineteenth century which was where, to judge by the appearance of Büyükada, or Big Island, they remained. I might have been back in a car-free Constantinople. Where the waterfront gave way to shaded lanes scented with blooms, pairs of grey horses stood between the traces of phaetons whose bright reds and yellows appeared lifted from children's picture books, the awnings hung with sun-bleached tassels. I peered beyond high iron gates festooned with scrolls to admire the extravagant belle-époque get-up – the colonnades, balconies, belvederes, louvred shutters, fretworked porticos and trellises – of timber mansions, often dilapidated, overrun by riotous gardens and left to shed blistered bits of their former grandeur. They seemed most vivid in their dying, these houses, the poignant exhalations of sepia-tinged pasts putting me in mind of cigarette holders, whisky sours, bridge fours, parquet floors and stockinged feet tapping to the sounds of wind-up gramophones.

A friend, lucky enough to have made the island his home, lived in such a house; a clapboard villa whose many doors were wedged open in what I took for a summer-long state of semi-permanence. Accessible not only to the elements but to visitors too, the house appeared designed to lure intriguing types, islanders especially, of the sort that nourish the minds of writers like Owen.

Though I was no islander, and dubious as to my own entertainment value, Owen had been kind enough to put his caique at my disposal as I was interested in visiting an outlying island which no ferry served; a little boat, then, to a little island where nobody had lived for years. At the bottom of the sloping garden we reached the landing stage where *Clio*, trim and freshly varnished, tugged at her tether. We puttered away, making south-west, the slicked waters barely disturbing the wake which unspooled behind us. Owen had visited Yassıada – Flat Island – on several occasions.

'I've always been transfixed by the place,' he said. 'Nowhere else like it. More ghosts than you could ever imagine, and such an unlikely assortment of them.'

We had left the larger islands to the north when Yassıada and the steep-sided Sivriada (Sharp Island) resolved out of the glare. It was not hard to see why the pair of islets had been dubbed the Hayırsız – Good For Nothing – Islands. Yassıada was low, only a few hundred metres in length, and littered with visibly derelict structures – squat bunkhouses, Nissen huts, a hangar-like concrete building and the odd low-rise office building – at odds with Büyükada's elegant dilapidation. The exception, which drew my eye, was the castellated folly at the water's edge. It saddened me, this older structure, because it seemed to tell of what someone had once made of this island – an idyllic vision, an Arcadian retreat – which the later buildings so brutally forswore. A violation had taken place here.

Photographs of the folly, which Henry Bulwer had commissioned in the 1850s, show it to have been far more extensive in its original form. Bulwer, British ambassador in Constantinople, was the brother of Edward Bulwer-Lytton, a novelist chiefly remembered for the opening line 'It was a dark and stormy night'. The adage 'The pen is mightier than the sword' was also Bulwer-Lytton's – as indeed was the ancestral family pile at Knebworth, in Hertfordshire, which his brother's startling island residence in the Sea of Marmara was said to imitate. Set amidst lemon groves tended by an army of gardeners, and thick with rumours of the grand romances Bulwer enjoyed, notably with a glamorous princess of Samos, this baronial spread appears to have been an outlandishly extravagant affair, to judge by the few surviving accounts. The historian Sir Edwin Pears, a long-term Constantinople resident, recalled the folly's extensive panelled library full of 'dummy' books whose titles – *Cursory Remarks on Swearing*, *Lamb's Tails* and *Percy Vere* (in ten volumes) – suggested a man serious about keeping himself amused, especially if it allowed him a sideswipe at his sibling's literary accomplishments. Pears, evidently a more practical type, assessed the folly as 'delightful for a recluse who might have half a dozen visitors' but 'open to the objection that it could not be approached except in very fine weather', with 'neither a beach nor a harbour for anything but a small boat'. Sir Edwin's later memories of the summer picnic parties he enjoyed on the island, when the folly was already falling into disrepair, the lemon groves untended and with just a caretaker in residence, rather bore out his reservations.

It was to be almost a century before another use was found for the island when the naval academy on nearby Heybeliada (Saddle Bag Island) acquired it as a training base. From the late 1940s the navy built dormitories, service buildings, training facilities and a gymnasium, in the process demolishing much of Bulwer's folly, before it too abandoned the island. Yassıada did short-lived service in the 1990s as a research centre for the University of Istanbul before again falling into disuse except, it was said, as a popular trysting place for itinerant prostitutes and local fishermen. In its architectural

incongruity and its disorder the little that remained felt decidedly
sinister, the more so when the chug of *Clio*'s outboard roused three
resident dogs, ravenous-looking alsatians, which emerged from
tottering doorways to confront us as we closed on the rust-stained
and crumbling quayside.

The snarling dogs made a fair fist of repelling us, but only until
we had gained the land, when they promptly signalled their surrender by tangling among our legs in craven bids for whatever scraps
we might have brought them. They scampered ahead as Owen and
I passed between the peeling towers of the folly's impressive gate-
house, the crenellations close as teeth. A concrete lane, which
numerous saplings had since forced, led between the shells of naval
buildings. Block and concrete walls rose to broken roofs whose
tiles had slid to the sills, gathering there like the coppers in an
arcade machine. Beyond the absent doors, sagging roof panels
revealed rusted ducts and the crumbling wattle rims of swallows'
nests. The plastered walls were punched with neat round holes,
with cables protruding, where filched light switches had once been
bedded. We stood in empty rooms, and through paneless windows
choked by vegetation listened for the slow suck of the sea. Nissen
huts, their corrugated-iron roofs long gone, were down to their
semicircular end walls. The only romantic flourishes – a keyhole
door in the Moorish style, its ornate portal dressed in pink and
turquoise plasterwork flowers – were to be found in outlying
remnants of the folly.

At the top of the island stairs led down into a series of partially
collapsed vaults where small cells were fronted by rusted grilles. In
these mildewed dungeons we thought no more of picnics nor of
grand romances, the more so from the moment we reached the
hangar-like building we had spotted from the sea. Beneath a roof set
with skylights stood what remained of the navy's sports hall. Concrete
seats were tiered along walls scrawled with graffitied exclamations
like 'No Pasarán!' and 'Let Yassıada be renamed Democracy Island!'
A navy marine in heroic pose was painted beneath the words 'Above
all – the Nation'.

The graffiti confirmed that the idyll – the library, the liaisons, the lemons and leisurely picnics – had long since vanished. Yassıada, 'a sort of Turkish St Helena', an Alcatraz or Château d'If, had become a prison island. Within days of the 1960 coup some 150 members and associates of the Democrat regime, initially held at various army barracks and at Ankara's military academy, were transferred to the island. By the end of June 592 of the so-called 'former and fallen' had been sent to Yassıada, which was to be their place of confinement for sixteen months.

*

Not long after the coup Baysan Aygün, who had been in close corres-pondence with the Baileys since their visit the previous summer, received a letter from England containing photographs of the families' time together. Baysan, who had just left school and whose fiancé was away on military service, found these evocations of an irretrievable idyll hard to bear.

'Your kind letter,' she replied, 'made me understand that there
are still a few good people in the world. Thank you very much for
remembering us when we all need to be remembered by our friends.'
In assuring the Baileys that her father and his friends 'will soon be
free if being honest and loving one's country will not be considered
great sins', Baysan made a brave stab at conjuring a brighter future
for herself.

She left much out of her reply, of course, not being one to
burden people with her problems and fearful besides that what she
wrote, liable to the censor's scrutiny, might only cause her father
further trouble. Overnight, life had become very difficult for the
Democrat families. They were condemned as outcasts and ignored
by old friends, their children subjected to teachers' scorn and the
spite of classmates whose playground gestures – on the tips of
their toes, hand clasped about the throat – mimed the fates popu-
larly supposed to await the former and fallen on their prison
island. Baysan's mother was not only frantic for news of her
diabetic husband's well-being but desperate for money; the
Committee, having accused the leading Democrats of systematic
embezzlement, had frozen the family bank account and stopped
Kemal Aygün's salary. In high summer, which usually saw them
decamp to the beach house in the prosperous Istanbul resort of
Florya, the Aygüns found themselves holed up in their stuffy
Teşvikiye apartment. They were loath to risk the street where
aggressive soldiers were posted every twenty-five metres, where
former acquaintances might no longer acknowledge them, and
where they were liable to the abuse of the crowd. The family came
to depend upon a loyal relative, who disguised herself as a cleaner
to make food deliveries. They learned to endure arbitrary visits at
all hours by soldiers who took officious pleasure in carting away
books and papers they considered suspicious or in resuming the
search for the guns the former mayor was accused of secreting in
the apartment, every failure to uncover the rumoured cache only
spurring them to ransack the cupboards ever more thoroughly.
Officials delivered sheaves of forms which required the family,

accused of illegal use of state funds, to declare their valuables and provide exhaustive accounts of their expenditure.

Baysan closed her letter by acknowledging the Baileys' special concern for the man who had invited the family to Turkey, though she was wise enough not to mention his name. 'I know for whom you are worried,' she wrote. 'But be sure nothing will happen to him, for all the people of Turkey adore him. God saved him from great dangers, now he will save him again. Don't believe the ugly lies you may hear about him. They are all made up because of jealousy.'

Adnan Bey's family, evicted from the prime-ministerial residence in Ankara, was taken in by friends who put them up in a nearby apartment and pressed emergency funds upon them. As for the Bayars, the family had barely had time to pack a few essentials – no jewellery, the soldiers insisted – before the former president's wife, daughter, three granddaughters and the family nanny were driven to the airport. After landing at Izmır they were taken to the Bayar's holiday villa in Ilıca where they found themselves under strict house arrest; a soldier let them know that he had orders 'to shoot anyone who walks out through the garden door'. They were to have no visitors, nor to go shopping or swimming. For weeks there were no letters. The telephone was cut off. They had access to the newspapers which in slavish service to the Committee were 'full of news and details about the corruption of the Democrats and the heroism of the Turkish army', and of scornful stories about the wonderful time the Bayar family were said to be having in their 'summer resort on the Aegean riviera, a house full of maids and servants'.

There was nothing wonderful about that summer. Akile, one of the granddaughters, remembered being in the garden when a group of youths swam past the house. The young men waved and laughed before running their hands across their throats. 'We will cut you to pieces,' they shouted. On another occasion Akile was lying in bed when she overheard the adults discussing their fears that the family might be killed, as the Iraqi royal family had been two years before, and considering possible hiding places in case the soldiers came for them. She retained a memory of Iraq's late king, Faisal, whom the family had hosted at the villa in the summer of 1955; a photograph showed him on one of the villa's bamboo chairs. Even as she recoiled at his murder, the haunted girl comforted herself with reminders that her family was not like his and that her country was a democracy. 'It cannot happen here,' she repeatedly told herself. 'It will not happen to us.'

*

At the end of May 1960 a young officer called Mehmet Taşdelen graduated from the naval academy on Heybeliada. Lieutenant Taşdelen was expecting to be assigned to a warship when he learned that his class had been selected for special duties. They were to be posted to Yassıada, an island he knew from training weekends, where they were to serve as guard officers for the former and fallen.

On arriving on the island on 28 June he was shown to his sleeping quarters before being assigned to Ward 1. It was in this large two-storey building, not far from the quay, that some ninety of the most high-ranking prisoners were held. The building's inmates were quartered according to the surveillance the Committee deemed them to require; the largest dormitory housed sixty-four men while most of the ministers slept four to a room, in bunkbeds. On the ground floor, directly opposite the duty officer's desk, were two single rooms whose occupants were kept under twenty-four-hour supervision by guards on hour-long shifts. Lieutenant Taşdelen's first such room duty took place at 10 p.m. on 29 June, in what the guards had taken to calling Room 1, where Adnan Menderes was confined.

Lieutenant Taşdelen found himself in a small square room with bare walls. There was a cupboard and beyond it the duty guard's armchair. Beneath the only window were the prisoner's table and chair. In the other corner was an iron bedstead, and the prisoner, with whom Lieutenant Taşdelen was under strict orders not to converse, except when it was strictly necessary. Advised that any such exchanges would be picked up by a hidden microphone, he spent the hour describing his surroundings in a notebook. Under the bed, he wrote, a beige suitcase which the prisoner's captors had labelled as belonging to The Former Adnan Menderes. On the table a brown glasses case, a letter from Berin Menderes and a full ashtray. A blue toothbrush. A white comb. A yellow bar of soap. A bottle of Pe-Re-Ja cologne. A tie, black with pink spots, which the prisoner had hung by the window. The black and white striped pyjamas that the prisoner wore when readying himself for bed. The three minutes he spent combing his hair. The courteous 'With your permission' as he climbed into bed.

On returning to Room 1 the following day at 2 p.m., Lieutenant Taşdelen continued with his note-taking. 'Welcome,' said the prisoner, restlessly pacing the room; seven steps, Taşdelen wrote, from one end to the other. The prisoner stopping to look out of the window. Then sitting on the bed to read a few pages from his copy of the Quran. When a mosquito distracted him, he swiped at it with a towel. He spotted a dead beetle under the table and smiled at Taşdelen. He told Taşdelen that his pills had not arrived. Pills he should have three times a day. Yellow pills. Perhaps the lieutenant could ask in case the doctor had forgotten. He smoked a cigarette. Then another. 'With your permission,' he then said, 'I'll have myself a lie-down.'

Lieutenant Taşdelen's next duty stint in Room 1 was on 2 July, beginning at 9 a.m., as the prisoner was getting out of bed. The prisoner fumbled for a cigarette and asked if the ashtray could be emptied. He looked tired; he had not slept, he said, on account of the sounds of footsteps from the upper floor. The sound of these shoes, you see, he said, I don't sleep. All day and night, footsteps to drive a man mad. The doctor gave me tranquillisers, but to no use. Why can't they wear slippers? I shall lose my mind.

That summer Lieutenant Taşdelen repeatedly returned to Room 1 where he kept up his notes. The days, he wrote, were so hot that the door was often left open to snag any breezes from the corridor, though it would then be closed to prevent any possibility of contact between the prisoner and passing colleagues among the former and fallen. The prisoner was not permitted to leave the room except for

visits to the toilet. The mosquitoes and the cigarettes, and the tran-
quilliser tablets – Equanil and Nembutal – which the prisoner was
prescribed every day. The letters and the telegrams which the prisoner regularly received, and the replies, limited to fifty words, which
the prisoner was permitted to write to his family. He hardly ate, and
even with the tranquillisers his sleep was fitful, the faintest of noises
from the patrol boats at the quay or the dull hammering sounds from
the gymnasium waking him in the middle of the night. On one occasion, Lieutenant Taşdelen noted how the sound of barking led the
prisoner to muse as to whose dog it might be, and on one hot afternoon in July he heard the prisoner murmur, 'I feel terrible; how long
is this going to last?'

Lieutenant Taşdelen would have answered, as this ordinarily
compassionate man would have answered anybody he knew to be in
such torment, if it had not been for the microphone.

*

A fortnight after the coup Rector Onar's professors published an
interim constitution, the preamble reasserting the legal basis for
revolution: the deposed government having abolished human and
civil rights, thereby imperilling the nation's very existence, the
army had acted on behalf of the people to restore legality. Under
the current arrangements all power was invested in the Committee of National Unity, which was free to make and amend laws.
The constitution was to be composed of twenty-seven articles in
commemoration, it was explained, of 27 May; the elevation of
a new date in the Turkish calendar, which special anthems and a
cigarette brand were soon to confirm, had begun.

The Committee was also authorised to administer justice. On the
insistence of the professors two special courts were established – one
to inquire into the former regime's possible crimes, the other to
prosecute any crimes deemed to have taken place. As to any suggestion that these courts might resemble the recent revolutionary
tribunals hastily assembled in places like Cuba and some Arab nations

– well, Turkey was not Iraq, as one officer indignantly declared. It was a cause for pride that the Committee, far from lining up the regime leaders like the Bolsheviks in 1917 or the Iraqis in 1958, had carried the whole thing off without shedding a drop of blood. The odd bruise might have been landed – Menderes was said to have been roughed up, his jacket torn, on the flight to Ankara on the morning of the coup, and the hated interior minister carried off to captivity at the military academy in a dustcart – but this was nothing compared with what the government and its cronies were supposed to have dished out in the final weeks.

As for the custodial arrangements, the former regime's leading figures were treated to enviable levels of comfort – the former and fallen president even enjoying a room with its own bath – at Ankara's military academy. These undeserved courtesies continued after the prisoners' transfer to the island, as the Committee was at pains to emphasise in the short documentary film it commissioned. *The Fallen on Yassıada*, screened in cinemas and schools across the country in the summer of 1960, showed detainees in apparently congenial surroundings – at the barber's, shopping at the island store, chatting in the dormitories or taking a walk with visiting loved ones in the grounds. Here was the former and fallen president relaxing in his room, the prime minister enjoying a hearty meal – a holiday village, in short, rather than a prison camp. For modern Turkey was a civilised nation, a member of NATO and a signatory to the United Nations Charter, where things were done by the book – in this case the country's civil code. Any trials which did arise from the ongoing inquiries would be strictly subject to the law of the land and to the long-established penal code which Turkey, committed to remaking herself along civilised European lines, had adopted from Italy in 1926.

These assurances might have brought comfort to the former and fallen and their families if it had not been for the mortal threat – in the form of a notorious insertion – which lurked in an otherwise proportionate penal code. This was Article 146, which dealt with attempts to upset the constitution by force, precisely the allegation that Onar's professors repeatedly cited in affirming the revolution's legal and moral legitimacy, and which Republican journalists, politicians and students had been levelling at the former regime for some time. The detained politicians had every reason to fear Article 146 for the ease with which its nebulous phrasing might allow a guilty verdict, the more so because of the capital sentence it mandated, without exception, in any such cases.

The changes to the penal code that the Committee announced in July only added to presumptions that a mass prosecution under the dread article – of 'not only a whole government, but a whole parliamentary majority' – was in the planning. Judges trying cases under Article 146, the amendment stated, were now given leave to hand down prison sentences where they felt a death penalty was inappropriate, which the man from *The Times* unhesitatingly interpreted as relieving 'the courts of the obligation to sentence to death all the 400-odd Democrat deputies who voted under the Menderes regime for laws now alleged to be unconstitutional'. The change brought comfort to some of the accused but not to the former regime's more prominent personalities, whom it appeared designed to target, including those aged over sixty-five, like seventy-seven-year-old former President Bayar, who under a second amendment were no longer to be exempted from capital punishment.

*

Beyond the cities the country stewed in sullen gloom. In the villages the scratch of chickens, the prayer call and the low murmur from the teahouses were the only sounds. The fall of Adnan Bey was no cause for celebration, whatever the radio and the newspapers might be saying about him.

The Committee, intent on converting the countryside, arranged for the collection and free distribution throughout the villages of newspapers which city readers were urged to deposit in boxes left for the purpose on street corners. 'The peasants,' the Committee explained, 'must learn and understand what is happening, what

Mr Menderes, whom so many of them so misguidedly admire, really did.' This would depend upon an impartial press, of course, and in portraying the newspapers as publishers of record, purveyors of truth, the Committee appeared to have confused the high levels of rural illiteracy with credulity, as the man from the *New York Times* discovered one June day while reporting from the villages scattered across the pasture lands beyond Ankara's airport.

In Imrendi, Democrat 'almost to a man, except for the village teacher', the villagers wondered at the crimes the newspapers levelled at Adnan Bey; killing and mincing up students, helping himself to public funds, cosying up to the communists by seeking to trade the eastern end of the sacred motherland for much-needed Russian roubles and violating the constitution, whatever that might mean. These claims were greeted with bemusement and regret, but chiefly with downright suspicion, not least by the unschooled and the illiterate. In depending upon others to learn what was written in the papers and to make greater sense of the radio's announcements, these people had come to mistrust their educated neighbours almost as much as they envied them, even describing the worldly and their Kemalist leaders as 'literate thieves' on the placards some had once carried at Adnan Bey's rallies. For in the countryside the belief endured that literacy and secular education, though they conferred all the material advantages, also begot a loss of innocence. The only learning which did not lead to worldly corruption was that revealed in the sacred pages of the Quran whose essential truths were known to the village imam and the holy itinerants, those wandering preachers whom the secularists had proscribed but who in remoter spots persisted in their back-country ministries. These were truths that Adnan Bey had himself honoured by providing the money 'to build new mosques, to repair old ones' such as Imrendi's, its minaret newly painted in 'bright reds, greens and whites enticing as stick candy'. The villagers of neighbouring Orhaniye were yet more outspoken, despairing that the accursed abolishers of the caliphate had forced their way back to power, and in flagrant disregard of the clear choices the people had made in a succession of elections. In their confidence that most of the claims against Adnan Bey would turn out to be lies, the villagers left the man from the *New York Times* in no doubt as to what they thought of the broadcasts and publications of the godless.

So deep was the distrust of the media, and the lies it appeared willing to peddle on the Committee's behalf, that the villagers gave greater credence to the rumours which so readily circulated in the country, drawing hope from even the most improbable ones. One such claim was that Adnan Bey had escaped his island prison in a submarine which was to land him at the Black Sea port of Trabzon 'where he would lead the 3rd Army in a march on Ankara'. A legendary aura of invincibility, which the Gatwick escapade only confirmed, had clung to Adnan Bey since the Democrats' early years, in large part because country ears were strongly inclined to confound his party's unfamiliar name for *demir kırat*, or iron-grey horse; this was a trope of the old stories, the trusty mount of the medieval folk heroes who rode to the rescue of imperilled maidens and benighted villagers alike, scattering the lascivious landlords and rapacious bailiffs of the corrupt state. The welcome association of such valiant figures of yore with Adnan Bey – the man who defied the villagers' Republican persecutors to bring fresh water, electricity, generous wheat payments and the freedom to worship – so delighted the Democrats that they adopted the iron-grey horse as their party logo.

Under the Committee's absolute rule these rural resentments manifested, initially at least, as little more than scattered acts of defiance such as the distribution of clandestine tracts hostile to the Committee in the south-east of the country and the public insistence of a man in the north-east that Menderes was a descendant of the Prophet. Arrests were also made after pro-Menderes messages were scrawled on the signs along the road between Izmır and Aydın, and a coffee seller was detained in Eskişehir for writing 'Menderes forgive us' on a statue of Atatürk.

Not that the lack of overt resistance implied an indifference to the fate of the fallen prime minister, as events at Çakırbeyli were to prove. The farm, which Adnan Bey had run so capably through the

early years of his married life, where Berin Hanım and he had begun
their family, had stood empty and untended since the coup. On the
first day army officers had appeared with orders for the farm's
closure and for the confiscation of the horses and other removable
assets. Gangs of Republican partisans also turned up at the farm to
hurl stones, earth clods and imprecations. The farm managers and
workers could only stand by while the outbuildings were vandalised,
the walls scrawled with curses. Over the weeks they learned to
endure insults and taunts from the Committee's militant supporters
who dismissed them as *kuyruk* – a tail brutally detached from its
body – and whose graphic gestures evoked the end they took pleasure in predicting for the Democrats' fallen leader.

Rather than the usual placards, messages of defiance or clandestine pamphlets, the people of the Aydın region expressed themselves,
finally, by an eloquent act of maintenance; dealing with the weeds
whose unchecked advance threatened to choke Adnan Bey's cotton.
When word reached them that there was work to be done, they came
from neighbouring farms, villages and towns in their hundreds.
Those who did not have it in them to stand by while a cotton crop
was lost, those who knew Adnan Bey and wished him well, and those
who had determined to register, if only with themselves, the injustice they saw in the maltreatment of a man they considered 'a sincere
and patrotic leader who worked day and night for the good of the
people and the prosperity of his country', all came to the farm. With
their hoes and rakes they gave days of themselves to his fields. In the
high heat they bent beneath the white flosses to grub out the night-
shade and cocklebur, pigweed and purslane, watering the turned
earth with their sweat. They left the fields looking as spruce as they
had back when Adnan Bey, riding out at dawn and dusk to inspect
the spread, had himself run the farm.

Saving the crop was not about to save the man, but the villagers'
actions confirmed that the officers' attempts to turn the country
people's regard for Adnan Bey to disenchantment had come to
nothing. The Committee appeared rattled, its comments turning
increasingly intemperate in the broiling heat of summer. 'I hear

gossip that that man will come out again and take the lead,' declared
General Gürsel on a visit to Istanbul in July. 'I tell you clearly, no
force can turn us aside. So far, we have acted bloodlessly but if the
need arises, we shall make it flow in floods.' On 8 August the Committee issued an order that all shotguns and hunting rifles, which the
authorities had returned to their owners shortly after their initial
surrender, were once again to be handed in.

*

Mehmet Taşdelen was waiting for me outside the Park Hotel, where
Adnan Bey had regularly commandeered the first floor as his Istanbul base while masterminding the city's redevelopment in the late
1950s. By the time Mehmet came to know him, of course, Adnan
Bey's spacious world had shrunk to an island cell which he could
cross in seven short strides.

The young lieutenant was now a slight hale man in his late seven-
ties. After a short career in the navy, where he ran its photography
unit, and a subsequent one importing camera products for Polaroid,
Mehmet Bey had retired to the suburb of Pendik. But he kept a
basement near the Park Hotel where he hoarded a lifetime's memorabilia. As we made our way there, weaving between the cats which
cruised the steep lanes below Taksim Square, wantonly running
their flanks against our legs, Mehmet Bey reminisced.

'Back before I met him how I despised Menderes!' he exclaimed.
'We all did, us cadets, for jailing journalists and for the way he dealt
with the student protests in the spring of 1960, when it looked like
he was taking the country back to a dictatorship.' Turning a key, he
led the way into the basement, showing me to a chair while he brewed
tea and arranged a plateful of biscuits.

'So it surprised me to discover how courteous he was, even to the
lowest conscript guards. He always asked how we were – even if
the ban on conversation meant we could only nod in reply. He
congratulated me that I'd married my fiancée one weekend while on
leave from the island after somehow noticing that I'd moved my ring

in the way we Turks do from my right hand to my left. Not, I suppose, that there was much else to keep him occupied.

'Even though I was only twenty-two, I soon realised that something important was taking place on Yassıada. That's why I began keeping the diary; I took to hoarding things destined for the rubbish bin – like the scraps of paper on which Adnan Bey scribbled requests for forty kuruş postage stamps and the like. And although I knew it to be forbidden, I began taking photographs.' It was these photographs Mehmet Bey showed me over tea and biscuits in his basement.

His interest in photography had developed at the naval academy.

'My father's early death had left us very poor, which was why I was always on the lookout for ways to make money. At the academy there was a boy with a camera who soon began to profit from his classmates' greed for their portraits; he charged a lira a time, which made him twenty kuruş on each photograph. Small change, but there were lots of us at the academy, and vain enough to want all the photographs we could afford of ourselves. When it occurred to me that the boy was in his last year, I made arrangements to replace him by borrowing money to buy my first camera – a Pentax Zenobia – from a soldier who'd got his cheap while serving in Korea. I paid off the camera, provided myself with a useful income, and I learned how to take photographs.

'Not that this taught me anything about taking photographs in secret. I would have been in such trouble, a court martial most probably, if they'd found out. It helped that the Zenobia was small enough to hide under my shirt. But it was fiddly, and I had a job making the necessary shutter and lens adjustments without being found out.'

Many of the shots were certainly hasty, even out of focus, but I was drawn to these snatched glimpses of the former leaders' confinement for their intimate poignancy and the sympathy they communicated, the more so because a young man had risked much to get them. For safety's sake he had tended to places he could expect to have to himself, like the dormitories while the prisoners were out at lunch or at exercise, where he produced still lifes which were not merely

competent but often moving: prisoners' cupboards, the doors stuck
with family photographs, with woodland scenes and paintings by
Degas and Vermeer; tables topped with books, ashtrays, water jugs
and fly swats; bedside portraits of loved ones and of Atatürk, the prisoners determined in their devotion to the man they were charged
with betraying; a sink stuck with a handwritten sign insisting that
only fruit was to be washed there; tidily stowed bunks and lines of
washing rigged at the windows to catch the drying sun; and views
over the prison buildings to the busy quayside and the gun emplace-
ments, barrels aimed in readiness at any unwarranted approach.

In time the lieutenant grew bolder, surreptitiously peopling his
photographs: sentries standing to attention in the corridors, rifle
butts to the floor, the barrels held at an angle; shirtsleeved prisoners stretching their legs on the island lanes, or gathering round a
newspaper to read of the latest things that were being said about
them and their probable fates, or pointing skywards at the helicopter
hovering beyond the frame. He began sneaking shots of official
documents, even memoranda marked secret, and of his special

charges: Bayar deep in a book, his legs resting on the seat of the chair
he had drawn up opposite, and a drawn-looking Adnan Bey stooped
over a sink, barely able to face the man in the mirror, and in mourn-
ing for the wide world – from the cotton fields of Çakırbeyli and the
lanes of Izmır, Istanbul and Ankara to foreign capitals like Baghdad
and London – which he had once roamed so freely.

One day Lieutenant Taşdelen, keen to see for himself what was
going on, made for the sports hall with his secret camera, timing his
visit when he would have the place to himself. Stepping inside the
hall, which smelt of fresh wood sap, he found himself in a construction site. Along two sides tiers of seating were being raised above the
concrete bleachers. At the head of the hall they had built a dais, with
a desktop running the entire length. Against the rear wall a scaffold
had been erected where an inscription of sorts was being installed,
and in front of the dais a low rail enclosed a large dock. It was to be
a courtroom. After considering a range of venues – Ankara's National

Assembly building, the High Court in Istanbul, various military
institutions and barracks buildings – the Committee had decided
that the fates of the former regime members were to be settled on the
island.

*

After leaving Mehmet Taşdelen I followed stepped paths and back
lanes down to the Bosphorus. From a high window an old woman
called down to the child in her charge who had just mastered the
pedals of a yellow tricycle, exhorting the tousled toddler to keep at it
but especially to take a greater interest in working out what the
handlebars did, if only not to bowl over passing foreigners. With a
sidestep I emerged unscathed onto the traffic-choked waterfront
road within sight of the Dolmabahçe Palace.

By the mid-nineteenth century the sultans had tired of the old
palace at Topkapı; for though when occasion demanded they might
yet bend the knee before that monument to their dynasty's glory

days, they were done with living there. Calling time on the old seraglio, all medieval gloom and scattered single-storey pavilions, they
put their mainly French creditors to ruinous expense by building a
clutch of new palaces along the shores of the Bosphorus. Armenian
architects and interior designers fresh from decking out Paris's opera
house were tasked with giving the sultans the modern fixtures,
fittings and comforts they had been denied at Topkapı – sumptuous
spreads to compare with those of Europe's royals, complete with
upper floors and sweeping staircases, the balustrades of Bohemian
crystal; grand state apartments and reception halls hung with the
world's biggest chandeliers; tiled stoves from Sweden and fireplace
surrounds of Sèvres porcelain, modish *trompe l'oeil* murals and
alabaster-clad bathrooms and, finally, the sunlit vistas their forebears,
pale and etiolated, had barely known in Topkapı's cloistered confines.

The waterfront Dolmabahçe, the most extravagant and extensive
of the new palaces, also gave its name to the adjacent mosque. The
mosque was an inelegant building, with oversized cartwheel arches
and ministry-style wings; and, to judge by its proximity to the palace
gates, built for no more exalted purpose than to convenience sultans
who would minimise the time they must devote to such tiresome
official obligations as the public performance of Islamic devotions.

But it was this forgettable show structure that I had come to see.
At the entrance I levered off my boots before pushing past the
weighted entrance drape. Beyond a wide vestibule I stepped into
the prayer hall, hardly registering the painted dome – an indigestible
riot of baroque scrolls, rosettes, false arches and lily flowers – for the
remarkable windows. These were large, and of unstained glass, an
unusual arrangement which not only flooded the prayer hall with
light but allowed the views which most mosques tended to screen
off, no doubt for fear that worldly vistas might distract from the
allure of their own interiors and the devotional reflection they
invited. That this one so gloried in the life beyond its windows I took
as my cue to do the same. I looked out on a passing ferry, its passengers tossing bread scraps into the tornado of seagulls wheeling above
the stern. A shabby fishing smack pitched wildly on the swell caused

by a speeding police launch, the captain steadying himself to fling
out an arm in the Turkish gesture of grievance. Guests leaned from
the windows of a pleasure boat to snatch drags on shared cigarettes,
and out in the channel a rusty freighter made north, perhaps for her
home port of Odessa, the smoke streaming flat from its stack. I liked
the little-visited Dolmabahçe mosque for this – and for the colourful
and diverse life it was to experience after the sultans.

In the 1940s the mosque, having stood empty since the fall of the
Ottomans, came to serve as as Istanbul's naval museum. The secularist view that this waterfront building made a fitting repository for
maritime artefacts evidently had not found favour with the religious
authorities. In returning the mosque to service, their erasure of all
reference to its godless phase left me to rely upon the entry I'd
happened across in a 1950s Istanbul guidebook which described the
figureheads and coats of arms, and plans of the Golden Horn's Ottoman arsenals, displayed in the vestibule; the shell cases of British
torpedoes salvaged from the Battle for the Dardanelles on the stairways; and in the prayer hall models of submarines and of the great
ironclad *Hamidiye*, along with assorted artefacts from Atatürk's
private yacht *Ertuğrul*, a dragon-shaped culverin captured during
the Siege of Vienna, bowsprits, framed battle scenes and belongings
said to have come from Barbarossa, scourge of the Venetians.

Then, in the summer of 1960, the Committee suddenly announced
that the naval museum was to be put to yet another use – as the ferry
terminal for Yassıada, where preparations were in hand for the trial
of the former regime leaders. The welcome inference – that the
recent intervention was no less an act of national defence than
the Dardanelles and the other historic feats commemorated at the
museum – no doubt commended the building to the Committee. But
a more practical reason was the private quay, a crucial security
consideration given the crowds that were to attend the trials.

The Committee had decided that the greatest trials since Nurem-
berg, as Turkey's press billed them, should be held in public, with
the sports hall adapted to take as many spectators as possible. The
proceedings were to be filmed, with newsreels reaching global

audiences, while a dedicated nightly radio bulletin called *Yassıada Hour* would broadcast recorded excerpts to listeners across Turkey. The world should not doubt the Committee's determination to ensure fair and transparent process in holding the former regime to account, as the commemorative stamps – all scales of justice and maidens bearing flaming torches of truth – were at such pains to emphasise.

But while the Committee was confident that it could rely upon the tribunal of presiding judges to reach the right conclusions, it worried that the public might prove impressionable, even wayward, unless people were constantly reminded of the defendants' crimes. Recent signs of growing sympathy, which the Committee had been quick to scorch off, convinced it that there could be no let-up. To this end the officers commissioned new photographs of life on the forbidden island, though this time the shots were to show the inmates in remorseful mood, as if reflecting on the gravity of their abuses. At a public event staged at the Dolmabahçe quayside the photographs were auctioned off to the highest bidders, with the press paying spectacular prices for shots casting the former and fallen in the most abject light; the photograph which topped the bidding, of a clearly discomfited Menderes mopping his brow while being subjected to questioning by the island authorities, appeared on the front page of *Hürriyet* (Freedom) a few days before the trials opened.

On 13 October, the eve of the trials, millions of Turks tuned into *Yassıada Hour* to hear the most thoroughgoing summation of the Democrats' crimes. A sombre presenter began by evoking Turkey's National Assembly, that solemn institution where those elected to office were sworn in beneath the sacred slogan 'Sovereignty Belongs to the People, Without Restriction, Without Condition'. The presenter then asked how those who had given such an oath could have betrayed it by serving the former regime.

'Who are these people,' he continued in tones of deepening outrage, 'who caring no longer to lead the country but to live the high life have chosen to rip sovereignty from the hands of the citizens . . . these people who instead of attending to the happiness of their charges have attacked the lives and interests of citizens not of their party? Who have said of the opposition: *the time to crush them has come?* These people, president and premier, ministers and MPs, who bought the best whiskies and champagnes with public money before settling down, drunk, to ogle at belly dancers? These people who turned our beloved Istanbul into a building site? Who set the army against their own brothers? These assassins who meant to arm murderers with weapons funded by American aid to kill patriotic Turks? Who hatched plans to destroy our military academy, shrine to our martyrs and altar to all our military glories? Who squandered the national fortune and tarnished the noble Turkish nation's international reputation? Who decked out their houses with furniture and crockery lifted from the palaces of Istanbul? Who to make money stooped to haggle over the price of a dog? Who are they, these people, who rather than attend to affairs of state wrote billets-doux to their mistresses? Who killed their children, fruit of illegitimate loves? Who dragged university professors to the ground? Opened fire on our student Youth, imprisoned our brave journalists? Who trampled on our constitution? Who fraternised with gangsters, pimps and black marketeers? The historic trial about to begin at Yassıada will unmask them one by one. Justice will be done.'

*

With these words ringing in their ears lawyers, journalists, diplomats, witnesses, international observers and members of the public gathered outside the naval museum the following morning. Passes were checked before armed guards subjected passengers to rigorous searches for penknives, cameras and other forbidden items. Typewriters were confiscated, despite journalists' complaints that they depended on them – no less, they pointed out, than the soldiers did their guns. Visitors were required to surrender their identification papers, passports and press credentials in exchange for the numbered clearance cards which they were to pin to their lapels. 'Cleared, searched and docketed', they made their way through the museum to

the quayside where armed guards were posted at the ferry gangplank. Female officers in armbands marked PROTOKOL showed
visitors to seats where they were requested to stay for the duration of
the voyage. Beyond the windows a pair of gunboats waited to escort
the ferry to Yassıada.

Since the arrival that summer of the former and fallen, Yassıada
had been in lockdown. Twenty-four-hour naval patrols zealously
enforced a three-kilometre exclusion zone by impounding any
vessels found to have strayed within it and arresting the owners. All
air traffic was strictly forbidden from crossing Yassıada below 7,000
feet, and any island visitor foolish enough to approach the prisoners'
barbed-wire compound was in danger of being shot without warning
– if they had not already been blown up by a mine.

Only once teams of frogmen had checked the hull for signs of
sabotage was the ferry cleared to leave Dolmabahçe. The gunboats
circled and took up station on the ferry's flanks for the forty-five-
minute journey to the island. The convoy headed up the Bosphorus,
passing the Karaköy quayside, the first statue of Atatürk and the
wooded prominence of Topkapı, as officials distributed an educational pamphlet among the passengers. The pamphlet, emblazoned
with an insignia of crossed bayonets, a flaming torch and a pair of
scales, contained a series of photographs entitled 'Reasons for the
Revolution': a policeman, pistol drawn; a student being frogmarched
away by baton-wielding policemen; mounted police officers char-
ging crowds; a student's body, naked and bruised, on a slab; Istanbul
University's rector, with his heroic black eye; a funeral procession;
the former and fallen prime minister, 'the main reason for the revolution', according to the caption – 'the violator of our constitution';
and the former and fallen Bayar, along with Zorlu, at a black-tie
dinner 'quaffing whisky . . . while our people were being slaughtered,
our Youth shot and our rector beaten up'.

The cartoons posted on the walls of the ferry saloon struck a
more derisory note, recasting the former regime's leaders as stock
villains from history and legend. Here was Bayar in the guise of the
old despot Abdul Hamid, and Zorlu as a bank-busting Al Capone;

the interior minister as a Gestapo officer, Polatkan as the tyrannical khan of Crimea, and assorted others as plundering Cossacks, pharaohs in thrall to their divine grandeur, serial murderers and various fairy-tale baddies.

Amidst this gallery of rogues the former prime minister appeared in buckled shoes, breeches and fur-lined sleeves beneath a powdered wig. Flourishing a dandy's cane and a lover's handkerchief, he prowled among a bevy of ringlet-haired beauties in low-cut dresses. In the show that was about to open at Yassıada, the Committee had finally settled upon a role for the main character whom they had cast as an amoral libertine – Casanova.

CHAPTER TWELVE

15 September 1961

The Yassıada sentences are announced

In summer of 1910 the island of Sivriada had taken delivery of its own captive population when a hastily assembled flotilla of caiques and coasters ferried huge numbers of Istanbul's stray dogs to the steep-sided islet. As these events took place precisely fifty years before the Democrat leaders were sent to neighbouring Yassıada, they might have been a presentiment – a reminder at least that the one thing the Good-For-Nothing Islands were good for was the disposal of unwanted outcasts.

Istanbul had long been noted for its dogs, though they were not held in the regard their feline rivals enjoyed; blame the Prophet, peace be upon Him, who was said to have cut away his own sleeve rather than disturb the cat which had deigned to curl up there. Dogs did not get to doze on the divine sleeve, nor even to enter houses, at least not Muslim houses, which Islam's protecting angels were said to avoid if dogs lurked within. They were dirty; clothes soiled by dog drool were to be washed seven times, and vessels they had licked hastily packed off to be re-tinned. Dogs, according to the Quran, were not to cross the threshold.

For all these Islamic prohibitions, dogs nevertheless enjoyed the affection of many Istanbul residents. They were said to be descended, after all, from the noble hounds which had accompanied Mehmet the Conqueror's besieging armies in 1453 – an illustrious lineage, which commended them as welcome presences on whatever Istanbul threshold appeared to offer the best prospects for a dog intent on winning the household's attachment and the street's trust. Quick to learn, staunch protectors of the local hens and babies, if not the cats, they also proved their worth as sentinels. Their barking served to warn of fires, a constant threat among the city's tight press of timber houses, and the presence of thieves, con men, would-be lovers and other undesirable prowlers. In return the dogs could expect scraps of food and bowls of water, the occasional scratch behind the ear and, if things went well, names all their own. Kindly locals might salve the dogs' wounds and raise them shelters, even kennels, on the streets. It was a life lived beyond the leash, where neighbourhood responsibilities did not exclude time-off forays with the pack, and a good one.

From the nineteenth century, however, Istanbul began looking for ways to better itself. To administrators intent on remaking their city along European lines, with trams, street lighting and public hygiene programmes, nothing signified Istanbul's oriental squalor quite as visibly as the dogs. Imams and Islamic scholars, incensed to find dogs skulking near their mosques, found themselves aligned, for once, with modernisers determined to rid the squares and streets of the mange-ridden, rabid and ever-excreting packs. The dogs being Istanbul's most visible bar to Western progress, the authorities ordered them to be culled.

But many residents resented 'the cruel destruction of their favourites', citing all manner of military reverses, earthquakes and ominous astrological indications, however imaginary, as evidence of Allah's displeasure at the eradication programme. The authorities instead tried transporting the captured dogs across the Bosphorus to the Asian side, with 'a certain quantity of bread . . . daily exported for their support'. When voices on the Asian side objected to being overrun by the displaced packs of Pera and Şişli, the creatures were removed to cages set up in the abandoned moats beyond the old Byzantine fortifications, their captors mindless of the irony that these were the same walls the dogs' forebears were supposed to have scaled centuries before. So overcrowded did these cages become that the dogs' incessant howls soon wakened the city's conscience to their plight. There was nothing for it, the authorities decided, but to remove the dogs to a place where they could neither be seen nor heard.

Tramps, beggars and gypsies, traditionally assigned the tasks others considered cruel, base or beneath their dignity, were issued with grab sticks and quotas, and instructed to deliver their catches to the transports awaiting at the Karaköy quayside. In May 1910 the first of these overladen craft set off for Sivriada where the captain, rather than risk running alongside the rickety landing stage, ordered his men to drive the dogs overboard, using whips on the unwilling. The animals that made it to the shallows found themselves to be castaways on an island without food, fresh water or shade.

That same summer a visiting French caricaturist called Georges Goursat, alerted to the dogs' plight, persuaded a friend to take him to Sivriada in his yacht. They were yet a mile from the island when the wind went slack, and the air turned foul. At the wheelhouse Goursat found his friend with a handkerchief pressed to his face. They pushed on until the island was in full view. From shore to summit Sivriada appeared as a seething mass of dogs in degrees of extreme distress or decomposition, some tearing at the corpses of their fellows while others appeared maddened by thirst and heat. Those that had resigned themselves to die rose to their feet as the yacht drew near, their faith in the mercy of humans pathetically intact, and confident even then that the craft had come to carry them home, some paddling frantically in its wake as the captain, stifling a retch, turned the wheel back towards the city.

*

As the ferry warped up to the Yassıada quayside on that first morning of the trials, a loudspeaker instructed passengers to stay seated; only when the codes on their clearance cards were called should they step ashore. By strict category – special visitors including Committee members and diplomats, then journalists, general spectators and finally kin of the accused – they disembarked, leaving the quayside via a gateway in a castellated facade where their route was lined by closely stationed guards armed with sub-machine guns. A short walk brought them to the courthouse, 'a very modern building looking rather like an aircraft hangar inside and out', where they found themselves beneath a vaulted ceiling of turquoise tiles, set with triangular skylights. They made for their allocated seats among the high timber tiers which took up two sides of the hall, and looked out over the court.

Before them was a large railed dock crammed with hundreds of chairs, the defence lawyers arranged along either side. Beyond the witness stand clerks, secretaries and prosecutors bustled about the bench as the nine judges in high braid collars and black silk gowns fringed in red and gold took their seats; there was to be no public jury. From the rear wall, where an inscription declared 'Justice is the Foundation of the State', the image of Atatürk looked down on the proceedings.

On that October morning the heat was unseasonal, the audience closely packed, and the rustle of vigorously fanned propaganda pamphlets, magazines and journalists' notebooks only added to the hubbub of expectant chatter. At precisely 10 a.m. the noise of marching boots at the doors brought the audience to silence. The ceiling strip lights flickered into life, and with a series of clicks and whirrs the four cine cameras began to roll. Steel-helmeted soldiers, sailors and airmen (the three services united in common cause) marched into the court building. The choreography continued as the former and fallen, flanked by more guards, entered in single file, and in strict order of their erstwhile seniority – Bayar, Menderes, then the ministers, among them Zorlu and Polatkan, followed by hundreds of MPs. It was fully half an hour before all 403 defendants charged under Article 146 with the main allegation, of 'altering and abrogating the constitution', had taken their places in the dock. The audience was reminded of their school days as the defendants dutifully rose to their feet on hearing the calling of their names.

For more than three hours the clerk of the court read the main indictment, the arraignment interrupted by 'much marching and counter-marching' with every change of the guard, as well as by the intermittent removal of defendants and guards overcome by the heat, which gave the galleries the opportunity to scrutinise the cast at their leisure. The *Times* man, who had last seen the prisoners 'at some official function in Ankara, surrounded by acolytes and toadies, wearing that sated look of those long in power, with yes-men leaping to satisfy their idlest wish, condescending to speak to a few favoured guests', described Bayar as 'slow, dignified, elegantly dressed' and carrying an 'ancient grey felt hat'. Menderes, also characteristically well dressed 'in a brown suit and gay tie', nevertheless looked 'worn and thin'. 'His clothes,' according to one report, 'appeared to hang from his body.' The British consul went further, describing Menderes as 'a complete physical wreck'. 'With sunken cheeks and eyes, with the bones of his jaw showing,' the consul continued, 'he gave one the impression of a very sick man.' After the reading of the indictment Menderes was granted permission to address the court. Walking with difficulty to the stand, and 'in a weak and trembling voice, often stammering, he said that he had almost forgotten how to speak', having been unable to talk to anybody, not even his officer on guard, during his four months' confinement. 'This is inhumane,' he said.

The former prime minister, the arraignment confirmed, was to face more charges than any other defendant. These included not only serial constitutional violations under the main charge but also responsibility for the brutal suppression of that spring's student demonstrations, impeding the opposition leader's constitutionally guaranteed rights to visit Kayseri and inciting violence against him at Uşak and elsewhere; instigating the Istanbul riots against the minority Greeks in 1955; the unlawful eviction of residents during the redevelopment of Istanbul; using the national radio for partisan political aims; misusing public funds and engaging in sundry other acts of corruption, malfeasance and violence – not least ordering the murder of his illegitimate child.

First, though, in keeping with his seniority, it was to be the turn of the former and fallen president. When the court reconvened at

four o'clock that afternoon, all the chairs in the dock had been
removed save for those reserved for Celal Bayar and the former
minister of agriculture, co-defendants in the opening case, which
related to the misuse of public funds in relation to the sale of a dog.

*

Akile Gürsoy remembered the dog, which had caught her grandfather's eye in the grounds of the royal palace at Kabul during a state
visit to Afghanistan in 1959. The Turkish president, an old hand
when it came to the regional codes of hospitality and the obligations
they imposed, should have known better than let slip his admiration
for the creature, which he had no sooner done than the dog was his.
Gifts from the king of Afghanistan were not to be refused, of course,
and when the president went back to Turkey so did the dog.

'It was a breed of Afghan, naturally, a very special and handsome
dog with beautiful eyes, somewhat silent,' said Akile. 'As I was only
a small child, it struck me as very tall. I loved all animals and of
course wanted to keep it. But my grandmother, being a practising
Muslim, would not have dogs in the house. The family were
concerned that we would not be able to take care of it properly. I
dare say we didn't keep it for that long. I often wonder what happened
to it in the end.'

Those in the Yassıada galleries had their own reasons to wonder,
not least that trials of such gravity should have opened with a case
concerned as to the arrangements made for the removal from the
presidential residence of an Afghan hound. 'One hardly knows
whether to laugh or cry,' wrote the bemused correspondent for the
Observer. Even the most partisan Republicans, whom the ticketing
arrangements so favoured that they were to dominate the public
galleries throughout the trials, were forced to concede that the main
defendant had a point when he declared the proceedings to be
beneath his dignity. 'I cannot imagine a more humiliating punishment for myself than being brought before this courtroom to be tried
for so insignificant a crime,' thundered Bayar. He even offered to

plead guilty if that would put an end to a case only the prosecution were inclined to take seriously. Even the court officials appeared unconvinced, their mumbled explanations commending the case as 'the sort of thing which has greater impact on the masses than charges of violating the constitution'.

Whatever the reservations, the case would be heard, and the former president was obliged to detail how he had arranged for the disposal of a dog which his wife would not have in the house. He recounted instructing the agriculture minister, whose portfolio appeared most closely fitted to the purpose, to deal with the creature, telling the minister that this was no common stray but a rare species of great value to Turkey, and one which the Ankara Zoo would no doubt wish to acquire.

Except that the zoo was not so sure; and even less so, according to the testimony of the zoo's director, once the agriculture minister mentioned 20,000 lira, a price which the deputy undersecretary and various presidential aides confirmed in a series of increasingly insistent phone calls. 'We needed money for salaries and we were in debt,' the zoo director complained to the court. 'Besides, we were being offered a crocodile we wanted to buy for 4,000 lira.' Being forced to buy the dog, another zoo employee testified, had necessitated the sale of 200 curly-haired sheep on a nearby state farm also managed by the zoo.

Nor was the dog said to be worth anything like the money – whether it converted to five crocodiles or 200 curly-haired sheep – that the defendants demanded. To establish its value, the prosecution commissioned a committee of experts who concluded, in a report solemnly read to the court, that the creature was useless for breeding as it was not accompanied by a female of the species. The experts therefore arrived at a value of 1,000 lira – which an enterprising businessman promptly trumped by offering Ankara Zoo all their money back, and some, with a bid of 22,500 lira. The businessman's plan for Buster – the dog having apparently acquired a name in the process – was to bring the celebrity hound to Istanbul and put him on show there, at twenty-five kuruş a look.

So the proceedings descended into farce, providing rich entertainment for the galleries but disappointing those whose purpose in bringing the case had been to expose 'the degraded mentality' of the former president; a case that Ahmed Emin Yalman, as supportive of the Yassıada trials as he had once been of the men arraigned there, described as 'a nice skit on our bad period. It will help us and the whole world see the kind of administration we have left behind'. The 'dog trial' backfired, disastrously so, not only in reducing the proceedings to ridicule but prompting revelations which reflected favourably on the former regime. Chief of these was the disclosure that the 20,000 lira received for the dog, rather than disappear into the defendants' pockets, had paid for the installation of a much-needed public fountain in an Izmır village whose residents, famed for their heroism during the War of Independence, were as deserving of a fresh water supply as any. The former president, whom the Committee meant to portray as a bullying extortionist, unfit for the land's highest office and impious enough as to have a dog in the house, turned out to be committed to public infrastructure projects, and in the can-do way of the Democrats, which was more than the godless had ever managed.

For the prosecutors it had been an unmitigated calamity. Clambering from the wreckage of the opening case, they dusted themselves down and resolved to try again, hoping to have more luck with the next man on their hit list.

*

During my 2016 visit to Ankara I'd visited the cemetery at Cebeci where two of Adnan Bey's three sons lay at rest. But I had been in search of yet another son of his, an illegitimate one, who was also buried here.

For some time I'd wandered through this huge cemetery's grid of lanes, lost in the bewildering layout of the hundreds of numbered blocks, each home to hundreds of graves, before two men with watering cans came to my aid.

'560,' I told the attendants who nodded and bade me follow them through the pines and the plane trees. It was raining, and the blocks were overgrown and dilapidated, the marble casings of the high-sided graves cracked or patched with rough render, the headstones askew. We tacked through the lanes, the attendants' watering cans sloshing about their disintegrating rubber boots, until one turned. 'Block 560,' he said. 'What number?'

'688,' I replied, and followed them into the tightly packed tombs. We forced a muddy path between the graves, the men murmuring our progress like taxi drivers hunting street addresses as we passed the identifying numbers I now spotted on the headstones. At 688 they halted and set to work with their watering cans, washing the grave of dirt, leaves and pine needles before plucking weeds from the recessed bed of decorative saxifrage. When they were done, each man laid a hand upon his chest in a gesture of respect before stepping back to allow me some privacy. I was pondering the headstone when there was a cough at my back.

'Knew him well, did you, sir?' asked one of the men, holding out a palm.

'Not in the least,' I replied, puzzled to discover that 560/688 appeared to be occupied by somebody called Sultan Yıldırımoğlu.

Nearby at the cemetery's administrative building a man in a boiler suit was mopping the entrance hall's tiled floor. He looked up to fix my muddy boots with a severe gaze. But I was not about to be deflected, and pausing only to attempt a Cossack's kick, knocking what mud I could from my boots, I strode across the gleaming floor. To the sound of excessively energetic mopping, I approached a shawled clerk at her computer terminal.

'I'm wondering what you can tell me about Block 560,' I said, raising my voice above the noisy mutterings at my back. 'Plot 688.'

She tapped at the keyboard. 'Sultan Yıldirımoğlu,' she said. '26 August 1984.'

I nodded. 'But I understand a baby boy was buried there much earlier,' I said. 'On 19 June 1955.'

'1955? Let's see. Back then 560 had not been adopted for general burials. It was reserved for paupers and destitutes, the details not officially recorded. But as Ankara's population grew, outlying blocks were allocated for general use, as 560 was in 1984. Your baby boy. How old was he?'

'Nine hours,' I said.

'So by 1984 . . .' she replied with a little shrug, her abandoned sentence eloquently expressive of the pliant solubility of newly born babies' bones. 'Anything that did survive of him, may he rest in peace, would have been removed to the cemetery's ossuary – the domed building you'll have passed on the way here. But as they didn't keep records for the blocks until they were officially adopted, there's no reference to him at all.'

It troubled me that this baby boy, having lost his life after nine hours, should also have lost his grave; and that those entrusted with his burial had laid him to rest on the margins of the cemetery – not to save money, for there was plenty of that, but to dispose of him discreetly, without the usual funeral rites, and without the headstone which should have carried the name Dunyam Menderes.

'Was he a relative of yours?' asked the woman at the computer terminal.

'No,' I replied. 'He was your prime minister's son. By Ayhan Aydan.' Across the room heads rose from desks.

'Ah.' The woman smiled fondly. 'Adnan Bey's beloved.' As I offered my thanks and left, the cleaner slipped into my wake with a disgrunted sigh to erase all trace of me.

*

Philandering in the 1950s, worldly Turks liked to say, was like committed drinking, gum chewing, listening to swing music and putting up Christmas trees; activities which were supposed to signal Western sophistication. But amidst the revolutionary austerity fomented by the coup, such moral licence was decried as evidence of the former regime's unpardonable decadence, particularly the prime

minister's, even if his numerous affairs were pursued in so recklessly precipitate a manner that his adultery seemed less like an
urbane affectation than a desperate attempt to plug the perforated
hull of his foundering self. Of the many stories which circulated
about the former prime minister's indiscretions the best bits – the
complex arrangements to ensure that the husbands were away, and
that the local street lights were temporarily extinguished as cover for
his nocturnal movements – tended to tell of Adnan Bey's doomed
attempts at discretion; contrivances which did manage to hoodwink
some while amusing many others, but not the newly censorious
Committee, which pounced upon Adnan Bey's serial liaisons, trusting that such revelations might finally turn his supporters' devotion
to disenchantment.

To that end the Committee approached the mufti of Istanbul who
obliged the officers by issuing a fatwa against adultery, which he
denounced as 'the biggest sin', and punishable by stoning. As for
the identify of the fornicator at whom the fatwa was directed, the
Committee even went so far as to offer the wronged wife induce-
ments to file for public divorce on grounds of adultery, but the
stubbornly steadfast Berin Menderes was hardly the sort to be
co-opted in such a business. No matter, there were other routes to
proof, like calling Ayhan Aydan to the stand.

The two had met at a reception near Ankara in 1951. The prime
minister, with his pronounced weakness for artistic free spirits like
chanteuses, musicians and writers, was instantly drawn to the young
opera singer. As the gracious and magnetic Adnan Bey was in the
first flush of his premiership, buoyed by the nation's rapturous
regard, the attraction was powerfully mutual. Within days Ayhan
Hanım – Madam Ayhan – was eagerly awaiting Adnan Bey's private
telephone calls and opening the door of her Ankara home to deliveries of bouquets. The two began a passionate affair which the prime
minister barely attempted to conceal, commonly leaving sessions at
the National Assembly to stroll through the city centre to his lover's
house on First Welfare Street. His chauffeur-driven car, which bore
the words ADNAN MENDERES on the front bumper's official red

plate, was often observed outside the house long after what passers-by considered bedtime.

They loved without restraint or precaution, and Ayhan Hanım conceived in 1952, only to lose the baby to an emergency abortion after complications, as she did again the following year. When for the third time she conceived in the winter of 1954, and the pregnancy proceeded smoothly, she soon developed a deep attachment for the unborn child whom she took to referring to as Dunyam, or My World.

Without warning, and a month early, the contractions came one June afternoon in 1955 when Ayhan Hanım was playing poker with friends at home. In distress she called her trusted gynaecologist in Istanbul, Dr Fahri Atabey, a distinguished doctor at Turkey's leading children's hospital as well as an old friend of the family, who promised to leave immediately after warning his patient that it would be hours before he reached Ankara. She tried without success to contact Adnan Bey, also in Istanbul, before calling two Ankara doctors whom she knew. One arrived in time to assess the mother, whom he judged too advanced in her labour even to reach hospital, and to help with the home delivery, which proved difficult and lengthy, the other to confirm the sickly condition of the newborn; the umbilical cord, wrapped around the dangerously premature infant's neck, had all but asphyxiated it. Rather than announce itself with a lusty bawl, the baby vomited blood; the doctor, detecting a faltering heartbeat, attempted to massage some life into the failing baby, which elicited no more than a thin whimper.

The boy died in the night, as Dr Atabey learned from the distraught mother and the friends who had remained with her through the ordeal, when he finally arrived the following morning. As the only sign of Adnan Bey was his official car, which the prime minister had put at Ayhan Hanım's disposal, Dr Atabey volunteered to take responsibility for the necessary arrangements. The doctor had Adnan Bey's driver take him to the Cebeci cemetery where he completed the brief formalities and saw to the baby's burial.

This was the account Atabey gave one November day in 1960 to the Yassıada court in denial of the prosecution's more lurid version of events; that the doctor had murdered Ayhan Aydan's newly born child on the say-so of the father, co-defendant in the case. It was the sort of thing Ayhan Hanım might have recognised from her opera roles, a prominent public figure's attempt to evade scandal by arranging for the murder of his newly born love child; a preposterous concoction even without taking Dr Atabey's excellent character into consideration. Indeed, the lack of evidence was such that the court was minded not to proceed with the case – only for the Committee to insist that it be heard. It was of no concern to the Committee that the case should fail – so long as it succeeded in establishing in the process the adultery of the main defendant.

Fail it did. Successive witnesses, close friends of Ayhan Hanım, testified that Dr Atabey had not even arrived at the house until some hours after the baby's death. Then the medical council charged with examining the baby's exhumed remains reported finding no signs of external harm. Even the partisan audience, its ranks typically thick with 27 May supporters, often the staff and students of Istanbul University, did not query Dr Atabey's aggrieved assertion that he had driven through the night to help in the birth of a friend's baby, not to murder it. But their silence was as much out of indifference as respect. They were not there that day to hear the protestations of a patently decent doctor. They were after scandal and sensation, and the prosecutor did not keep them waiting for long.

To establish the degraded character of the main defendant, as the prosecutor put it, objects recovered from a safe in Menderes's office were presented to the rapt court. These were some items of women's underwear, including panties and stockings, and an envelope marked 'historical documents' which turned out to contain some mildly titillating photographs. To the defendant's claim that he had been given these unsolicited items by a colleague, and thought it best to lock them away, the prosecutor replied that this was not the sort of thing to be expected of a man who liked to call himself 'the first Muslim prime minister of Turkey'; the type of man, as the prosecutor would subsequently characterise the main defendant, 'who chases women in the street'.

If the Committee members in the audience observed all this with
mounting satisfaction, not least on account of the embarrassment
caused the main defendant, they nevertheless hoped for more from
the testimony of the chief witness whom the judge was to call that
afternoon. In confirming the affair, as she surely must, Ayhan Aydan
might even disown the main defendant – as much out of bitterness
that her former lover had begun an affair with another woman, an
Istanbul novelist, in the months before the birth of their child as
because she had been led to understand that it was in her interests to
do so. The Committee had let the young woman know that, with so
much of her life and career ahead, the line was there for her to grab
– that she had been forced into the affair by a powerful man whom
she now knew to be a worthless serial predator.

A hushed silence fell over the court as the chief witness was
summoned. A small and attractive figure in cloche hat, 'fully fashioned stockings and matching high-heeled shoes', the soprano strode
past the dock where her former lover and her family doctor sat. At
the stand she gave her name in 'clear and ringing tones' and listened
attentively while the judge spoke of her affair with the defendant,
whom he described as 'the married Adnan Menderes', and of the
pregnancy Menderes had not wanted, and the doctor he had hired to
get rid of the child. She digested the judge's version of events before
making her measured reply.

'I met Adnan Menderes in 1951,' she said. 'I loved him so much.
And I so wanted a child. All my efforts went into bearing his child.
But it was not to be.' She went on to flatly reject any idea that her
previous abortions had been the result of pressure from Adnan Bey;
described Dr Atabey, whom she had known for eighteen years, as a
very good friend; confirmed that Atabey had arrived hours after the
death of the baby; and scorned suggestions that he could have
contemplated murdering her baby or that Adnan Bey might have
ordered such a thing. As to any question of her own honesty in these
matters, what monster of a mother would have connived in, or
covered up, the murder of a child she had so longed to bring into the
world?

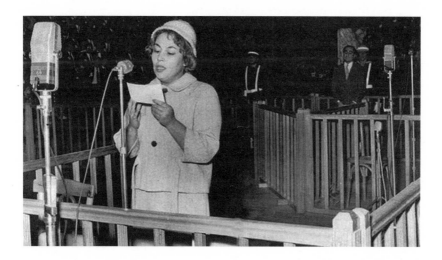

Even the newspapers admitted to being impressed. 'It takes great courage or a genuine, very deeply rooted love to face the world and boldly declare the true depths of private, personal feelings,' wrote one commentator. 'The brave woman did just that, and in doing so won the admiration of all those present.' In refusing to disown the man who had deserted her, she defied the soldiers. It seemed the man the Committee meant to cast as a cheat and a lecher had inspired a deep and lasting love, a love which only encouraged Adnan Bey's followers in their estimation of the man. Once again, the trials had missed their mark.

On 23 November 1960 the defendants Menderes and Atabey were cleared of the charges in the case. The doctor was returned to the Dolmabahçe quayside in a motor torpedo boat where jubilant friends and supporters had gathered to take him out for a celebration dinner. No such pleasures awaited Adnan Bey, though he was at least to see his dear Berin who had obtained permission to visit Yassıada the next day with one of their sons, Mutlu. As prison officials insisted on being present throughout the family's fifty-minute reunion, the first since the coup six months ago, there was little opportunity to speak freely. It nevertheless gave Adnan Bey strength that Berin had stood by him as Ayhan had done, despite the wrongs

he had done the two women; strength he would need in the months
to come as the trials proceeded apace, and his first acquittal proved
to be his last.

*

Beyond the island the world was in the grip of momentous political,
social and technological change. 1961, which began with the inauguration of President Kennedy, saw the Soviets put the first man in
space before resuming nuclear missile testing after the US's failed
Bay of Pigs invasion of Fidel Castro's Cuba. Newly independent
Cyprus joined – and South Africa left – the British Commonwealth.
The 'Freedom Riders' boarded buses to carry the civil rights message
into the segregationist South. In Jerusalem Adolf Eichmann went on
trial. Britain applied to join the European Economic Community, as
the EU was known at the time. The Beatles played their first concert
at Liverpool's Cavern Club. And in Berlin the East Germans started
work on a wall.

On the island the inmates gleaned what news they could from the
Turkish newspapers and radio, as well as of the latest crimes for
which they stood condemned, when they were not busy with the
daily round of practical concerns. Like learning how to keep themselves and their clothes clean when the time permitted for washing
was as limited as the water, which was mostly cold. Like preparing
fruit without knives, which were banned to guard against suicide
attempts; an enterprising MP called Ahmet Kocabıyıkoğlu solved
the challenge by customising a loose bed spring which he lashed to
his toothbrush before lending it to his ward mates. Like ensuring the
goodwill of those who might otherwise take spiteful pleasure in
withholding the supply of vital medications such as the painkillers
for Kocabıyıkoğlu's troublesome teeth, the insulin for the diabetic
Kemal Aygün, or the tranquillisers on which Adnan Bey increasingly
depended. Like coping with the boredom of confinement by fash-
ioning packs of playing cards from cardboard biscuit packets, or
embroidering such details as seagulls, bayonets and barbed wire into

the needlepoint of island life with which the seven MPs in the women's ward kept themselves occupied.

Then there were the letters the inmates were permitted to write, but on forms which limited them to fifty words, where only platitudes would pass the censor. These letters often arrived at their destination all but redacted out of existence, and scrawled with threats or obscenities, as did the replies. The prisoners nevertheless craved these reminders of home, touching them as they knew their loved ones had done, drawing the rudely slit envelopes apart to bury their noses there for the faintest scent from their former lives, and poring over their contents in case coded clues were concealed within the text. In these ways they did all they could to keep themselves clean, healthy and composed while they awaited trial.

Many of them, having appeared before the court on the opening day, were not to return there for more than six months. The court's decision to deal first with the various subsidiary cases, mostly involving a limited number of defendants, saw to it that the main case, with its cast of hundreds, did not open until 11 May 1961. On that morning the Committee signalled the significance of the moment by dispatching air-force jets to fly low over the little island. Yassıada, wrote the man from *The Times*, in lyrical mood after leading the foreign press corps in a successful demarche to be allowed to retain their typewriters, 'was unusually beautiful today, carpeted with spring flowers. The rosy bluffs of the Princes' Islands, falling into the smooth blue of the Sea of Marmara, with the minarets of Istanbul on the skyline, made for a setting of natural beauty for the course of Turkish justice.' Exactly 397 defendants crowded into the dock together to hear the prosecutor call for thirty-seven death sentences, and up to twenty years' imprisonment for the rest, on the charge of violating the constitution.

The case alleged eight such violations, though the prosecution chose to focus on the one which had become emblematic of the Democrats' infamy: the commission of investigation into the opposition which the former regime had established in April 1960 and which triggered the protests leading to the Democrats' downfall.

Many of the death sentences demanded were for those who had sat on the commission or been instrumental in establishing it. Hundreds of prison sentences were sought for those who had simply voted in favour of the commission – an act which itself amounted, it was alleged, to a violation of the constitution.

This was a contentious claim, as Professor Ali Fuad Başgil asserted in appearing for the defence. A foremost expert in constitutional law, Başgil did concede that establishing the commission of investigation was politically unwise, as he had cautioned Bayar and Menderes at the time. But he was clear that any law passed by a democratically elected parliamentary majority could not be called unconstitutional – Article 17 of the constitution unequivocally stated that MPs could not be held legally accountable for their voting decisions – and that any judgement to the contrary amounted to an abuse of the democratic process. Other expert witnesses were also of the opinion that the Democrats had been within their rights to vote for the commission of investigation, but had violated the constitution by granting it extraordinary powers normally exercised by the judiciary, which one likened to dressing butchers and barbers in judges' robes. Another, as if to emphasise the diversity of opinion, was in no doubt whatsoever that the Menderes regime had violated the constitution. All of which should have made for dull drama, this 'lawyer's banquet of Byzantine subtlety', if it were not for what everybody understood – that in this case 'men's heads' depended upon the outcome. So it was that differing opinions on fine points of constitutional law, juridical abstractions and legal interventions carried all the force of Nero's thumb, the partisan galleries giving rein to their bloodlust by booing those who might bring comfort to the accused and cheering those whose expert opinions would condemn them.

*

Through the summer of 1961 a young man called Erhan Kocabiyikoğlu regularly returned to the naval museum to queue for one of the few trial passes available to the families of the accused.

'We had left our home in Ankara, my mother and I, to stay in a friend's Istanbul apartment so that we could take it in turns to attend my father's trial,' Erhan told me. 'Seeing him, even at a distance, even if it was not possible to have a single word, brought us some comfort. And him too, we liked to think, even if he only caught brief glimpses of us. To be sure of getting one of the thirty daily passes allocated to the families, we generally had to be at the naval museum by midnight. That summer I spent many nights dozing by the low wall opposite the ticket office – the old kiosk where the imams used to calculate the times of the call to prayer.'

Erhan, now a retired architect, had agreed to meet me at the Koç Transport Museum at Hasköy on the northern shores of the Golden Horn. These restored docks, warehouses and quays are home to a grand collection of vintage cars, locomotives and carriages, trams, aeroplanes, motorcycles, submarines, lifeboats – and the *Fenerbahçe* ferry, which throughout the trials carried passengers like Erhan to Yassıada.

'I was not eighteen, the minimum permitted age for visitors,' Erhan recalled. 'So I needed a fake ID, which our sympathetic local mayor provided. We the families of the accused were always the first on board and the last off – I guess so that others would be spared any sight of us.'

The *Fenerbahçe*, built in Scotland in the early 1950s, spent her life plying the Bosphorus routes before being decommissioned in 2008, when she dodged the scrapyard to be retired to her final quayside on the Golden Horn. She appeared immaculately maintained, in a fresh coat of white paint with a mustard trim, the railings neatly hung with red and white lifebuoys. The saloons were elegantly finished, with decks, railings and stairways in varnished teak, the floors of the open-sided upper deck scattered with round tables, some on high chrome stands, and topped with retro ashtrays in frosted glass. The winter cabins were panelled, with leather banquettes.

'Not that I saw any of that,' said Erhan with a wry smile as we made our way to the bridge. We had an appointment with Tuncer Şensoy, the *Fenerbahçe*'s captain since 1994, who had been retained as the ferry's custodian into her retirement. We found Tuncer poring over back copies of the ship's log.

'I was just looking up the entry for 27 May 1960,' he said, greeting us. '*Army took over. Crew didn't come to work. Everybody ordered to stay at home till four o'clock. Ship stayed in dock.* Now, let me show Erhan Bey what you wanted to see,' he said, grabbing a bunch of keys and leading the way to a locked door off one of the decks. Beyond the door a flight of steps led down into a dark and airless hold where the teak gave way to the exposed hull's riveted ribs, the rust showing through the old paint. We followed Tuncer onto the stairs, and down to a place Erhan had last been as a young man fifty-five years before. At the foot of the stairs he looked about him.

'This was where we spent the journey,' he said. 'The defendants' parents, often elderly and feeble, their wives and husbands, siblings and grown-up children. There were some chairs, I remember, but no views, of course, and armed guards stationed at the door. At the end of the crossing, after all the other passengers had disembarked, they led us to the courthouse and to seats right at the back, as far from our loved ones as possible. We got no more than glimpses of them; if my father tried to turn and catch sight of us he could expect a cuff from the nearest guard. Once, though, they did let me see him during the lunch break. It was a short visit, and my father was tearful, and there were officers on hand so he couldn't tell me how he was being treated, but they did let him kiss me. As they led me away, we happened across Bayar, Menderes and some others who had been organised into a line before entering the court.'

'See how well we have them trained!' boasted the officer accompanying Erhan back to his seat. 'Monkeys couldn't do better.'

Erhan's father had been the Democrat MP for the city of Balıkesir since 1950. 'Like so many of the others, he faced the main charge of violating the constitution,' explained Erhan. 'In his case it seemed that would mean a long prison sentence if he were found guilty, though it was hard not to imagine an even worse outcome. In my father's absence it was up to me to reassure my mother that it would all turn out all right.'

*

As the summer advanced, so temperatures rose in the Yassıada court-house. The crowded galleries wilted, brows beading and heads nodding as audiences struggled to keep pace with the labyrinthine arguments, conflicting constitutional interpretations and legal intri-cacies that the main case entailed. But the proceedings had their full attention whenever the former prime minister was on show, which was often, and in a progressively enfeebled state.

In earlier exchanges Adnan Bey, taking courage from Ayhan Aydan's example, had gallantly fought his corner. Drawing deep on his legal training and natural oratory, he combined trenchant argu-ment with trademark flashes of defiant eloquence: 'physically shrunken but still well groomed', as one witness put it, 'evasive in his answers but witty and courteous'. Recently, however, the fight had gone out of him, as if the trials had proved too much for his vulner-able personality. But if the ordeal had done for Adnan Bey, it was as much because he had had by far the worst of it; far more cases to answer, more appearances in court, more convictions and more calls by the prosecution for his head – eight in total – than any other defendant. Of all the accused, it was he the judges and prosecutors attacked especially, belittling his achievements in office: the only reason he had participated so wholeheartedly in the restoration of Istanbul, they claimed, had been as cover for his libidinous activities in the city. Their relentless taunts and jibes, invariably greeted by cheers from the hostile galleries, made each court appearance as unendurable as the solitary confinement which followed it. There were many reasons, then, for Adnan Bey's increasingly broken state; but it seemed there might have been still more, as an old schoolfriend discovered when he was given leave that summer to visit Adnan Bey on Yassıada.

'And how are you?' the friend asked.

'You may judge for yourself how I am,' the prisoner whispered, covertly unbuttoning his shirt to reveal a torso patterned with his captors' cigarette ends.

For the Committee, who had thrown everything at Menderes in their attempts to discredit him, bringing him down had become a matter of urgency. Beyond the cauldron of the courthouse, support for the revolution had cooled while the opposition grew increasingly outspoken. The teahouses rang with muttered threats against General Gürsel and his officers, who were suspected of plotting to cut the wheat payments and close the mosques. Posters of the Committee, depicting the members in a reverential wreath, were repeatedly torn down or defaced. Announcements that 27 May was to be a national holiday were met with banners condemning the so-called Festival of National Unity and Freedom as a communist innovation. Not that the communists were any more supportive; even the exiled Nazım joined in the criticism, claiming in one of his radio broadcasts that 27 May 'was born dead, and has merely replaced one dictatorship by another'. Plots against the Committee and planned acts of sabotage, in one case to destroy a key Istanbul power station, were reported to have been uncovered. Every day brought fresh rounds of arrests as the Committee clamped down on those suspected of planning to liberate Menderes, even those whose audacity extended only to making public declarations of their devotion to Adnan Bey by, for example, raising glasses to his health in restaurants.

As the gestures of solidarity with the fallen Democrats and their leader grew more strident, so the officers came to recognise their dependence upon Menderes's public capitulation, and at any cost, counting on that abject spectacle to sap the spirits of his supporters. Things began to look up for the Committee as the trials' later stages saw Menderes's performances suffer a drastic deterioration, the old thrusts and sallies giving way to base defences like timely bouts of forgetfulness or citing the lamentable deficiencies of subordinates; and when the defendant was reduced to addressing the presiding judge with 'elaborate courtesies and oriental titles', which observers took to be craven pleas for his life, the officers could barely conceal their delight.

In early August, as the trials finally approached the end, the leading defendants were given leave to make closing statements. There

CHAPTER THIRTEEN

17 September 1961

Execution

M etin was in combative mood.
'Menderes?' he muttered, stubbing out a cigarette. 'The worst thing that ever happened to this country.'

We were back at his favoured haunt, the Nazım Hikmet Centre in Kadıköy, where I had hoped Metin might help me make better sense of the divisive figure at the centre of this story. This was a promising start.

'Your Nazım certainly thought so.' I nodded. 'I'm aware of the hatred. Then and now. But I've also heard from people who think nothing of the sort. In fact, the opposite, that Adnan Bey—'

'Don't call him that.'

'—gave them and their people the means to live better lives. Transformed the villages. Took them out of their rough sandals – isn't that the phrase? – and put them in shoes.'

'What he did,' said Metin, 'was use the people to get into power. Then bribed them – with the likes of mosques and wheat subsidies – to keep him there. Just like the current one.'

'But that's not quite true. We know that Adnan Bey wavered towards the end, even tried to resign, only for tough old Bayar to dissuade him. Obviously, he liked being in charge, and would have been loath to go, but it wasn't power at any cost.'

'But it was the same cynical way of staying in charge – bowing to the people's backward ways, whatever it cost the country.'

'But they were new to democracy, the Democrats. Call him naïve, but I think he sincerely believed it was only about giving the people what they wanted. Even if—'

'By bankrupting the country.'

'—even if, as I was about to say, he wasn't on top of the economics.'

'And the people who happened to disagree with him, the journalists, academics and students – he certainly didn't give them what they wanted. He imprisoned them.'

'Oh, heavens, he was far from perfect,' I replied. 'Sensitive, spiteful and unstable, overemotional and with an enormous autocratic streak that surprised, I think, even himself. But wasn't that for the voters rather than the army to decide? As they had done in three consecutive elections. How did the officers think that ousting and imprisoning the elected leaders, then defaming and destroying the great hope of so many people, was going to go down with the Democrats' supporters? Did they really think that Adnan Bey, for all his failings, and I accept there were plenty towards the end, deserved what they did to him?'

'It's our way of doing politics,' said Metin, lighting a cigarette. 'It's called getting even.'

'It's called vengeance. Which explains where we are now. I mean, isn't 27 May where it all began? After that, and Yassıada, retaliation was inevitable. You talk of getting even – isn't that what Erdoğan's been doing for years now?' Metin lit another cigarette.

'Anyway, whose side are you on?' he asked.

'I'm trying to be on neither,' I said. 'I'm not sure taking sides helps. I'm only showing you the man that you think of as your hated enemy.' Metin threw back his head, tutting and blinking all at once in the unmistakable Turkish gesture of disagreement.

'Not taking sides,' he said, jabbing a finger, 'that's simply not a Turkish position.'

*

Two days after the coup an army major, fresh from tying up Istanbul, had left for the capital to attend a meeting of the Committee of National Unity.

In the circumstances national unity was an optimistic ambition, even if the country at least appeared at peace from the window of the train, where the major spotted no disturbance more noteworthy than a runaway pony cart, a dog frenziedly snapping at the spooked beast's fetlocks, farmhands in laboured pursuit across the spinach fields. Proud that 27 May had gone off without a hitch, and of his part in it, the major sat back and imagined the hearty pats on the back he could anticipate as he took his seat, a dossier in his name indicating his place at the polished conference table.

But at the Ankara offices of the deposed prime minister the major found no committee – only men intent upon being on it – and no kind of unity. Officers in full regalia bustled through the crowded offices and corridors, jostling to advance revolutionary credentials. Colonels squared up to squadron leaders, navy commanders to majors, besting each other's claims to membership of the Committee. Officers from Istanbul reminded the Ankara men where the action had begun, only for their comrades to point out, fingers jabbing, that Ankara was the capital and that its capture, a more testing challenge, was what had finally clinched it. Rank, in normal circumstances the only arbiter, suddenly counted for nothing, with captains in their twenties and majors in their thirties shouting down colonels in their fifties and generals in their sixties, veterans of Korea and even the War of Independence, on the basis of their superior contributions to 27 May. The coup had been carried out with such secrecy that few knew who had been in from the start and who had come in only when the outcome appeared assured, who had made the difference and who had merely milled about, loosing off rounds into the night. Who, in short, was to say who had done what – risked his neck in the cause – if one did not say it oneself? And more loudly than the next man.

For seven hours the officers strove in vain to form their Committee. One proposal that six or eight individuals be appointed to select the membership was shouted down by those who saw no friends of their own among the likely appointees, by junior officers who expected to be overlooked in favour of their superiors, and by naval

officers who knew how little army men tended to think of their boat-
ing counterparts. Another proposal, that the Committee be restricted
to twenty members, was opposed by those who doubted, on the basis
of a quick head count, that they would make any such cut. Not until
the early hours was it agreed that the Committee – under General
Gürsel, its chairman as well as head of state, prime minister and
commander-in-chief – should comprise thirty-eight members.

Later that summer the number dropped to thirty-seven when a
traffic accident claimed one member; then, on a dramatic night in
November, it fell to twenty-three. In the early hours the Committee
swooped upon fourteen members whom it suspected of plotting a
takeover. This cabal of young radicals, who had shown no enthusiasm for the Committee's pledges to restore democratic rule at the
earliest opportunity, had lately been agitating for the period of dictatorship it considered essential to shore up Atatürk's sacred reforms
after the grievous damage done to their foundations by Menderes's
accursed Democrats. The fourteen men, mostly majors and captains,
were held under house arrest before being assigned as special attachés
in Ottawa, Delhi, Tokyo and other far-flung Turkish embassies. In
the Committee of National Unity there was disunity; and in explaining that 'such different ideas, such disagreements have emerged that
committee discussions have become battlefields more than means to
solve problems', General Gürsel appeared to have woken up to the
fact that there was more to the business of government, and maintaining national unity, than the Committee had allowed.

When further internal disagreements led to the resignation of
another member in June 1961, twenty-two members remained.
These were the men charged, by their own laws, with ratifying the
death sentences passed by the Yassıada court. On 15 September they
duly gathered at the National Assembly in Ankara to await the arrival
of the judges' decisions from Yassıada where the papers were signed
before being locked in a satchel which was entrusted to the care of
two officers. A helicopter flew the officers to the airport where a military jet, with fighter escorts, was waiting to fly them to the capital.

*

At six o'clock that same morning Lieutenant Taşdelen replaced the
duty officer on the ground floor of Ward 1 where the leading
members of the ousted regime had been confined for fifteen months.
The former prime minister remained under twenty-four-hour
observation though he no longer had to share his cramped and often
stifling quarters with a guard. Under the new arrangement, which
brought a degree of privacy and peace to Room 1's nerve-wracked
occupant, the duty officer kept watch on the prisoner through a
window fitted in the door. Being stationed in the corridor came as as
much of a relief to Lieutenant Taşdelen, who took no pleasure whatsoever in being obliged to observe at close quarters the acute distress
of a man he was expressly forbidden from comforting. For reasons of
his own, though, he did plan to spend a few minutes in Room 1 that
very morning.

From his first days on Yassıada, Lieutenant Taşdelen had been
quick to adapt to island routines and to acquaint himself with the
personalities and habits of inmates, colleagues and senior staff
officers alike. Alert to their caprices and moods, he kept out of
trouble, and continued his secret activity without bringing his naval
career to a premature end in a courtroom or prison cell. He had
succeeded in taking hundreds of photographs. These photographs
were a source of pride and not only because of the technical chal-
lenges that their discreet taking entailed, but because they were not
like the propaganda shots – the officers at their heroic best, the
inmates their remorseful worst – which the newspapers slavishly
devoted to the Committee plastered across their front pages. Lieutenant Taşdelen liked to think that his work captured something of
Yassıada's truth; that his photographs might one day shed light on
what he sensed, even then, to be a defining episode in the history of
his young country.

But he needed better shots of the man at the heart of it all:
Menderes. As the trials drew towards a close, Lieutenant Taşdelen

began to despair of having missed his opportunity. On the very last morning his luck changed when he was assigned the duty slot which exactly served his purposes, 6 a.m., which was late enough, he judged, to provide the necessary natural light and early enough that senior officers were unlikely to be around. He would take this last best chance. When Lieutenant Taşdelen made his way along the corridor to replace the duty officer that morning there were two cameras – a Kodak Retinette as well as the Pentax Zenobia – slung beneath his loose-fitting shirt.

The duty officer nodded at his replacement and with a yawn he sauntered off, straightening his cap. Lieutenant Taşdelen watched him out of sight, alert to the sounds beyond the fading boot-falls. Hearing only the slap of the sea, the gulls and the bark of a distant dog, Lieutenant Taşdelen wasted no time. He turned to the duty private stationed near Room 1, dispatching him on an errand the private might have managed in barely a minute but which, the lieutenant had no doubt, he would complete at the pace of any soldier presented with a welcome alternative to standing interminably at attention; time enough, at any rate, for what the lieutenant had in mind. He watched the private out of sight before slipping into Room 1, fully expecting the prisoner, the most fitful of sleepers, to stir even as he turned the door handle. But his luck held; Lieutenant Taşdelen, ready with his rehearsed lines in case of the prisoner's reluctance – something about a historic record that would outlast them all – was surprised to discover him, on this of all mornings, in the deepest of sleeps.

He was dressed in cotton pyjamas, striped white at the cuffs, and lying beneath a sheet, head on the pillow, a forearm folded across the chest, in an attitude of uncharacteristically tranquil repose. A Quran, an ashtray heaped with crumpled cigarette butts, a newly written letter addressed to his wife and an empty water glass were on the bedside table. Without wasting a moment, Lieutenant Taşdelen unbuttoned his shirt to remove his cameras. In the dawn light he began to take photographs at different angles and distances, thinking no more of the subject's failure to stir, even at the repeated click of the shutter, than that it was to his further good fortune. Here was a man at peace; the elusive peace which the generously disposed lieutenant had often wished for the former prime minister and which these photographs might finally capture.

Only when Lieutenant Taşdelen drew near the bed to shoot some final close-ups did he notice the spittle. Bending close, he could barely discern breathing; only the bubbles freshly forming between the prisoner's lips. The lieutenant hurried into the corridor and beckoned to his colleague at the nearby duty desk. Gently, they shook the prisoner by the shoulder. 'Sir,' they said, 'sir,' before shaking him more vigorously. When there was still no response, they raced to the duty desk and telephoned the infirmary and the commander's office.

The private, having spun out his errand as Lieutenant Taşdelen had predicted, was returning to his post when he heard the raised voices. He reached Ward 1 to find the ground floor overrun with alarmed officers in unlaced boots and hurrying nurses shrugging on their white coats. In Room 1 the doctors were wrestling with flailing rubber tubes as they prepared to pump the prisoner's stomach.

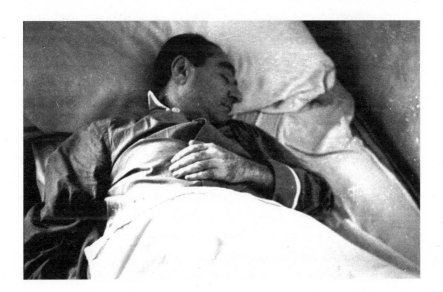

*

That same day an Istanbul imam, returning from Friday prayers, stopped for some groceries before climbing the lane that led from the Bosphorus. At his house he pushed through the door, puffing heavily.

'The mufti's been trying to reach you,' called his wife. 'There was a man round. Something about some job.'

'Bread,' replied the imam, depositing the shopping on the table before settling heavily into a chair. 'Onions. Aubergines. Peppers. Leeks. Tomatoes. Yoghurt. All God's gifts. The ones you asked for, at least. A job?'

'Didn't say any more; the mufti will fill you in at the office. Unless this is him in person,' she said, tucking strands of hair beneath her headscarf as she made to answer the door, 'and aren't we busy today.' The imam was wondering what they could want with him when his wife returned. 'An officer,' she said, an eyebrow raised. 'For you.' The imam struggled out of the chair and made his way to the door.

'*Salaam aleikum*,' he said.

The officer, declining to return the traditional Arabic greeting, nodded curtly before scanning his clipboard. 'Under the authority of the Committee,' he said, 'I'm to advise you that you've been selected for special duties. You're to come with me. As quickly as possible, and with an overnight bag.'

The imam scratched his head. 'A job,' he queried. 'Nights away, then.'

'No time to lose,' said the officer impatiently. 'You'll be told more in due course.' Minutes later the officer led the way to a khaki-coloured truck, gesturing to the back where the imam found himself among a dozen or so men, several of whom he recognised as clerics.

'*Salaam aleikum*,' he said, settling among them.

'*Aleikum salaam*,' they chorused.

'So many of you!' he exclaimed before dropping his voice to a whisper. 'Rounding up the religious reactionaries, are they?' he

chuckled. 'The counter-revolutionaries? In case it all kicks off after
the island sentences?'

'Nothing of the sort, apparently; they say it's to do with some
Islamic delegation newly arrived from Pakistan.'

'That we're to host. Show around the city.'

'Is that where they're taking us now?'

'Down to the water,' replied the officer from the front seats.

'The Bosphorus ferry?' asked one of the imams.

'Not quite the Bosphorus ferry,' said the officer. 'But yes, we've a
sea voyage ahead of us.'

The imams, who had no more expected to put to sea than to
spend the weekend with a delegation from Pakistan, exchanged
bemused glances as the truck jolted down a cobbled lane to the
Dolmabahçe waterfront.

*

In the course of the trials, and to the mounting alarm of the defendants' families and friends, the prosecutors had asked for a total of 228
death penalties. The tally was also a source of concern to the foreign
diplomats who, in the weeks before the sentences were announced,
repeatedly reminded their Turkish contacts of the harm that executions risked doing to the country, not only condemning it to deep
political division and factional hatreds but doing lasting damage to
its international standing. Grass did not grow under the gallows.
These warnings were met with airy assurances that all the talk
amounted to nothing more than belligerent bluster; the officers had
made so much of their bloodless coup, after all, that it was inconceiv-
able they would stain it at the end. The man the Committee had
installed at the foreign ministry, Selim Sarper, judged there was no
more than a half-chance that the judges would pass any death
sentences, 'and an 80/20 chance against executions' even if they did
so. For the power was with the Committee to commute them.

But vengeance was in the air. 'In all my service,' wrote US Ambassador Warren, 'I have not found elsewhere the hate which is among

the intelligentsia and military today for Menderes and his leaders.'
As the day of the sentences drew near, the diplomats began to lose
faith in the Turks' assurances. The ambassadors hurriedly conferred
to establish who had the best contacts on the Committee, and what
leverage they might have with the self-appointed final arbiters. The
Germans suggested financial sanctions, favouring a blunt warning
that executions would affect Turkey's access to international aid and
its reported ambitions for membership of the European trading bloc,
only for the Brits to counter that the Turks were 'oriental enough to
enjoy standing on their honour against sordid economic consider-
ations'; they should nevertheless be left in no doubt, the British
ambassador added, that the revolution would 'largely be judged
abroad by whether the Committee of National Unity have the moral
courage and magnanimity to keep it bloodless'. The Pakistanis, quick
with reminders that their own recent coup had merely seen the
deposed ministers banned from politics for a decade, approached
the Committee with an offer to take in any leading figures whom the
Turks saw fit to exile. The Libyan ambassador not only spoke fluent
Turkish but was 'an old friend of several of the leading Turkish
soldiers' whom he vigorously reminded of the case for clemency.

Early September saw a succession of ambassadors descend upon
Ankara's foreign ministry with letters from their national leaders –
presidents and prime ministers, kings and queens, chancellors and
shahs – for General Gürsel. Among these was the British ambassador whose letter from Prime Minister Macmillan respectfully
reminded General Gürsel of his administration's public commitment
to Western values, describing any such executions as 'inconsistent
with the high ideals of the Western community to which you and we
are proud to belong'. Foreign Minister Sarper promised the ambassador that he would pass on the letter and continue doing everything
in his personal power to press for clemency. Sarper confided to the
ambassador that as the matter appeared likely to come down to a vote
he had taken to counting heads on the twenty-two-man Committee;
he was fairly sure that the three most senior members would vote for
clemency, and 'also confident of the votes of five other Committee

members, making eight altogether'. That left four extra votes required for a majority.

If there was encouragement in all this, the ambassador was disturbed to hear Sarper refer for the first time to a 'shadow committee' in the Turkish army. This group, Sarper explained, had taken upon itself to 'express to the Committee the views of the armed services', not least of the colonels, many of whom 'still fanatically supported the view that death sentences should be carried out'.

In a further meeting a week before sentencing was to take place Sarper informed the ambassador that the Committee – 'eight in favour of clemency, eight in favour of executions', the rest undecided – remained resolutely split. The more sinister development was that the 'shadow committee' had acquired greater definition – as 'some thirty or forty officers in the army outside the Committee, mostly colonels or one-star generals, who were insisting actively on their view that a certain number of executions must take place to ensure the future security of the country'. By way of asserting that view, these officers were in the habit of descending, conspicuously armed, upon the National Assembly, where the Committee had taken to meeting, to prowl the corridors. The ambassador felt bound to ask 'whether the efforts being made by this group were directed towards influencing the Committee or whether there was any idea that they might act in any other way, outside the legal framework'; how far, baldly put, were these men prepared to go? Sarper could not say, though his admission that 'the Committee were to some extent no longer the ultimate source of power' only confirmed what the ambassador was hearing from other contacts. His information officer in Istanbul had recently reported a meeting in which a colonel had told him that the army now exerted 'considerable influence over the Committee – to the point of dictating its terms'. It had, moreover, been 'fairly reliably' reported that elements in the Yassıada garrison were vowing that some prisoners, whatever the decisions of the Committee, would 'never get out of Yassıada alive, since this would be too dangerous for the army personnel who have been guarding them there'.

The British ambassador was forced to the unpalatable conclusion that they might be trying to reach the wrong people. Just as the Committee had assumed power, by force, so it was now being relieved of it by elements outside its control. After what was effectively another coup, nobody could say any longer who was in charge, nor who held the lives of the Yassıada defendants in their hands.

*

On 15 September, when the court broke for lunch, the Yassıada commander gathered the members of the press and offered to show them the former prime minister.

Under heavy guard more than a hundred journalists followed the commander along the trail beyond the barbed wire to Ward 1. In single file they were shown into Room 1 where the medical orderlies and attendants made room for the journalists at the foot of the bed. The *Times* correspondent described the comatose patient's face as 'a greyish-blue colour', with an oxygen tube up his nose and a drip feeding a lemon-coloured liquid into his wrist, and the *Daily Express* wrote of the patient's 'pitiful, deathly-marble colour'. The commander, unusually harassed, emphasised that the patient had been seen by several doctors, and the contents of his stomach sent to Istanbul for analysis. 'I'm letting you see him so that,' he repeatedly insisted, 'you will know no one has beaten him or hurt him in any way.'

At four o'clock that afternoon, while the patient remained in a coma, and in no condition to be moved, the fourteen other condemned men were taken from the island. The former president, the foreign and finance ministers were among those placed in handcuffs and led down to the quay where a patrol vessel was waiting to take them to İmralı.

The island of İmralı lay thirty miles to the south. Once home to Greek grape growers and silk farmers, it was abandoned after the community's expulsion in the 1920s' population exchanges. By the summer of 1961 it housed a prison whose governor had lately received instructions that he should prepare to receive an

unspecified number of high-profile political prisoners over the weeks
ahead. At the same time the military authorities ordered the govern-
or to arrange for the delivery of a quantity of timbers, and to put
some earthworks in hand. When the consignment arrived, the govern-
or told the prison staff that the timbers were for building repairs,
adding that he would also need some trenches dug in readiness, he
said, for the planting of a new olive grove.

*

On the afternoon of 15 September a drifter by the name of Kemal
was in Üsküdar, Istanbul's old port district of Scutari, where he had
repaired to one of his regular drinking holes. He was seeing off a
bottle of rakı when Hasan rushed into the *meyhane*.

'Soldiers!' gasped Hasan. 'Asking for you all along the street.' He
wagged an accusing finger. 'You been up to something, you no-good
ruffian?' he laughed. Kemal belched, his breath fetid with aniseed,
anchovy and red onion.

'Soldiers?' he asked, draining his glass and clambering to his feet.
'Better make myself,' he hiccuped, 'scarce.'

'Bill!' the landlord bawled, slapping the counter.

'Later!' said Kemal, dodging the landlord's outstretched arm and
raising a promissory palm as he steadied himself at a passing table
before lurching through the back door of the *meyhane*. In the glare
he squinted, stumbled over a dozing dog and paused to light a cigarette before weaving his way down the lane. Not his favourite people,
the uniforms, who could hardly be said to have time for people like
him; a gypsy layabout, they called him, a worthless good-for-nothing,
and truth was they had a point. It hadn't all been bad, of course –
Kemal had been a dependable night watchman in his time, and an
honest enough porter – but he'd also made off with stuff that wasn't
his, and done jobs he wasn't proud of, whatever came along, which
was all that was left when the tolerable tasks had gone and there was
nobody else for them to ask. Like the dog job he'd lately done, on the
quiet, the man from the municipality slipping him some lira for

putting out the baits to make a dent in Scutari's growing population
of strays. Odd thing about this was that it was always the police on
his case. He couldn't think what the soldiers should want with him
– unless the baits had done for one of their officers' dogs. Perhaps
even the officer who now brought Kemal up short, arms folded and
feet spread as he blocked the fugitive's escape route.

'It's Kemal Bey, isn't it?' said the officer equably, brushing dust
from the brim of his cap. 'We've been looking for you.'

'What do you want?' asked Kemal, backing away. 'If it's about the
dogs, I didn't mean no harm. They told me to put out the baits. They
ordered me to do it – I couldn't know I'd do for yours, sir.'

The officer held up his palms. 'Enough about dogs,' he said.
'Don't worry about any dogs you've done in. Doing in's what you do,
after all. Talking of which, I've a job for you. An important one. For
you and Hasan and whoever else. Pull a crew together and there's
150 lira each in it for you. We'll see you at the waterfront, and as soon
as you can.'

*

Imralı's governor had been advised to expect the boats later that day.
The sun was low by the time the first of them appeared from the
north. The patrol vessel drew alongside, churning the waters as sailors leapt onto the quayside, running ropes to the bollards. As the
rumble of the engines fell silent armed guards stepped ashore,
motioning for their cuffed charges to follow. They looked about
them, these men in their crumpled jackets but straight ties, before
they filed across the gangplank and along the quay into the custody
of the prison authorities.

The second boat was not far behind, the disembarking passengers pale after their time at sea. On their way ashore they took in
the surroundings, the low grey buildings, fence-lines and cypress
trees, and the soldiers, and wondered what business fifteen Turkish
imams and their Pakistani guests could possibly have in such a
place. By the time the third boat arrived in the gathering dusk,

Kemal blinking and unsteady as he led his hastily assembled mob ashore, the imams had learned that they were not on the island to entertain Pakistanis, just as the prison staff had discovered there were to be neither building repairs nor olive groves – the timber baulks being for gallows, the trenches graves.

*

At about the same time twenty-two officers gathered around a table at the National Assembly.

'The door,' instructed one, turning a key in a satchel before removing the contents. The room was silent as he scanned the sheaf of documents. 'As we understood,' he eventually said, laying his palms upon the table. 'Fifteen.'

'But only on our say-so,' said another, gesturing at a stack of telegrams. 'Just delivered by Sarper. In person. The views, in case any of us needed reminding, of the Americans and the British, the French and the Germans. Plus the Pakistanis and Indians, the Swedes and the Swiss, even the Guatemalans and God knows who else. Personal interventions, minutes old, from Kennedy and Adenauer, and Winston Bey, no less, reminding us of "the beneficial effect it would have on all who wish you well, and throughout the world, if your government were to show clemency in commuting the sentences of death recently promulgated."'

'We all know what our foreign friends think.'

'And we also know that Ismet Paşa agrees with them. Those of us, that is, who've bothered to read his letter – where he says any executions, however few, will be against the national interest . . . that even the civilians who suffered most under the administration of the guilty would find such executions excessive and saddening . . . executions would create an irreparable loss of trust towards the army . . . executions for political crimes simply don't take place in civilised countries today.'

'All very well. But I don't see Ismet Paşa, with all respect to him, among the heavies hanging about in the corridor,' said an officer, thumbing at the door. 'Our more, how to put it, resolute colleagues from the air force.'

'I was under the impression we were the Committee. That the revolution was ours. I thought we were in charge.'

'Seems they want their say, which is that they insist on executions to confirm the revolution. To warn others against straying from the path of political moderation.'

'And that if we don't do it, then they will, whatever the decision we make in this room. Perhaps even by bombing the island. Then who knows how many end up dead? Plus, then we're looking at nothing less than the armed forces at each other's throats.'

'Are we really going to do this? Remember the pride we all took in our bloodless coup! There are people out there who'll never forgive executions. Especially if we hang *him*. And if not him, we can hardly hang anybody.'

'But after Gatwick, what will they think if we don't hang him? It will only convince them that we didn't because we *couldn't*.'

'We don't have a choice. We can't risk outright rebellion. We have to give the hard-liners something.'

Hours later the committee agreed on a compromise to put before a vote; if the vote passed, they would ratify the death sentences in those cases where the nine Yassıada judges had been unanimous, but exempt the former president on grounds of age. At almost nine o'clock that evening the proposal to commute twelve of the death sentences passed by fourteen votes to eight, the Committee hoping that the men lurking in the corridors would be satisfied with three.

*

On hearing the news that evening from Turkey, Margaret Bailey agreed to a visit by the London newspapers; it might just help save him, the newsmen explained.

Margaret, dressed in a white raincoat and a neatly tied headscarf, led the journalists and photographers into Jordan's Wood. In the clearing where the Turkish Airlines flight had come down two years earlier, among the broken trees and the scarred earth, the farmer's wife stood in silence. Clasping her hands before her, she prayed for the man who had somehow survived and who was now to die. 'We had hoped that in the end Mr Menderes would be set free,' she said over the clicks of the cameras. 'He is such a kind, considerate man.' She told the newsmen that she would write that night to Berin Menderes – 'as one woman to another' – but wondered what more she could do.

A woman prays

The following morning Ismet Paşa, shocked to learn that the Committee had roundly disregarded the contents of his long and considered appeal, as they had ignored the letters from Kennedy, Churchill, Adenauer and the rest, set off for the ministries where he hoped to shake some sense into Gürsel. The general proved elusive, though he did eventually take a telephone call from Ismet Paşa who repeated his warning that the Committee's decision would prove disastrous for the country. 'If Menderes and his colleagues are executed,' he said, 'it will be impossible to achieve peace and harmony in the country and among the political parties.'

Later that morning Ismet Paşa learned that Zorlu and Polatkan had already been executed, and that Menderes was to follow them the moment the doctors pronounced him fit to hang. When Berin Menderes visited his house later that day to plead for the life of her husband, all Ismet Paşa could tell the distraught woman and her youngest son Aydın was that he had no say in the matter. The 'men with guns' would have their bloody reckoning. For all his former influence Ismet Paşa found himself powerless to do anything other than splutter dire warnings about Turkey's future, and perhaps rue his own part in shaping it.

*

A few days after the coup the former interior minister, among the fallen regime's most reviled figures, had abruptly exited a fourth-floor window at Ankara's military academy, with predictable consequences. The loss of such a key individual was a warning to the Committee – whatever the nonsense subsequently spouted about tunnels, rescue submarines and winged horses – of their captives' likeliest escape route. Many proud Democrats, despairing of their predicament and the humiliations their enemies had in store for them, were inclined to favour death at their own hands, especially those who had fallen furthest of all and whom the authorities could least afford to lose: the two solitaries they kept under round-the-clock guard in Ward 1.

These fears were realised one day in September 1960 when Room 2's occupant set about strangling himself during a visit to the bathroom. Despite causing copious bleeding from the ears, the former president failed in his attempt. Of yet greater concern was the former prime minister whose mental state led the Yassıada authorities to take every precaution, even ones which bordered on the farcical. An anonymous tip-off claiming that the prisoner's Quran had been steeped in a poison so powerful that the owner need only chew on a page or two to see himself off led to the prompt replacement of the volume in question, the least possibility that the prisoner's holy book might also provide his way out, and thus contribute to the powerful mystique about the man, being one that the authorities were not prepared to countenance.

It was a profound shock to learn, then, that Menderes had so nearly spoiled the show on the very day of the sentencing. The authorities demanded an explanation. On 16 September, shortly after the prisoner had regained consciousness, Lieutenant Taşdelen and his fellow guards were summoned to Room 1 where they found the commander in an angry mood.

'Tranquillisers,' he thundered, flourishing the medical report which he slapped against the foot of the patient's bed. 'A potentially fatal overdose of tranquillisers. And you three – you were supposed to be guarding him!' Lieutenant Taşdelen and his comrades, with no idea where the prisoner had found the tranquillisers, did not reply. 'I insist on knowing the facts. Otherwise, you three are to face court martial.'

'You have no reason to reproach them.' The patient was sitting up in bed, smoking. He was pale, and the little vigour he mustered in his defence of the young lieutenants left him short of breath. 'They were not to know that for weeks now I've been hoarding my daily tranquillisers – the Equanil, the Nembutal—'

'It was their job to notice,' the commander snapped.

'We watched the prisoner swallow them, sir, every time.'

The prisoner smiled, savouring his tiny triumph. 'You thought you did. In fact, I kept the pills under my tongue and removed what remained once you had left. They were like a paste, but not entirely dissolved. I hid them down the hole I'd ripped under the collar of my suit jacket. Let me show you.' He gestured at the cupboard where the jacket hung. The commander handed the jacket to the prisoner who turned back the collar to reveal a hole which he forced open with two fingers before shaking the fabric to release some residual white powder.

'See? I managed to collect enough to fill a matchbox. Not quite enough, it seems, to see me off. Though if the young lieutenant had not been so vigilant' – he smiled wanly at Taşdelen – 'then I might have escaped my sentence. Whatever that may be.'

For despite asking shortly after coming round, he was yet to learn. The prison staff told him, unsure themselves whether this was out of compassion or cowardice, that sentencing had been deferred. In all Turkey he was the only person not to know, then, that he had been sentenced to die; that the Committee had ratified his sentence, along with those of two colleagues; and that the sentences on Fatin Rüştü Zorlu and Hasan Polatkan had been carried out on Imralı in the pre-dawn hours of that same morning.

First they came for Zorlu. He listened calmly while they read him the execution order. He was given leave to write final letters, to perform his ablutions before dressing with his usual care, even fastening his cuffs with links. He attended to prayers, gently offering a correction when the imam stumbled across an Arabic phrase in the Quran. Then they dressed him in a white smock, hung the execution order about his neck, and led him out into the courtyard.

The tripod gallows stood in a corner, beneath a tall tree which was yet to shed its first leaves. A makeshift scaffold, a table topped by a chair, had been placed beneath the hanging noose. The executioners handed the prisoner up, but not before he had wiped the dirt from the soles of his shoes. 'You seem nervous,' he told one of the executioners. 'Better leave that to me.'

Kemal, sober now, clambered onto the table only for the prisoner to wave him aside as he set the noose about his own neck.

'I kiss the hand of my mother,' said Zorlu. 'May my daughter marry and be happy.' He removed his wedding ring and requested that it be returned to his wife. Then he nodded, gave the night sky a glance, took a barely discernible breath, and kicked away the chair.

Minutes later, when his turn came, Hasan Polatkan left the last action of his life to Kemal.

*

Mehmet Taşdelen was not to see Menderes again, though it happened that another man with a camera was on hand at the end. I tracked down Ismail Şenyüz, now in his mid-eighties, to his Ankara apartment where he recalled his time as an official army photographer.

'My job was mostly portraits of senior officers, official visits, ceremonial dinners and NATO exercises,' said Ismail. 'And the Yassıada trials. The photos they wanted for the newspapers, photos of the trials. I was often dispatched to the island for days on end. I must have been twenty-eight at the time.

'On 16 September, the day they'd hanged Zorlu and Polatkan, I was at the office near Dolmabahçe when I got a call. A rumour was going round that Adnan Bey, despite being barely alive, had been hanged with the others. The rumour worried the Yassıada commander who needed shots to prove that the prisoner was alive. They were sending a boat for me.

'But when I got to the island that evening they told me that Menderes was sleeping, and that I was to stay over and come back to his room in the morning. I did so to find Adnan Bey having breakfast and the commander explaining that there were to be some photographs. Adnan Bey courteously replied that he didn't want his photograph taken. The commander promised Adnan Bey that the photographs were not for the newspapers but to reassure the family of his well-being. Taking the commander on trust, he agreed to one photograph. I snapped him in his pyjamas, attempting a smile.

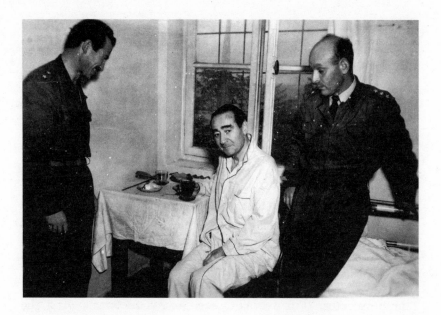

'A little later six doctors arrived to examine the patient. It was by all accounts a thorough examination; on the orders of the commander I photographed one of the doctors as he peered into the patient's mouth. I remember how polite Adnan Bey was, even using his white handkerchief to wipe the thermometer before he returned it to the doctor. I'm not sure when it dawned on me that all these tests were to confirm the patient's fitness to hang. Certainly, he didn't seem to suspect when they explained that he was to be taken to hospital. After asking him to dress, they cuffed him, put him in a jeep and drove him down to the quayside.

'I must have known, I suppose, by the time the commander told me that a boat would take me to Imralı. I remember it as an uncomfortable journey; the weather had broken, the end of summer. It was raining and the sea was choppy. Our boat left some time before Adnan Bey's so that I would be on Imralı to photograph him coming ashore. I think he must have known by then; known at any rate, that they had not taken him to a hospital.

'They led him to a room where the prosecutor was waiting to read the execution order. That's when I learned I was to photograph the execution. They put him in a white gown, hung the execution order around his neck, and walked him to the gallows between two guards, with the rest of them following behind. He was unsteady and unwell, and the guards lent him their support until somebody told them not to; they needed, they said, a photograph of the prisoner walking unaided. I was given instructions only to photograph Menderes and the two guards from the back, which I initially took as a gesture of respect for the man's privacy. Only later did I realise that none of the others wished to be included – implicated – in the shot. It was as if they already knew – the prosecutor, the officers, the prison governor and other officials – that they were party to a crime.

'He had regained his composure by the time he reached the gallows where he smoked a cigarette before turning to ask a favour of the prosecutor. "I'm worried about my son entering politics," he said. "Try to dissuade him. Politics abandons us to fate."'

I was not about to ask this kind old man what he had seen at the end, nor whether Adnan Bey had found the courage to kick away the stool; I took it that Ismail Şenyüz had turned away. It was said that the prisoner took a long time to die, suffering a gradual asphyxiation after his executioners bungled the preparations. After it was over, Ismail Şenyüz was ordered to take more photographs; the Committee saw to it that the former prime minister's swinging corpse appeared on the front pages of several Turkish newspapers the following morning. The newspapers published other photographs, including the one the commander had given his word that the public would not see – of the wan smile that Adnan Bey had summoned for the comfort of his family.

According to custom, the authorities arranged for the charge sheets which had hung about the condemned men's necks to be nailed to the doors of their homes. They permitted the return to the families of the executed men's possessions, at a charge, but the bodies were committed for burial in the hillside trenches which the prison governor had ordered to be dug on Imralı. The governor, who was in attendance as the bodies were washed according to Islamic ritual, happened to notice circular marks on Adnan Bey's chest which he later understood to be from lighted cigarette ends.

'These men weren't the traitors,' said Ismail Şenyüz, seeing me out. 'The men who killed them were.'

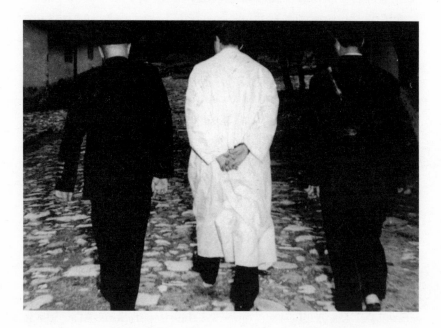

CHAPTER FOURTEEN

15 October 1961

Elections

International revulsion greeted the events in Turkey, with appalled observers likening them to the darkest days of the Soviets and the Yassıada verdicts to those of 'the people's courts in Bulgaria'. One Italian newspaper described the executions, their graphic coverage in the Turkish press only adding to the brutality, as marking 'the savage and bloody dawn of the new Turkey'. The editor of an Athens newspaper condemned Prime Minister Menderes's 'tragic and barbarous end . . . these unpardonable photographs . . . these demonstrations of medieval barbarity, these shrouds, these frightful pictures of the medical examination'. Writing to the Baileys a few weeks later, Baysan Aygün called the hangings the 'greatest murder story of the last years'. 'No wonder we are called barbarians by the Europeans,' she lamented. 'We don't even know where their graves are, we don't know where to send our prayers for the rest of their souls. Dissolved in the history, they lie in our hearts, in the hearts of nearly 20 million people.'

As for Baysan's own family, the Aygüns were still coming to terms with Kemal's life sentence. The exhausted and careworn Mrs Aygün, whom Baysan described as 'a living corpse', was in Kayseri where she had been permitted two brief prison visits with her husband whom she could barely make out beyond 'a thick and dirty glass'. 'They are going to put Daddy in a single room for eight months beginning from tomorrow,' wrote a distraught Baysan. 'He is ill, but who cares,' she added bitterly. 'Then for the rest of his life he will be in jail. But this is only what they say. We still hope. On 15 October the elections will take place.'

The date, as so often in Turkey, was chosen with care; by scheduling the elections for exactly one month after the announcement of the Yassıada sentences, the officers framed the verdicts as part of an orderly and legitimate progression that was to culminate in the resumption of democracy, along with the dissolution of their Committee.

The elections would not include the Democrat Party, of course, long since liquidated by the Committee. The party's absence from the ballot paper led some to look forward to a handsome victory for Ismet Paşa's Republicans, but this was to reckon without the other parties which for some months had been hatching, albeit under the Committee's close supervision, in readiness for the country's return to democracy.

The Committee, mindful that it relied upon the revolution's continued high standing for its own reputation, legislated to prevent any of these parties from making a play for the Democrats' orphaned constituency. It forbade the use of the word 'Democrat' or any of its variants in their names, and ordered campaigning politicians to refrain from expressing the least sympathy for the imprisoned Democrats or criticism of the 27 May coup, but to no avail. Chief among the new contenders was the Justice Party which sidestepped these restrictions by the simple contrivance of basing its party logo on the Democrats' iron-grey horse. This brazen but effective borrowing made it plain to all, then, that the justice the new party sought was for the former and fallen – alive or dead. Baysan, whose new husband was standing for the Justice Party, certainly left the Baileys in no doubt, describing the new party in her letter as 'where the old democrats and Menderes lovers are'.

The *Times* correspondent witnessed the 15 October elections in a village near Ankara. Polling took place in a mosque 'with a gleaming new red-brick minaret' apparently provided by Adnan Bey. The journalist's informant added that news of their leader's recent execution had caused the villagers to weep for three days, which appeared to indicate at least how the locals would vote. In the event, the same turned out to be true at the national level as the Justice Party and the other parties in contention for the former Democrats' support took more than 60 per cent of the vote. The results, a disaster for the Republicans, bore out one commentator's characterisation of the executions as 'an offence calling for vengeance, if not physically, in the vendetta tradition, certainly in the political arena'. The Republicans, on the receiving end of what was described as 'little less than a legal counter-revolution', were left with no choice but to enter into uneasy coalition with their political adversaries in the Justice Party.

The results, which saw Baysan's husband elected as a Justice Party MP, at least gave the Aygüns and the hundreds of other families reason to hope for leniency in the treatment of their loved ones, even to believe that the sentences would not stand. The prison staff showed every respect to the new prisoners while the Kayseri community considered it a point of honour to treat them as their guests, delivering inmates' favourite dishes to the prison gates on birthdays and other special occasions. Distinguished figures including foreign ambassadors were regular visitors to the prison. In the event, the growing political clout of the Justice Party, which would form administrations of its own in the years to come, saw to it that the prisoners were to serve much reduced terms; every last one of them, even those serving life sentences, were amnestied within five years.

For Kemal Aygün freedom came on a snowy evening in March 1963 when he was released from the Ankara hospital where he had been transferred on account of concerns over his diabetes. On hearing the news the rest of the family – Baysan now with a baby boy – drove through the night from Istanbul to be reunited in their Ankara home. The celebrations were extensive and tearful. 'A whole week,' Baysan told the Baileys, 'our house was like a holy place and hundreds of people visited him.' In her letter Baysan enclosed some photographs which the developing studio, having refused any dealings with the family since the coup, had lately delivered to them. The photographs, from the Baileys' visit in 1959, were a poignant memory of happier times but their prompt return on Kemal Aygün's release also held out the promise of a better future. With the end of the former mayor's incarceration, the family's years in the wilderness were at an end. Life might begin again. Friendships might be rebuilt. Some wounds could start to heal.

As for Adnan Bey and his two ministers, only their reputations could be revived.

*

Now that they had done it, not only proving but advertising Adnan Bey's mortality in the most graphic manner, there was the question of guarding against his posthumous return. This was a concern, as it had been in the case of Said Nursi, to judge by the drastic steps the Committee had taken against the holy man six weeks after the coup. On a July night in 1960 army units closed all roads into Urfa before moving tanks and armoured vehicles into position. The authorities cleared citizens from the streets and cordoned off the hallowed courtyard of the Halil-ur Rahman mosque. Soldiers armed with hammers and crowbars were directed to a domed alcove in a corner of the courtyard where three months before Said Nursi had been lain to rest beneath a slab of inscribed marble. The soldiers broke into the tomb, the hammer blows putting up flocks of the white pigeons which frequent the neighbourhood, and removed the shrouded remains to a coffin which they carried to a waiting army truck. At the airport the coffin was placed on a military aircraft and flown to the city of Afyon in the interior of western Turkey where the remains were taken to a secret location and reburied in the lost hours before dawn. By causing the holy man to disappear, the Committee meant to check the veneration, even erase all memory of the Wonder of the Age.

To the same end, the officers refused the families' requests to release the remains of the three men hanged on İmralı. They were buried on that off-limits island, on a slope above the sea, where no mourners could reach them. No public expression of sympathy for the men was to be tolerated; the anniversaries of their executions and other significant occasions were not to be acknowledged.

Newspapers were suspended, their offices attacked by student mobs and their editors jailed for printing photographs of Menderes or those associated with him; among these was a newspaper which marked 17 September a few years after the executions by running a photograph of Margaret Bailey praying for Adnan Bey's life in the Gatwick woods.

But these blunt attempts to obliterate the executed men, as if the least invocation of their memory constituted an insupportable insult to the sanctity of 27 May, only served to breed an aggrieved obstinacy in even the meekest of their supporters, fuelling a determination to remember. A clandestine trade in sacred keepsakes sprang up, with hawkers touting postcards of the 'three martyrs', often alongside their reprieved president, amidst the minarets and chimneys which were their honoured legacy. Such images endured, as I was to see for myself on the wall of Mehmet's ramshackle village house more than fifty years later.

The release of the imprisoned Democrats, then the official pardons extended to some of them, could only presage the restoration, however gradual, of the executed men's reputations. With the years, politicians with an enduring attachment to Adnan Bey and those with an eye on his intact and considerable constituencies began to risk the displeasure of the officers by publicly honouring the memory of the man. The newspapers, alive to every shift in the public mood, courted suspension by acknowledging anniversaries of his execution. The death of General Gürsel, which by chance took place days before the fifth anniversary of the Imralı executions, especially emboldened the press, with one newspaper even claiming that 'the inclination of the Turkish people to rejoice over General Gürsel's death was overshadowed only by their sadness in recalling Mr Menderes's death'. In the towns and villages around Aydın, the man's home territories, mayors even began raising the first statues and honorary busts of Adnan Bey. In 1986, fully twenty-five years after the executions, Prime Minister Turgut Özal offered a public apology to the three families. Özal also passed a law allowing for public roads, structures and institutions to be named after the three

men. Dams, boulevards and universities, many of which were the
result of Adnan Menderes's own building programmes, duly took
his name. It was decided that the new airport at Izmır should be
named for the former prime minister. Neither the preference of
others for 9 September, the date the army drove the Greek forces
from the city in 1922, nor the compelling objection that no airport
should be named after a man closely associated with an air disaster,
was about to prevent Izmır from so honouring its own son.

The laws of physics held, of course, that his rise must bring about
the fall of others, the rehabilitation of Adnan Bey and his two ministers inevitably leading to a decline in the standing of the 1960
revolution and its leading figures. Once lauded, 27 May fell into such
disrepute that Süleyman Demirel, who served as prime minister for
the Justice Party, succinctly dismissed it as 'the name of the action by
which the Republican Peoples Party got the army to crush its rival'.
In 1982 the 27 May national holiday, which many people had opposed
from the moment the Committee introduced it in 1961, was abolished. Six years later the authorities decided to decommission the
Freedom Martyrs' Memorial precinct at Anıtkabir, shrine of the five
martyrs of the revolution, whose eternal elevation into the national
pantheon now turned out to have been on a more conditional basis
than those present at the ceremonial interment on 10 June 1960
might have supposed. In the presence of a handful of witnesses the
martyrs were discreetly exhumed, along with the remains of General
Gürsel who had lain alongside them since his death in 1966. These
evictions and the re-interment of the remains in less exalted Ankara
graveyards incensed the army and its supporters, with the family of
General Gürsel declining to attend. The general's son condemned
the downgrade as a disgrace, predicting that the time would come
when the villainous Menderes took his father's place at Anıtkabir.

*

It was not long before others followed the example set on 27 May;
just months after the 1961 elections, on 22 February 1962, a group

of radical officers under Colonel Talat Aydemir attempted to overthrow the government. Aydemir, who had been actively involved in
the early planning for the 27 May coup, was frustrated by the political direction of the country which he considered unready for
democratic rule. The attempt, which sought to install a revolutionary Kemalist dictatorship, narrowly failed. Aydemir, pardoned along
with his associates, was not discouraged. In May 1963, further
incensed by the early release and public lionisation of the Democrats, he tried – and failed – again. Aydemir, convinced to the last
that his failure to secure the national radio station was all that kept
him from success, was hanged by the government in July 1964.

The next intervention took place on 12 March 1971, a time of
widespread civil unrest, political extremism and high inflation, when
a five-man military junta issued the government with an ultimatum
over the national radio. The so-called 'memorandum' left the ruling
Justice Party in no doubt that it must resign if its members were not
to face consequences like those which had befallen the Democrats a
decade earlier. A partial military takeover ensued.

On 12 September 1980, in yet another period of civil disorder and
street violence, the military intervened on the pretext of restoring
democracy. The army abolished all political parties, imposed martial
law and ordered mass arrests. The ensuing years, which saw a spate
of extrajudicial killings and state executions, were among the darkest
in the Republic's history.

And on 28 February 1997 the army, outraged by the government's
increasingly overt religious agenda, issued a series of policy direct-
ives which the prime minister was not about to mistake for anything
other than a thinly veiled threat – his cue, in other words, to resign.

All these dates, grimly familiar to Turks, may be traced back to 27
May 1960. The legacy of the first coup has been disastrous, serving
as an example, even an inspiration, for a series of interventions by a
few men who thought they knew best, and had the guns in case
others disagreed. These men considered themselves the ones with
the answers when it came to dealing with the reaction, radical
extremism, civil unrest, economic mismanagement or constitutional

abuses – Turkey's usual issues, only a different combination each
time round – besetting the country. Incalculable damage has been
done to the democratic development of Turkey, not to mention to its
image, with coups so closely associated with the country that they
are to Turkey, regrettably, what farmers' strikes are to France, missile
tests to North Korea and school shootings to the United States.

   Turkey's reputation was a problem I had long experienced in my
writing, putting me on the defensive in my articles about the country. Tasked with evoking the best of the place – the beaches strewn
with classical ruins, the winning ease and generosity of the people
and their genius for food, and the gloriously diverse cultures – I
found myself forever beating back that crowd of competing visions,
all rendered in a grim palette of gloaming greys and military-issue
khakis, which 27 May had spawned: the tanks on the streets, the
curfews, the emergency radio broadcasts, the mass detentions,
the unsolved disappearances, the grisly executions. I spent my time
persuading friends, associates and readers alike that they should
shoulder aside these dark preconceptions for the brighter ones which
more accurately reflected my favourite country. For though they
were unwelcome, these images, I thought of them only as ghosts,
never believing that they could come again.

                                  *

I had one more journey to make. In the late spring of 2016 I left
Istanbul for Adnan Bey's heartlands. It was hot in the south, the air
scented with figs and grapes, the brick chimneys of old factories
topped with storks' nests. At the town of Aydın, Adnan Bey's statue,
arm outstretched in a beckoning gesture, stood beside the highway.
Beyond the banks of the sluggish Meander River the cotton heads
were flaring in the fields. The old Menderes farmstead stood dilapidated in overgrown gardens. A bust of Adnan Bey dominated
Çakırbeyli's shaded village square, and in the village mayor's office a
life-size waxwork of an industrious Adnan Bey, dapper as ever in suit
and tie, sat at a desk scattered with red carnations.

Izmır, where the young Adnan had survived the loss of his family, overcome illness, grown up and fallen in love, was my last stop. For it was in that ruinous Aegean port, its waterfront backed by shabby hillsides veined by broken alleys, the sagging roofs spilling their tiles across the pavements, that Adnan Bey's one grandson had settled. One afternoon I took the tram to visit Dr Adnan Menderes, a reconstructive surgeon at the 9 September University Hospital, at home in the city's western suburbs. He lived with his family in an airy and attractive modern villa on a potholed lane which led down to the sea. The fifty-year-old Adnan and his wife Menice led me out into the gardens where long lawns were set with fruit trees. While the two young children ran about, their son Mutlu gathering platefuls of mulberries and cherries to deliver to the adults, we talked over tea. Adnan remembered the occasion in his early twenties when his grandfather and his two ministers were finally pardoned and given the state funerals their families had been seeking for decades.

'In 1990, on the day before the anniversary of his execution, they laid on a ferry to take us, some friends and dignitaries to Imralı,' Adnan explained. 'I was there with my Uncle Aydın. From the waterfront we walked up to the graves where a memorial service was held. Then they began digging up the remains, uprooting the geraniums planted there. Once they had uncovered my grandfather's bones, it fell to me to remove them from the grave with my bare hands. This was how we recovered him.'

On the following day, 17 September, the three coffins were draped in the Turkish flag and carried on soldiers' shoulders through Istanbul. Crowds bore placards – 'Menderes Holds the Torch', 'Martyrs Never Die' – behind the cortege. The procession passed down the wide boulevard which Adnan Bey had had built as part of the city's redevelopment and which now bore his name. Just beyond the old walls, on a cemetery bluff not far from the old bus station, they laid him to rest between his two colleagues beneath a monumental granite pagoda.

'My father named me after my grandfather, as we named our son Mutlu after his,' explained Adnan. 'That makes it obvious who I am.

To thank me for whatever I've done for my hospital patients, and also to honour my grandfather, people often present me with keepsakes passed down through their own families.' Among the gifts Adnan had received were photographs signed by his grandfather, letters and cards in his handwriting, and commemorative plates featuring his image.

What caught my eye was the personalised cigarette packet. It was an elegant box with a hinged lid, the low sides banded in a gold floral motif. A Star and Crescent occupied one corner while the name A. Menderes was inscribed in another. I opened the lid to find a single cigarette lying in the foil, the tobacco scent faint but present.

Of the pack, lately received from a grateful patient, Adnan Bey's grandson knew only that its last cigarette had gone unsmoked. But as Adnan Bey was limited to ordinary cigarettes after the coup – Yenice being the brand that he smoked at the gallows – it could at least be assumed that the pack dated from his high days. Left, I wondered, on the back seat of the Buick with the personalised number plates? In a compartment on the Ankara train? On some balcony, after the prime minister had given a speech, and found by a party worker lingering above the dispersing crowds? Pocketed by a waiter who discovered the pack while clearing the table of ashtrays, glasses and crockery after an official dinner? In the pocket of a suit sent for cleaning? In a hotel room? On the table beside a bed not his own? If the facts were lost, the circumstances counting for little, it at least signified that somebody had thought the pack worth preserving. The presentation of the cigarette packet so many years later not only thanked Dr Menderes for the care rendered his patient but told of an older, enduring affection.

As Mutlu continued enthusiastically delivering fruit to the table and Berin, named for her great-grandmother, broke from grooming the dog to collect her swimming things, we reflected on the family's misfortunes. It might have been said that Adnan Bey was the lucky one, given all that Berin was left to endure; not only his execution but the suicide in 1972 of her oldest son and the death in a traffic accident of her middle son Mutlu when his own son Adnan was nine. Even the youngest son Aydın, though he was to survive his mother, fell victim to ill fate, also suffering a traffic accident which was to confine him to a wheelchair for much of his later life.

So it lifted my spirits to find myself among these scenes of contentment. After all that I had learned of the Menderes clan, I was happy to find the last of them leading peaceful lives. The quiet-spoken and courteous Adnan put it down to his decision to steer clear of politics. Unlike his father and his uncles, all of whom had defied their own father's last words, Adnan had avoided public life. There were other ways, he felt, to serve the country. So the past could rest and the family heal.

And as families healed, so perhaps could countries.

It was time for Adnan to take Berin to her swimming lesson. It was also time for me to leave – for Adnan Menderes International and my flight back to Gatwick where this story began.

EPILOGUE

15 July 2016

Failed coup

In the weeks after returning to England I watched, appalled, as the news from Turkey worsened by the day. In June twelve people were killed in a bomb blast near Beyazit Square. Later that month forty-eight people died, and more than 230 were injured, when gunmen ran amok at Istanbul's airport. The continuing carnage saw off the final vestiges of the tourism sector, wiping out the season and with it millions of jobs. As the conflict with the Kurds intensified, Erdoğan's increasingly intolerant regime continued to seize media outlets and to persecute its critics.

Even so, the rumours that I first heard on the evening of 15 July were scarcely believable. Social media told of troop units in Istanbul and of tanks taking up position on the Bosphorus bridges, which led some to advance, without conviction, the explanation that military exercises must be taking place in the city. Then eyewitnesses reported troops and gunfire on the streets around Taksim Square. TV news channels confirmed explosions in Ankara after helicopters and air-force jets were sighted overhead; it was reported that soldiers in the capital had seized the General Staff HQ and the offices of the ruling party.

Any doubts as to what was happening in Turkey were dispelled when shortly after midnight troops broke into the state broadcaster, TRT, and forced a presenter to read out a declaration on air. The statement told of the subjection of Turkish citizens to constitutional and legal abuses; of a country governed by an autocracy based on fear, where fundamental human rights were trampled on, and which could no longer guarantee the nation's security; of systemic corruption and of a judiciary unfit for purpose. 'The government, which has lost all legitimacy,' the statement concluded, 'has been dismissed from office.'

But if the game was up, then the government begged to differ. Within minutes one of Turkey's numerous private television channels, CNN Türk, trumped the TRT footage by carrying a live interview with a defiant – and patently at large – President Erdoğan. An enterprising journalist had succeeded in contacting the president who, in an extraordinary move, FaceTimed the nation via the journalist's mobile which she held up to the studio's television camera. The president condemned the plotters and called on the people to resist by confronting the rebel units on the streets and at the airports, whatever tanks and armaments they might face there. 'I acknowledge no authority above the National Will,' Erdoğan thundered.

It turned out that the president, on holiday in the resort of Marmaris, had fled his hotel earlier that night after being alerted to the attempt against his government. As word spread of Erdoğan's message, which TV channels played on continuous repeat, people hurried from their homes, many still in pyjamas beneath the flags draped over their shoulders, and gathered on the streets. The mosques, under the control of the loyal religious authorities, roused the faithful by issuing prayer calls throughout the night. In the streets and squares the crowds upbraided the soldiers. Ignoring the warnings, they advanced on the troops blocking the First Bosphorus Bridge, where they were met by gunfire. Scores of civilians were cut down while in Ankara rebel helicopters and fighter jets bombed police departments, killing many occupants, and the National Assembly. Meanwhile, Erdoğan had reached Dalaman Airport where he boarded the presidential jet for Istanbul.

The indications, in an admittedly chaotic picture, were of mounting opposition to the coup attempt. Rebel soldiers ran into resistance at the presidential palace in Ankara where loyal units repelled, then detained, the attackers. The crowds, despite the fatal gunfire, continued their advance across the First Bosphorus Bridge to confront young soldiers who had been assured that they were to participate in a training exercise. Many of these soldiers refused to follow their rebel commanders' example and fire on the crowds, choosing to shoot into the sky and even hand over their weapons as the crowds engulfed them. Corridor by corridor, police units and citizens succeeded in regaining control of the TRT building. Loyal troop detachments managed to secure the release of the high-ranking officers whom the rebels had abducted earlier that day. In Ankara civilians faced down tanks or slowed their advance by leaving vehicles in their paths. Crowds converged on Istanbul's airport where units of the special operations police set about reclaiming key buildings from the rebels. With the main runway and control tower back in their hands, the authorities cleared the circling aircraft to land. It was the presidential jet. Shortly after disembarking, Erdoğan gave what he called a 'victory press conference'.

That night's events amounted to a national tragedy, costing hundreds of lives and inflicting yet more grievous wounds upon the country; but they also felt like the coda, however improbable, to the story I had been investigating for so long. At no point in my researches into the Menderes years had I imagined that the parallels, however glaring – the same social divisions, economic ills, building sprees, brawls in the National Assembly, the leaders' resort to talk of the National Will, even the jokes against them – might be leading to the same outcome.

Even if with the alternative result. For in the dawn scenes from Istanbul and Ankara, the bombed buildings smoking in the pale light and the streets strewn with corpses, crushed cars and abandoned tanks, I saw the discarded weapons, helmets, boots and fatigues of the soldiers. This time it was the soldiers who had lost, who were ordered to strip to their underpants by police officers whose exultant colleagues mounted the surrendered tanks to stand arm in arm with flag-draped, selfie-snapping civilians. This time those who had resisted the coup were the martyrs, those who had attempted it the disgraced.

In hindsight, the coup's failure was inevitable from the moment it kicked off on a busy Friday evening; coups that hope to go un-opposed invariably begin in the early hours, as 27 May had done. Plotters serious as to their prospects are careful to enlist the support of key generals and commanders, in some instances years before the action, as they had in the case of 27 May – rather than opt to wait until the last moment. The 15 July putschists appeared to presume that any objections the country's most senior officers might have to their forced abduction – some from an Istanbul wedding reception which they appear to have been thoroughly enjoying – would vanish on learning of the glorious roles assigned them. In this they were hopelessly wrong, as they were in neglect-ing to detain even one of the regime's leading figures, something the 27 May officers had accomplished within hours. An attempt was made to capture Erdoğan but on a night of spectacular incom-petence the snatch squad tasked with the job was reduced to asking bemused Marmaris holidaymakers for directions to the president's hotel which they finally located, only to be informed that their quarry had left hours earlier.

The night's events gave Turks ample reasons for reflection – not least to wonder what had become of their renowned army. The attempt appeared so amateurish that many wondered if it could have been for real. One rumour circulated that the government, alerted to the impending coup, had let events play out for its own purposes – another that it had in fact staged the entire action as a pretext for moving against its growing numbers of opponents. It would be years, it appeared, before the full facts behind the events of that July night were ever brought to light.

The coup attempt, whatever the truth, was promptly turned to Erdoğan's advantage. Famously calling it 'a gift from God', he set about elevating 15 July and the martyrs who had fallen that night. Within weeks all manner of institutions and edifices, most notably the First Bosphorus Bridge but also Ankara's main metro station along with roads, state forests and bus stations, had been renamed for the latest significant date in the Turkish calendar.

Erdoğan then invoked emergency powers to set in train a wholesale purge of the army, the civil administration, the judiciary and
other national institutions. Chief among his enemies were the
so-called Gülenists, the followers of US-based cleric Fetullah Gülen
whom Erdoğan promptly accused of masterminding the coup. The
elderly and influential Gülen, in his youth a devoted follower of Said
Nursi, had more recently been Erdoğan's close ally in the Islamic
cause, though the relationship had ended in acrimony some years
before. In acknowledging his former close association with Gülen,
the president claimed that he had been tricked into trusting the
cleric whom he now considered the head of a terrorist movement.
Under the emergency powers anybody suspected of Gülenist affiliations or sympathies was to go. In the subsequent witch-hunt at least
100,000 public employees were sacked, and tens of thousands imprisoned. Dissenters – journalists, activists, writers and members of
human rights organisations and action groups such as the Academics
for Peace signatories – were prosecuted. Brutality and persecution
reigned. Justice was subverted. I had never known the country more
divided, never known its best people so demonised.

Yet, remarkably, there was cause for hope. The coup attempt
might have failed for numerous reasons, but the one that counted
was that the people had not supported it. Those who confronted the
soldiers on the streets, bridges and at the airports, many losing their
lives in the process, were not exclusively supporters of the regime.
There were among them many whose dearest wish was to see the
back of Erdoğan, who might even have clamoured for his removal,
but who would not let it happen this way. It was for the people, not
the soldiers, to decide when Erdoğan went; and they would do that
at the ballot box, a process which the president, though he might
dominate the media, was unable to subvert in its entirety. While
another coup attempt after all these years might have been the worst
thing for Turkey, the best thing was that Turks now knew it. Here,
then, was the defining difference with 27 May. At the country's darkest moment it seemed to me that Turkey might just have come of age;
that this latest coup attempt might have been the last.

*

Since 2016 I have spent a lot of time in Turkey where Erdoğan's regime persists in imprisoning writers, human rights workers and others on risible, often surreal charges; in subverting the judiciary; in extending the state's control over the media; and in concentrating unjustifiably excessive powers in the office of the presidency. Other than the remarkable spirit of the people, I have seen little to suggest that the country can look forward to a brighter future.

Until, that is, 2019 when an opposition politician emerged to confront the old divisions and emnities, and challenge the apparent invincibility of Erdoğan's ruling party. Ekrem Imamoğlu, who had made his name as a competent and communicative district administrator, stood in the local elections as the opposition candidate for the office of Istanbul's mayor. A prestigious and powerful position, decided by more than 10 million voters, the mayoralty was considered a key stepping stone on the path to national leadership, as it had been for Erdoğan after winning it in 1994. The idea that after a quarter of a century the secular opposition might capture a post the ruling party was determined to defend, with the state-controlled media overwhelmingly on its side, appeared extremely improbable.

But given the dire state of the economy – high unemployment and double-digit inflation had made even vegetables unaffordable for many residents – the opposition was reckoned to be in with a chance. Voters disenchanted with the country's polarised politics took to Imamoğlu's conciliatory, inclusive and tactile approach. Rather than attack his political opponents, Imamoğlu famously urged people to 'find a neighbour who doesn't think like you, and give them a hug'. Imamoğlu – his surname translates as Son of an Imam – made no secret of Islamic beliefs which he combined with an open-minded and practical approach, campaigning in a calm and temperate manner that made a refreshing change from the ruling party's trademark belligerence. As Erdoğan staged mass flag-waving rallies in support of his candidate, recycling tired accusations that linked the

opposition with terror groups, Imamoğlu devoted his time to attending neighbourhood meetings, immersing himself in the concerns he
heard on Istanbul's streets.

The approach worked; to widespread celebrations, Imamoğlu
won the elections of 31 March. But the margin of victory was narrow,
the more so when the ruling party's complaints of voting irregularities led the electoral board to discount some returns. Imamoğlu had
served for just eighteen days as mayor when he was removed from
the post after the electoral board annulled the elections, ordering
that they be rerun.

The unprecedented decision sparked fury, with even influential
voices in the ruling party condemning a move liable to expose the
vacuity of the party's democratic credentials. Fears that the government meant to steal the elections, delivering a potentially terminal
blow to Turkey's shaky democracy, caused fright in the currency
markets which saw the lira plummet in the weeks after the annul-
ment. The announcement that the elections were to be rerun in late
June was interpreted as a cynical ploy, taking advantage of the fact
that with the school holidays already under way, many opposition
supporters would have left Istanbul for the summer.

But the opposition, not to be defeated, went out of its way to ensure
that those supporters returned. In the Mediterranean and Aegean
resorts eligible voters who were on holiday or working there learned
through social media how they could secure free return bus tickets to
Istanbul. Those intending to drive back to the city saw to it that any
spare seats were occupied. Students who had returned to their distant
towns and villages were also urged to return, with offers from hotels
and restaurants of free board and meals while they were in Istanbul,
even with the promise of flights. From resorts like Bodrum and
Antalya convoys of extra coaches were laid on as hotels temporarily
closed for the exodus. Along the holiday coasts poster and social
media campaigns, which framed the vote as a national duty, politely
advised eligible voters that they should not expect to be served in the
resorts on the day of the elections – in some cases not even be

acknowledged – but would of course be extended heroes' welcomes on their return.

From across the country they descended upon Istanbul in vast numbers, determined to be heard. They cast their votes and so they saw to it that Imamoğlu won again, in the process increasing his majority from just 13,000 to over 800,000 votes. With Istanbul as well as Ankara and Izmır now held by the opposition, the ruling party had lost control of Turkey's three biggest cities. This time the government was quick to concede, with even President Erdoğan having the good grace to congratulate Imamoğlu on the result. Then he added that the National Will had once more prevailed which appeared to acknowledge, remarkably, that that Will need not be his.

Democracy had been defended. The people had been heard. It turned out, after all, that the only route to power was by elections; and about that at least it seemed that Adnan Bey had been right all along.

POSTSCRIPT

27 May 2020

Shortly before this book went to press, at the height of the global Covid-19 pandemic, President Erdoğan honoured his idol by inaugurating a major memorial project on Yassıada. It was 27 May 2020, the sixtieth anniversary of Turkey's first coup.

From before the time of my visit in 2016 Yassıada had bristled with cranes and construction teams; at night, powerfully illuminated, it could be mistaken for one of the anchored freighters awaiting its turn to pass through the Bosphorus. For an island which had stood deserted for so long, it proved the rudest of awakenings as trees were flattened and old buildings torn down to make way for visitor and tourism facilities including a hotel, conference centre, mosque, cafes and restaurants. But the island's centrepiece was the restored sports gymnasium where a museum told of the overthrow of Adnan Bey's government.

Among the displays were waxworks of the judges, of Adnan Bey, even of Henry Bulwer, as well as mock-ups of the courthouse dock, of Adnan Bey's cell and of the shattered aircraft which he had escaped with his life in 1959. Artistic representations included a wall embedded with prisoners' suitcases and an oversized sheaf of prisoners' letters confined within an entanglement of barbed wire.

The gymnasium was named after Hasan Polatkan, the mosque after Fatin Rüştü Zorlu, and the conference centre after Adnan Menderes. As for Yassıada, officially renamed Island of Democracy and Liberties, President Erdoğan described its redevelopment as a triumph of the National Will. Turkey, and the world, now knew what had happened all those years ago.

Acknowledgements

Over the years it has taken to research and write this book, I have been assisted by countless kind people. I like to think that I care as much for Turkey as they do, even if this book may appear to some as a strange way of showing it. Immense credit to them, then, that they all put aside any reservations about my subject, contentious to some, to submit to interview, respond to queries, translate documents, arrange introductions, open doors or otherwise make this book possible. My heartfelt thanks.

In Turkey those who gave their time to reminisce included: Oktay Aksoy and Benku Kırsan Aksoy, Mehmet Arif Demirer, Oktay Ekşi, Seva Erten, Selçuk Esenbel, Mehmet Nuri Güleç and Şükran Vahide, Akile Gürsoy, Emine Gürsoy Naskali, Güner Karatekin and Ülkü Karatekin, Dr Adnan Menderes and his family, Filiz Önder, Asya Saydam and Emre Tansu Keten, Murat Seçkin, Ismail and Selçuk Şenyüz, and Tuğrul Sezen. Erhan and Gülümser Kocabiyikoğlu gave their time and hospitality in Istanbul and Alaçatı. Baysan Bayar, née Aygün, proved delightful and illuminating company who was kind enough, besides, to allow me to quote freely from her wonderful letters. The inexhaustible Mehmet Nuri Taşdelen went out of his way to help, answered my detailed queries about his published memoir and allowed me the use of his Yassıada photographs. He also travelled to the island with me, a visit made possible by Selçuk Altun who opened other doors besides, not least the guarded ones of Istanbul University. Owen Matthews put his elegant boat *Clio* at my disposal on my first visit to the island.

I'd also like to thank Jane Akatay, Sabahattin Alkan, Keith Anderson, David Barchard, Professor Faruk Birtek, Alex Christie-Miller, Ayten Col, Nicholas Danforth, Alex Dawe, Mehmet Demir, Ertuğrul

Duru at the Rasım H Koç Museum, Şaban Erdikler, Associate Professor Dr Dilşen İnce Erdoğan, Andrew Finkel, Selim Kalafat, Richard Newton, the late Andrew Mango, Ziya Nazlı, Necati Ortabaş, Mehmet Özçakır, Iffet Özgönül, Zeynep Öziş, Sabahat and Osman Poshor, Özan Sayın, Çiğdem Sungur, Pat Yale and Yusuf Yilmaz. Annie Onursan heaped me high with a number of notably fruitful introductions. Ömer Koç was as generous with his contacts as with his hospitality, not least at a series of wonderful Istanbul dinners.

My hiking companions on what would prove that formative visit to Kargıcak recounted at the beginning of this book are now friends: Yunus Özdemir, Altay Özcan and Dean Livesley. So too are Edward Charlton-Jones, who was good enough to read a draft and provide a stream of invaluable comments and corrections, and Yasmine Seale.

I am grateful to the staff at the newspaper library on Beyazit Square, the Istanbul Library in Sultanahmet and the National Library in Ankara.

In Britain, my thanks to Tony Bruce, Martin Bysh, Gulsema Cerezci, Christopher de Bellaigue, Professor William Hale, Philip Marsden, Wendy Thornton-Clark, Colin Thubron and Ally Watson. *Selamlar* to fellow Turkophile writers Barnaby Rogerson, Jason Goodwin, Justin Marozzi and Anthony Sattin with whom I have been fortunate enough to spend time in Turkey. Warmest thanks too to Margaret, Elizabeth and Tom Bailey, not least for their generous access to the family archive, an indispensable trove of cuttings and memorabilia from the family's lifelong association with Turkey.

I am grateful to the staff at the British Library, the London Library and the SOAS Library. I acknowledge the invaluable access to JSTOR, the online article resource, through the University of Exeter's alumni scheme.

Thanks to the Society of Authors for the welcome grant provided via the Authors' Foundation.

At Chatto & Windus I have been edited with quite exceptional attention and rigour by Poppy Hampson; thanks to her, and to Greg Clowes and David Milner, this is so much more than the book I originally delivered. Thanks too to Jane Randfield for her great map-making, and to Rob Shaw at Northbank, Bath. And to the late David Miller at Rogers, Coleridge & White, who helped find a home for this book before his untimely death.

More than any others, two people have been especially generous with their time and help. In Istanbul Melih Zulfu Aslan has repeatedly demonstrated a knack for bringing dead ends to life. In London Gul Greenslade, who translated my *A Fez of the Heart* into Turkish, has done more for this book than I can begin to describe. To them both, I am particularly indebted.

My loved ones, Ash, Anna and Lizzie; acutely aware as I am that this book has been preoccupying me for many years, I'd like to apologise if ever its presence caused you to roll your eyes. Thanks for your forbearance. It's done now.

Bibliography

Ahmad, Feroz: 'The Islamic Assertion in Turkey; Pressures and State Response'. *Arab Studies Quarterly*, Vol. 4 (Spring 1982), pp. 94–109.

Ahmad, Feroz: *The Making of Modern Turkey*. London, 1993.

Ahmad, Feroz: *The Turkish Experiment in Democracy, 1950–1975*. London, 1977.

Akpınar, Ipek: 'The Turkification of Istanbul in the 1950s'. *Traditional Dwellings and Settlements Review*, Vol. 12, No. 1 (Fall 2000), pp. 58–9.

Akyol, Mustafa: *Islam Without Extremes*. New York, 2011.

Azak, Umut: *Islam and Secularism in Turkey: Kemalism, Religion and the Nation State*. London, 2010.

Balcı, Ramazan: *Bediüzzaman Said Nursi: Wonder of the Age*. Clifton, New Jersey, 2012.

Başgil, Ali Fuad: *La Révolution Militaire de 1960 en Turquie*. Paris, 1963.

Birand, Mehmet Ali: *The Generals' Coup in Turkey*. London, 1987.

Blasing, Randy and Mutlu Konak (trans.): *Poems of Nazım Hikmet*. New York, 1994.

Brockett, Gavin D.: *How Happy to Call Oneself a Turk: Provincial Newspapers and the Negotiation of a Muslim National Identity*. Austin, Texas, 2012.

Brockett, Gavin D.: 'Provincial Newspapers as a Historical Source: Buyuk Cihad and the Great Struggle for the Muslim Turkish Nation (1951–53)'. *International Journal of Middle East Studies*, Vol. 41, No. 3 (August 2009), pp. 437–55.

Brockett, Gavin D.: 'When Ottomans Become Turks: Commemorating the Conquest of Constantinople and its Contribution to World

History'. *The American Historical Review*, Vol. 119, No. 2 (April 2014), pp. 399–433.

Brown, James: 'The Military and Society: The Turkish Case'. *Middle Eastern Studies*, Vol. 25, No. 3 (July 1989), pp. 387–404.

Brummett, Palmira: 'Dogs, Women, Cholera, and Other Menaces in the Streets: Cartoon Satire in the Ottoman Revolutionary Press, 1908–11'. *International Journal of Middle East Studies*, Vol. 27, No. 4 (November 1995), pp. 433–60.

Carver, Michael M.: '"A Correct and Progressive Road": US–Turkish Relations, 1945–64. A Dissertation'. Bowling Green State University, May 2011.

Çınar, Alev: 'National History as a Contested Site: The Conquest of Istanbul and Islamist Negotiations of the Nation'. *Comparative Studies in Society and History*, Vol. 43, No. 2 (April 2001), pp. 364–91.

Danforth, Nicholas: 'The Menderes Metaphor'. *Turkish Policy Quarterly*, Vol. 13, No. 4 (Winter 2015), pp. 99–105.

Demirer, Mehmet Arif: 27 *Mayıs, Masallar ve Gerçekler*. Istanbul, 2012.

DH: 'Strains and Stresses in Turkish Policy; Summer 1958'. *The World Today*, Vol. 14, No. 9 (September 1958), pp. 399–406.

Dündar, Can: *We Are Arrested*. London, 2016.

Ellison, Grace: *An Englishwoman in Angora*. New York, 1923.

Finer, Samuel E.: *The Man on Horseback: The Role of the Military in Politics*. Piscataway, New Jersey, 2002.

Frey, Frederick W.: 'Arms and the Man in Turkish Politics'. *The Land Reborn*, Vol. 11 (August 1960), pp. 3–14.

Göksu, Saime and Edward Timms: *Romantic Communist: The Life and Work of Nazım Hikmet*. New York, 1999.

Gül, Murat: *The Emergence of Modern Istanbul*. London, 2009.

Gündoğdu, Cihangir: 'The state and the stray dogs in late-Ottoman Istanbul: from unruly subjects to servile friends'. *Middle Eastern Studies*, Vol. 54, No. 4 (2018), pp. 555–74.

Gürsoy, Akile: 'The Coup of May 27, 1960', in Elizabeth Warnock Fernea (ed.), *Remembering Childhood in the Middle East; Memoirs From A Century of Change*. Austin, Texas, 2003.

Gürsoy Naskali, Emine (ed.): *Bebek Davası*. Istanbul, 2008.

Hale, William: *Turkish Politics and the Military*. Oxford, 1993.

HARP: 'Turkey Under the Democratic Party'. *The World Today*, Vol. 9, No. 9 (September 1953), pp. 383–92.

Harris, George S.: 'The Cause of the 1960 Revolution in Turkey'. *Middle East Journal*, Vol. 24, No. 4 (August 1970), pp. 438–54.

Harris, George S.: 'The Role of the Military in Turkish Politics'. *Middle East Journal*, Vol. 19, No. 2 (Spring 1965), pp. 169–76.

Heper, Metin and Jacob Landau (eds): *Political Parties and Democracy in Turkey*. London, 1991.

Heper, Metin and Sabri Sarayı: *Political Leaders and Democracy in Turkey*. Washington DC, 2012.

Heper, Metin: *Ismet Inönü: Turkish Democrat and Statesman*. Leiden, 1998.

Hikmet, Nazım (trans. Randy Blasing and Mutlu Konuk): *Human Landscapes from My Country*. New York, 2002.

Hotham, David: *The Turks*. London, 1972.

IHE: 'The New Regime in Turkey'. *The World Today*, Vol. 6, No. 7 (July 1950), pp. 289–96.

Ipekçi, Abdi and Coşar, Ömer Samı: *Ihtilalin Içyüzü*. Istanbul, 1965.

Jenkins, Gareth: *Political Islam in Turkey, Running West, Heading East?* New York, 2008.

Karpat, Kemal: 'The Military and Politics in Turkey, 1960–64: A Socio-Cultural Analysis of a Revolution'. *The American Historical Review*, Vol. 75, No. 6 (October 1970), pp. 1654–83.

Karpat, Kemal: 'The Turkish Elections of 1957'. *The Western Political Quarterly*, Vol. 14, No. 2 (June 1961), pp. 436–59.

Karpat, Kemal: 'Young Turks Again'. *Challenge*, Vol. 9, No. 6 (March 1961), pp. 17–20.

Karpat, Kemal: *Turkey's Politics: The Transition to a Multi-Party System*. Princeton, New Jersey, 1959.

Kinross, Lord: *Atatürk, The Rebirth of a Nation*. London, 1964.

Koelle, P. B.: 'The Rehabilitation of Adnan Menderes'. *Journal of South Asian and Middle Eastern Studies*, Vol. 35, No. 2 (2012), pp. 65–77.

Leder, Arnold: 'Party Competition in Rural Turkey: Agent of Change or Defender of Traditional Rule?'. *Middle Eastern Studies*, Vol. 15, No. 1 (January 1979), pp. 82–105.

Lerner, Daniel and Richard D. Robinson: 'Swords and Plough-shares: The Turkish Army as a Modernizing Force'. *World Politics*, Vol. 13, No. 1 (October 1960), pp. 19–44.

Lerner, Daniel: 'The Grocer and the Chief: A Parable', in D. Lerner, *The Passing of Traditional Society: Modernizing the Middle East*, pp. 19–42. London, 1958.

Lewis, Bernard: 'Recent Developments in Turkey'. *International Affairs*, Vol. 27, No. 4 (July 1951), pp. 320–31.

Lewis, Bernard: *Notes on a Century*. London, 2012.

Lewis, Bernard: *The Emergence of Modern Turkey*. 3rd edition. Oxford, 2002.

Lewis, Geoffrey: 'The Thorny Road to Democracy'. *The World Today*, Vol. 18, No. 5 (May 1962), pp. 182–91.

Lewis, Geoffrey: 'Turkey: The End of the First Republic'. *The World Today*, Vol. 16, No. 9 (September 1960), pp. 377–86.

Lewis, Geoffrey: *Modern Turkey*. London, 1974.

Lewis, Geoffrey: *Turkey*, London 1959.

Linke, Lilo: *Allah Dethroned*. London, 1937.

Mango, Andrew: *Atatürk: The Biography of the Founder of Modern Turkey*. London, 1999.

Meeker, Michael: 'Once There Was, Once There Wasn't', in Sibel Bozdoğan and Reşat Kasaba (eds), *Rethinking Modernity and National Identity in Turkey*. Washington, 1997.

Nursi, Bediüzzaman Said: *Emirdağ Letters*. Istanbul, 2016.

Oron, Yitzhak (ed.): *Middle East Record* 1960 (Vol. I) and 1961 (Vol. II). Tel Aviv, 1960–1.

Pears, Sir Edwin: *Forty Years in Constantinople*. New York, 1919.

Pelt, Mogens: *Military Intervention and a Crisis of Democracy in Turkey: The Menderes Era and its Demise*. London, 2014.

Pope, Nicole and Hugh: *Turkey Unveiled: A History of Modern Turkey*. London, 1998.

Reed, Howard: 'A New Force at Work in Democratic Turkey'. *Middle East Journal*, Vol. 7, No. 1 (Winter 1953), pp. 33–44.

Reed, Howard: 'Revival of Islam in Secular Turkey'. *Middle East Journal*, Vol. 8, No. 3 (Summer 1954), pp. 267–82.

Rustow, Dankwart A.: 'The Army and Founding of the Turkish Republic'. *World Politics*, Vol. 11, Issue 4 (1959), pp. 513–52.

Simpson, Dwight J.: 'Development as a Process: The Menderes Phase in Turkey'. *Middle East Journal*, Vol. 19, No. 2 (Spring 1965), pp. 141–52.

Simpson, Dwight J.: 'Turkey, Problems and Prospects'. *Foreign Policy Bulletin*, May 1958, p. 141.

Singer, Sean R.: 'The Struggle for Istanbul'. *The American Interest* (online), 6 June 2013.

Stephanov, Darin: 'Sultan Mahmud II (1808–39) and the First Shift in Modern Ruler Visibility in the Ottoman Empire'. *Journal of the Ottoman and Turkish Studies Association*, Vol. 1, Nos. 1–2 (2014), pp. 1290–48.

Tachau, Frank: 'The Face of Turkish Nationalism: As Reflected in the Cyprus Dispute'. *Middle East Journal*, Vol. 13, No. 3 (Summer 1959), pp. 226–72.

Taşdelen, Mehmet: *Yassıada, Menderes ve Muhafızları*. Istanbul, 2005.

Toprak, Binnaz: *Islam and Political Development in Turkey*. Leiden, 1981.

Ülman, Hilal (ed. Seva Erten): *Kadınlar Koğuşu Yassıada*. Ankara, 2013.

Vahide, Sukran: *Islam in Modern Turkey: An Intellectual Biography of Bediüzzaman Said Nursi*. Albany, New York, 2012.

Walsh, Robert: *A Residence at Constantinople*, 2 vols. London, 1836.

Weiker, Walter Fritz, and Robert D. Calkins: *The Turkish Revolution, 1960–1961*. Washington DC, 1963.

Wharton, Annabel Jane: *Building the Cold War: Hilton International Hotels and Modern Architecture*. Chicago, 2004.

Yalman, Ahmed Emin: *Turkey in My Time*. Norman, Oklahoma, 1956.

Yeats Brown, F.: *Golden Horn*. London, 1932.
Yeşilbursa, Behcet Kemal: 'The "Revolution" of 27 May 1960 in
  Turkey: British Policy Towards Turkey'. *Middle Eastern Studies*,
  Vol. 41, No. 1 (January 2005), pp. 121–51.
Yılanlıoğlu, Ismail: *Kocatepe Camii Nasıl Yapıldı?*. Ankara, 1988.
Zurcher, Erik Jan: *Turkey: A Modern History*. London, 2004.

Documentaries:
Coup / Darbe (Elif Savaş, Brian Felsen; 1999)
*Wind, Carry My Voice: A Modern Story of Exile / Sesim Rüzgara:
  Modern Bir Sürgün Hikayesi* (Emre Sarikus; 2010)
Demirkırat (Mehmet Ali Birand, Can Dündar, Bulent Çaplı; 1991)
The Fallen on Yassıada / Yassıada'da Düşükler (1960)

Newspapers and Magazines:
Turkish: *Cumhuriyet / Milliyet / Vatan*
English: *Turkish Times* (Istanbul) / *Daily News* (Istanbul) / *The
  Times / Sunday Times / Observer / Guardian / New York Times*
French: *La Republique* (Istanbul) / *Istanbul*

Notes

The full name of the author and complete title of the work are given with the first citation of any source. In subsequent mentions, authors' surnames and abbreviated titles are given. Where not otherwise specified, page references are from the editions given in the bibliography. Foreign Office files are indicated by the initials FO.

PROLOGUE

3: 'as if someone had taken a sheet of foolscap paper and crumpled it up': 'Mr Menderes Escapes in Air Crash', *The Times*, 18 February 1959.

3: 'It is a miracle,' a fire officer added, 'that anyone came out alive': 'Seven Brought Through Holes to Safety', *The Times*, 18 February 1959.

4: 'It is particularly sad,' Harold Macmillan . . . : 'Sympathy Given to Turkey', *The Times*, 19 February 1959.

7: Allegations circulated: FO371/144789, RK1382/10, 26 February 1959.

10: last time the two leaders would shake hands: Behcet Yeşilbursa, 'The "Revolution" of 27 May 1960', p. 67, footnote.

12: 'prayer-rug vote': Mogens Pelt, *Military Intervention and a Crisis of Democracy in Turkey*, p. 52.

12: 'appointed by God and his Prophet', 'God has Informed the Nation Very Clearly that He Protects You' and subsequent quotes: Pelt, *Military Intervention*, p. 58.

13: 'I am sacrificing my child for your having escaped . . .': Binnaz Toprak, *Islam and Political Development in Turkey*, p. 86.

14: 'the despair of his security police-guard . . . loves to walk alone . . .': *The Times*, 6 July 1952.

14: 'to an English farm and two charming people . . .': Pathe newsreel, 26 February 1959.

14: The 'very respected and highly intelligent Mr Bailey and his esteemed wife . . .' and subsequent quotes: from letters, telegrams and other correspondence in the Bailey family archive.

CHAPTER 1

22: 'They held a press conference for us at the airport . . .': All quotes by Margaret Bailey are either from the author's meeting with her or from her unpublished account, 'Our Holiday in Turkey'. Bailey family archive.

26: 'governments that do their work well . . .': 'Afraid of Criticism', *Time* Magazine, 9 July 1956.

28: 'such a strong weapon that the secret type . . .': *Vatan*, 27 March 1947.

28: In 'fluent and captivating speeches . . .': Kemal Karpat, 'Young Turks Again', p. 448.

28: It proved a message the peasants heeded . . . : General detail on the 1950 elections in in FO424 RK1017/4, 'Turkish General Elections' by Sir Charles Noel, 18 May 1950.

28: 'secret ballot–open count' principle: Metin Heper and Jacob Landau (eds), *Political Parties and Democracy in Turkey*, p. 103.

28: Turks 'put on their best suits . . .': 'Pledge to Turkey by Gen. Gürsel', *The Times*, 29 July 1961.

29: These birds put down in plague volumes: *Daily News*, 15 August 1961.

31: 'free as the wind off the Taurus Mountains': 'Thanks to Aid and Allah', *Time* Magazine, 19 February 1951.

31: cut down on unnecessary expenditure . . . : Detail on the new administration's economising in 'New Conditions in Turkey', FO 424/260 RK1015/8, No 19. See also IHE, 'The New Regime in Turkey', p. 296.

31: even to be seen on Istanbul's public trams and ferries: *Turkish Times*, 18 February 1952.

33: 'the voice of the Devil coming from his deep hiding place': Daniel Lerner, 'The Grocer and the Chief', p. 26.

34: 'mud hut becoming more and more often a whitewashed cottage': 'Turkey's Expanding Economy', *The Times*, 8 July 1953.

34: 'genial mien, always smiling' and 'of a man endowed . . .': Ali Fuad Başgil, *La Révolution Militaire de 1960 en Turquie*, p. 25.

34: 'great personal magnetism': Geoffrey Lewis, 'Turkey: The End of the First Republic', p. 378.

34: 'great energy, exuberance, eloquence, and genuine goodwill.': David Hotham, *The Turks*, p. 35.

34: 'a figure of the first magnitude. An energetic, alert man . . .': *Daily Telegraph*, 7 January 1953.

34: 'daring gamblers' and subsequent observations: Howard Reed, 'A New Force at Work in Democratic Turkey', p. 36.

CHAPTER 2

36: 'discoloured patches of wallpaper . . .': Bernard Lewis, 'Recent Developments in Turkey', p. 326.

37: had a medallion stamped with his own likeness . . . : Darin Stephanov, 'Sultan Mahmud II (1808–39) and the First Shift in Modern Ruler Visibility in the Ottoman Empire', p. 137.

40: 'the common struggle which both peoples have undertaken against the intervention of imperialism': B. Lewis, *The Emergence of Modern Turkey*, p. 283.

41: 'the entire frame of everybody's existence': G. Lewis, 'Turkey: The End of the First Republic', p. 384.

42: the proscription of the Ottoman national fez: For a detailed treatment of the episode, see the author's *A Fez of the Heart* (1995).

42: 'a disgrace to seek help from the dead': B. Lewis, *The Emergence of Modern Turkey*, p. 410.

47: 'to propagate the idea that the modern Turkish woman . . .', and subsequent observations: 'Reaction in Turkey', *The Times*, 16 April 1926.

47: 'Tribunal of Independence': 'Reaction in Turkey', *The Times*, 16 April 1926.

47: Atıf Hoca's crime . . . : Mustafa Akyol, *Islam Without Extremes*, pp. 177ff.

48: 'ignorant old men' and 'existence must not be pressed . . .': Lilo Linke, *Allah Dethroned*, p. 116.

51: 'chipmunk-cheeked': 'The Impatient Builder', *Time* Magazine, 3 February 1958.

CHAPTER 3

54: 'this one act of government interference . . .': B. Lewis, *The Emergence of Modern Turkey*, p. 416.

54: more painful, some peasants claimed, than the bouts of hunger . . . : Toprak, *Islam and Political Development in Turkey*, p. 79.

55: the 'old men, squatting on their heels, swaying forward . . .': Linke, *Allah Dethroned*, p. 21.

55: 'the freedom of religion and conscience . . . how we understand the meaning of true secularism': Umut Azak, *Islam and Secularism in Turkey: Kemalism, Religion and the Nation State*, p. 73.

57: a favourite cousin's husband, falsely implicated in a plot . . . : 'Typical Terrible Turk', *Time* Magazine, 6 September 1926.

58: a few lines of inflammatory religious poetry . . . : Erdoğan's arrest came after he quoted, not for the first time, nationalist poet Ziya Gökalp at a rally in 1997.

59: 'that time he compared democracy to a tram': Quoted in *Milliyet*, 14 July 1996.

62: 'a measure of their designs': Grace Ellison, *An Englishwoman in Angora*, p. 151.

64: 'My Son's Unjust Imprisonment': Saime Göksu and Edward Timms: *Romantic Communist*, p. 214.

66: Malatya, Ismet Paşa's seat: Malatya was the home town of Ismet Paşa's father.

66: 'abject homage to the sultan' and 'secretly read books and papers written against him': Ahmed Emin Yalman, *Turkey in My Time*, p. 15.

66: 'the views of the last person to stand him a drink' and 'principal publicists': FO424/290. Further Correspondence Respecting Turkey, 1950. Appendix 38. 'Leading Personalities in Turkey': Ahmet Emin Yalman, p. 26.

67: argued in *Vatan* for the release of a poet . . . : Göksu and Timms, *Romantic Communist*, p. 209.

67: **whose devotees were also said to include President Bayar**: FO424/290.
Further Correspondence Respecting Turkey, 1950. Appendix 38. 'Leading
Personalities in Turkey': Nazım Hikmet, p. 12.

68: **'private mosque construction and support . . .'**: Howard Reed, 'Revival of
Islam in Secular Turkey', pp. 271–2.

69: **'Making Known to the World the Beauty of the Turkish Lady . . .'**: The
line was in fact used in French-language Istanbul daily *La République*.

69: **the regional 'spirit of understanding'**: Yalman, *Turkey in My Time*, p. 255.

69: **'suddenly had the sensation of being showered . . .'**: Yalman, *Turkey in My
Time*, p. 255.

69: **doing all he could for Yalman**: Yalman, *Turkey in My Time*, p. 257.

72: **'Our nation,' he added, 'will not forgive those who betray our democratic and economic achievements . . .'**: 27 May 2015, Turkish government
online comment.

CHAPTER 4

74: **'marched between an unbroken avenue of festoons of laurels', 'every
ship lying in the harbour', 'the Anatolian forces made their triumphal
march . . .', 'pardonably flamboyant rhetoric', 'the absolute and crushing victory . . .' and 'second conquest'**: 'Second "Conquest" of Constantinople', *The Times*, 8 October 1923.

75: **All Ottoman insignia . . . streets commemorating sultans . . . Ottoman
archival documents . . .**: Murat Gül, *The Emergence of Modern Istanbul*, p. 75.

81: **'Turkish embrace of free conscience and religion'**: Sean Singer, 'The
Struggle for Istanbul'.

81: **the Conqueror's magnanimity towards a Byzantine girl . . .**: 'Ceremonies in Istanbul', *The Times*, 30 May 1953.

83: **'the new conqueror of Istanbul'**: Alev Çınar, 'National History as a Contested
Site', p. 382.

CHAPTER 5

90: **'The elections have clearly revealed . . .'**: Feroz Ahmad, *The Turkish Experiment in Democracy, 1950–1975*, p. 50.

90: **'counsel with his colleagues and with the parliamentary following on
which his position depends'**: FO424/293 (1953), WK 1011/1, 'Annual
Review of 1952', p. 1.

91: **'in Turkey and in the oriental countries in general . . .'**: Başgil, *La Révolution Militaire*, p. 28.

91: **'authoritarian tendency and intolerance of criticism'**: FO424/295
(1955), RK1016/7 No. 9. 'Further Set-backs for Democracy in Turkey',
p. 27.

91: **'*his* government, in a very real sense'**: FO424/293 (1953), WK1105/3
'Report on the Economic Situation', p. 35.

91: 'If the Hilton Hotel needs foreign exchange to buy toilet paper': 'The Impatient Builder', *Time* Magazine, 3 February 1958.

94: 'celebrities from the American and European world of movies', 'solid wall of humanity . . .' and subsequent quotes: Annabel Wharton, *Building the Cold War*.

94–5: 'the magic of this famed city of antiquity', 'friendly centers where men of many nations . . .', 'that the new republic chose to continue one element . . .' and 'friendship between nations, which is an alien word . . .': 'City on the Bosphorus', Conrad Hilton's inaugural speech, Istanbul Hilton, 10 June 1955; hotel display.

96: 'a provincial cleric': 'Turkish Case on Cyprus', *The Times*, 26 August 1955.

98: 'into the city, where mobs went howling . . .': 'The Great Riot of Istanbul', *Sunday Times*, 11 September 1955.

99: 'the police nor the garrison troops': FO424/295 (1955), RG10344/50, p. 32, 'Account of the Riots in Istanbul and Izmir on the Night of 6–7 September 1955' by Michael Stewart.

102: 'as if every third shop on Madison Avenue . . .': 'Rioting in Turkey Called Danger Sign', *New York Times*, 17 September 1955.

103: 'lugubriously danced at the centre of the curfew': 'The Great Riot of Istanbul', *Sunday Times*, 11 September 1955.

103: 'its alliance with Turkey de facto in a state of suspension': 'Foreign Affairs', *New York Times*, 17 September 1955.

103: 'in favour of Turkish claims on Cyprus': 'Rioting in Turkey Called Danger Sign', *New York Times*, 17 September 1955.

103: 'of a type more proper to the Middle Ages': 'Foreign Affairs', *New York Times*, 17 September 1955.

103: 'fabulous modern hotel': 'The Great Riot of Istanbul', *Sunday Times*, 11 September 1955.

104: 'In our civilisation . . .': Singer, 'The Struggle for Istanbul'.

105: 'Live Like a Tree . . .': The line, often invoked, is from Nazım Hikmet's famous poem 'Davet' ('The Invitation').

CHAPTER 6

109: 'for reading a book with two friends': Nazım Hikmet, *Human Landscapes from my Country*, p. 9.

111: a woman in a yellow dress hanging out washing . . . and subsequent descriptive details: Hikmet, *Human Landscapes*, p. 16.

112: American wholesale buyers responded . . . : 'Tobacco Boycott Alarms Turkey', *New York Times*, 17 January 1956.

113: 'an unduly high casualty rate among farm machinery': *Economist*, 18 October 1952.

113: 'as tragic for the Turks as no tea would be for the British': 'The Turkish Elections', *The Times*, 3 October 1957

314

116: 'to swing on his legs for several minutes' and 'the once-dreaded head lay harmless . . .': Francis Yeats-Brown, *Golden Horn*, p. 68.

117: 'Death – a body swinging from a rope': 'Letter to My Wife', *Poems of Nazım Hikmet*, p. 38.

119: a newspaper boy arrested in Ankara's Nation Square . . . : *New York Times*, 22 September 1956.

119: 'A copy of *Freedom*, please': 'Costly Joke', *Time* Magazine, 30 July 1956.

120: 'the shouts and criticism of a handful of intellectuals': Samet Ağaoğlu, quoted in Ahmad, *The Turkish Experiment in Democracy*, p. 44.

120: 'own brand of semantic confusion . . .' and 'more or less normal that the political power . . .': Yeşilbursa, 'The "Revolution" of 27 May 1960 in Turkey', p. 143.

120: 'conviction that he can plot Turkey's future . . .' and 'the democratic principles espoused . . .': 'Turkey Goes Backward', *New York Times*, 29 December 1954.

121: 'a town still chiefly composed of mud': 'Typical Terrible Turk', *Time* Magazine, 6 September 1926.

121: 'of possible interference from dreadnoughts': Ellison, *An Englishwoman in Angora*, p. 149.

CHAPTER 7

125: A story told of a diplomat . . . : Ismail Yılanlıoğlu, *Kocatepe Camii Nasıl Yapıldı?*, p. 5.

125: Ankara's was a skyline without minarets: Gül, *The Emergence of Modern Istanbul*, p. 85.

125: 'a tombstone underneath which there lies a Turkish village': Kemal Karpat, *Turkey's Politics: The Transition is a Multi-Party System*, p. 255.

126: Prime Minister Menderes lent his support: Ismail Yılanlıoğlu, *Kocatepe Camii Nasıl Yapıldı?*, pp. 5ff.

126: 'backed up against a wall . . .': 'The Impatient Builder', *Time* Magazine, 3 February 1958.

126: 'economists of international repute to raise their hands in horror': DH, 'Strains and Stresses in Turkish Policy: 1958', p. 402.

126: 'bus confronted with a swollen ford . . .' and 'an economist's nightmare': *Economist*, 15 June 1957.

127: its electoral pamphlets . . . in apocalyptic terms: *Köylu* (newspaper), 23 October 1957.

127–8: a place of Islamic pilgrimage . . . until a minaret was seen to stand beside every chimney: Karpat, 'The Turkish Elections of 1957', p. 443.

128: 'the bearded fanatic of the Anatolian villages': 'Intellectuals Gain Ground in Turkey', *The Times*, 8 August 1960.

128: Ahmed Emin Yalman . . . no less momentous than Gallipoli . . . : Karpat, 'The Turkish Elections of 1957', p. 440, footnote.

133: **army officers felt especially neglected**, and 'shiny uniforms but empty pockets': see Karpat, 'The Military and Politics in Turkey', pp. 1663ff.

133: **'lemonaders'**: Nicole and Hugh Pope, *Turkey Unveiled*, p. 91.

133: **A colonel's wife**: George Harris, 'Causes of the Revolution', p. 441, footnote.

133: **'at a restaurant filled with well-heeled politicians . . .'**: James Brown, 'The Military and Society: The Turkish Case', p. 388.

134: **the man capable of solving all problems**: see Karpat, 'Turkish Elections of 1957', p. 440, footnote 15. And Andrew Mango, *Atatürk*, p. 484.

134: **When dealing with Ismet Paşa, Adnan Bey . . .** : Başgil, *La Révolution Militaire*, p. 188.

CHAPTER 8

136: **'wide enough for three or four carts to pass'**: Ellison, *An Englishwoman in Angora*, p. 135.

137: **'with disloyalty in the minds of both rulers, and ruled'**: Ahmad, *The Turkish Experiment in Democracy*, p. 38.

137: **'Peasants who had never before dreamed . . .'**: 'Thanks to Aid and Allah', *Time* Magazine, 19 February 1951.

138: **'the greatest revolution in the history of Turkey . . .'**: B. Lewis, 'Recent Developments in Turkey', p. 326.

138–9: **A 'witch-hunt' ensued . . . loudspeakers outside the assembly building . . . and 'former rulers were little better than gangsters'**: FO424/260 RK1015/8, 'The First Weeks of Democrat Party Government', p. 30.

139: **'mere seekers after office . . .'**: Geoffrey Lewis, *Turkey*, p. 123.

139: **'as disgusting as the broadcasts of Moscow'**: Ahmad, *The Turkish Experiment in Democracy*, p. 48.

139: **some kind of disease**: 'The Turkish Case', *The Times* 15 October 1957.

140: **'a psychopathic case . . .'**: FO424/290, WK1016/23, 'The Turkish Government's Attitude Towards the Opposition', p. 36.

141: **'fisticuffs' and 'with the cold-bloodedness of a professional criminal'**: 'Turks' Assembly Halted by Brawl', *New York Times*, 16 November 1954.

144: **'A traveller who visits Turkey for the first time . . .'**: FO424/260, RK1015/2: No. 5. 'Conditions in Turkey', p. 7.

144: **'Beautifying Istanbul and Celebrating its Ottoman Past'** and subsequent quotes: Ipek Akpınar, 'The Turkification of Istanbul in the 1950s', pp. 58–9.

145: **'forests of unsightly shacks were swept away'**: 'Benevolent Bomber', *Time* Magazine, 12 August 1957.

145: **'through Istanbul's cluttered slums and crowded business sections'** and **'Bedrooms and bathrooms'**: 'Benevolent Bomber', *Time* Magazine, 12 August 1957.

146: **'Menderes jumped out of bed . . .'**: 'The Impatient Builder', *Time* Magazine, 3 February 1958.

149: **Bernard Lewis had overheard the same joke . . .** : B. Lewis, *Notes on a Century*, p. 99.

153: **'their hereditary oppressors and enemies':** FO371/115486. 1073/90, letter of 1 January 1955.

153: **'full of renewed dark references to Nuri Said' and 'between the methods of Nuri Said . . .':** FO371/136453, RK1015/40.

154: **the principle that soldiers were to have no part in running the nation:** See Lerner and Robinson, 'Swords and Ploughshares', pp. 21ff.

155: **'their boldness to such an extent as repeatedly to publish . . .'** and subsequent quotes: FO371/136453, RK1015/30 'Summary of World Broadcasts', part IV, Adnan Menderes' Speech of 6 September 1958, Balıkesir.

155: **'sixty or seventy miles an hour in safety and comfort'** and subsequent quotes: 'Turkish Premier Opens Power Dam', *New York Times*, 27 September 1958.

156: **how great was Adnan Bey's understanding . . . and 'his understanding of the Turkish officer was small . . .':** G. Lewis, 'The Thorny Road to Democracy', p. 186.

CHAPTER 9

157: **'clearly evocative of the ghosts of his former military triumphs':** 'Turkey's Stormy Democracy', *The Times* 24 August 1959.

158: **Himmetdede, a country halt on the wide steppe:** The incident is described in FO371/153032, RK1015/6 (D), 8 April 1960 and in *Istanbul*, 4 April 1960.

159: **'a completely illegal and unconstitutional act':** FO371/153032, RK1015/6 (D), 8 April 1960.

161: **no better than that of Balkan brigands . . . could not remain indifferent to such divisive strategies:** 'İnönü Visite Kayseri', *Istanbul*, 4 April 1960.

163: **a gold trowel in recognition of his work:** The dinner took place at the Liman Lokantası, Istanbul on 13 March 1960. *Istanbul*, 14 March 1960.

164: **would his trademark turban come off:** Şukran Vahide, *Islam in Modern Turkey: An Intellectual Biography of Bediüzzaman Said Nursi*, p. 189.

165–6: **'more backward than those of the sheikhs of Yemen':** The comment, attributed to *Dünya* (newspaper) editor Falih Rifki Atay, is quoted in 'Said Nursi and His Disciples', Umut Azak, *Islam and Secularism in Turkey*, p. 124.

166: **a selection of Texan-style brimmed hats:** *Istanbul*, 2 January 1960.

166: **a *yobaz* . . . 'the great dead weight which is dragging Turkey back out of Europe':** 'Intellectuals Gain Ground in Turkey,' *The Times* 8 August 1960.

166: **'You are trying to bring back Islamic law . . .'** and subsequent exchanges: *Akşam*, 9 January 1960.

167: **the day of Adnan Bey's conception the saddest in Turkey's history . . . a wild pig loose in Turkey's fields, a fire raging through its towns:** Hikmet, 'Insults to Adnan Bey'.

167: **a young soldier who had lost his life in Korea:** Hikmet, 'Blood Money'.

168: pompous, venal and mean-eyed, his clammy hands . . . : Hikmet, 'Blood Money'.

168: 'cutting the branch on which you're sitting': Hikmet, 'Turkey Receding, or Advice to A. Menderes'.

168: He denounced Menderes for his lies, compared him to a mad sultan . . . : Göksu and Timms, *Romantic Communist*, p. 304.

168: the overthrow of the 'little dictator': Göksu and Timms, *Romantic Communist*, p. 305.

169: 'of trial and tribulation during which more newspapers . . .': Ahmad, *The Turkish Experiment in Democracy*, p. 62.

169: 'criticise itself freely, because that is the most reliable promise . . .': Yalman, *Turkey in My Time*, p. 209.

169: 'governments that do their work well . . .': 'Afraid of Criticism', *Time* Magazine, 9 July 1956.

169: 'grotesque, almost farcical, as if the Editor of *The Times* . . .': 'New Turkish Pleas for Gaoled Editor', *Observer*, 13 March 1960.

169: 'I have been a journalist for fifty-three years': 'New Turkish Pleas for Gaoled Editor', *Observer*, 13 March 1960.

170: 'a normal regime of freedom and justice': 'Editor Aged 71 Goes to Jail', *The Times*, 8 March 1960.

171: He was credited with casting his party's overwhelming defeat . . . : Metin Heper and Sabri Sarayı, *Political Leaders and Democracy in Turkey*, p. 225.

171: the 'destructive and illegal' activities . . . : 'Turkish Ban on all Political Activity', *The Times*, 20 April 1960.

171–2: 'If a government ignores human rights and establishes a repressive regime . . .': 'Turkish Ban on All Political Activity', *The Times*, 20 April 1960. In Turkey these comments were published in *Vatan*, 20 April 1960. They are quoted at length in Metin Heper, *Ismet Inönü: Turkish Democrat and Statesman*, pp. 206–7.

172: 'do just about anything it – or Mr Menderes – wants to do': 'Istanbul Tense for NATO Talks', *New York Times*, 1 May 1960.

172: 'History,' Ismet Paşa reminded the Assembly, 'shows that no dictatorship . . .': 'Martial Law in Turkish Cities', *The Times*, 29 April 1960.

172: Ali Fuad Başgil crossed Beyazit Square: Başgil, *La Révolution Militaire*, pp. 132ff.

174: 'That would take me too long', and subsequent exchanges: Başgil, *La Révolution Militaire*, pp. 146–7.

175: badgered the international delegates for news: 'Istanbul tense for NATO Talks', *New York Times*, 1 May 1960.

175: relevant excerpts translated into Turkish: 'Tanks Used in Turkish Clash', *The Times*, 16 May 1960.

175: 'Turkish citizens will never accept a coercive regime': 'Troops in Turkey Break Up Protest by 2,000 Students', *New York Times*, 3 May 1960.

175: 'fighters for Turkish freedom': 'A "Fight for Freedom" in Turkey', *The Times*, 10 May 1960.

175: 'an oppressive regime can never be sure of the army': Ahmad, *The Turkish Experiment in Democracy*, p. 159. See also 'Danger of Rising in Turkey', *The Times*, 7 May 1960.

175: the pedestal in Taksim Square where Ismet Paşa's proscribed statue was to have stood: 'Troops in Turkey Break up Protest by 2,000 Students', *New York Times*, 3 May 1960.

176: 'We will not fight or resist our army:' 'Troops in Turkey Break Up Protest by 2,000 Students', *New York Times*, 3 May 1960.

176: a round of brotherly embraces: Başgil, *La Révolution Militaire*, p. 134.

176: 'the Turkish officer is fully aware that the army ...': Ahmad, *The Turkish Experiment in Democracy*, p. 159.

176: 'one of the most violent scenes in the history of the Turkish parliament': 'MPs Injured in Violent Scene in Turkish Parliament', *The Times*, 26 May 1960. Also see 'Turkish Deputies Battle in House', *New York Times*, 28 May 1960.

178: in this case, a visit to Greece: William Hale, *Turkish Politics and the Military*, p. 109.

178: It was a mortifying moment: Başgil, *La Révolution Militaire*, p. 24.

179: he reminded the Eskişehir crowds: Menderes's speech in *Istanbul*, 26 May 1960.

CHAPTER 10

180: a group of army officers in Istanbul: Abdi Ipekçi and Ömer Sami Coşar, *Ihtilalin Içyüzü*, p. 191.

180: Istanbul's military commander . . . had thrown a dinner party: FO371/153034, Ankara telegraph No. 23, p. 3.

180–1: 'We took over Istanbul in twenty minutes': Suphi Karaman, quoted in Savaş, *Coup/Darbe*.

181: to round up the leading members of the regime: Bayar's arrest is recounted in Başgil, *La Révolution Militaire*, pp. 177ff. Also in Pope, *Turkey Unveiled*, p. 95.

182: Some had not yet taken to bed; Foreign Minister Zorlu ...: FO371/153034, No. 1638, 10.19 p.m., 28 May 1960.

183: a dinner given in his honour ...: Başgil, *La Révolution Militaire*, p. 178.

185: From as early as 1954 the first cliques ...: For the plot's gestation see Harris, 'The Role of the Military in Turkish Politics', pp. 171ff; Yeşilbursa, 'The "Revolution" of 27 May 1960 in Turkey', p. 125; Karpat, 'The Military and Politics in Turkey 1960–64', p. 1664; and Hale, *Turkish Politics and the Military*, pp. 100ff.

186: One of the more active plotters ...: Hotham, *The Turks*, p. 40.

187: 'military dissidence spread with explosive speed': Harris, 'Causes of the 1960 Revolution in Turkey', p. 451.

188: **even forming societies of defiant radio refuseniks**: Erik Jan Zürcher, *Turkey: A Modern History*, p. 251.

189: **busying himself with watering the garden**: G. Lewis, 'Turkey: The End of the First Republic', p. 383.

189: **'taken control of the State and overall command . . .'**: The announcement quoted in *Istanbul*, 27 May 1960.

189: **Subsequent communiqués reported . . .** : See *Istanbul* editions for 27 and 28/29 May 1960.

189: **sabres and swords dating from the First World War**: Communiqué No. 3, *Istanbul*, 30 May 1960.

190: **'The professors talk about their universities . . .'**: Menderes's attacks on the law professors in '4,000 Students in Ankara Clash', *The Times*, 20 May 1960, and 'L'Allocution du Premier Ministre at Turgutlu', *Istanbul*, 19 May 1960.

190: **assembling the legal delegation which he now led to Ankara**: Zürcher, *Turkey: A Modern History*, p. 254.

193: **Legality of rule, the report asserted**: For detail see Ahmad, *The Turkish Experiment in Democracy*, pp. 162ff.

194: **'closest rapport with the fervour of our Youth . . .'**: *Istanbul*, 9 June 1960.

195: **They gathered at the plinth where Ismet Paşa's statue . . .** : *Istanbul*, 21 June 1960.

195: **recommending the Turkish army for the Nobel Peace Prize**: *Istanbul*, 14 June 1960

195: **'in shop windows, in restaurants, on the front pages of the newspapers'**: G. Lewis, 'Turkey: The End of the First Republic', p. 377.

195: **'executing power' of the great action**: 'Gen. Gursel Visits Army Units', *The Times*, 6 June 1960.

195: **'Your approval of our actions . . .'**: *Istanbul*, 4/5 June 1960, and 'Atrocities Laid to Ousted Turks', *New York Times*, 4 June 1960.

195: **'in violation of Atatürk's firm principle . . .'**: G. Lewis, 'Turkey: The End of the First Republic', p. 377.

195: **'mutual consideration and respect, regardless of party affiliations'**: Communiqué No. 13;1, *Istanbul*, 28/29 May 1960.

195: **'Those who shouted for Menderes . . .'**: *Istanbul*, 9 June 1960.

195: **slavering dogs, their mouths crammed with dollar bills**: *Istanbul*, 14 June 1960.

195: **with flags soaked in their own blood**: Yitzhak Oron (ed.), *Middle East Record* 1960, p. 443. Gürsel officially discouraged Turks from sending him such flags on 29 June 1960.

195: **the official held responsible for the stoning at Uşak**: Başgil, *La Révolution Militaire*, p. 124, footnote.

196: **'Terrible feelings of revenge'**: 'What Lies Ahead for Turkey?', *The Times*, 15 June 1960

196: **'journalists who, without fear, put their pens . . .'**: *Istanbul*, Communiqué No. 22, 28/29 May 1960.

196: **'I had little inkling this would happen'**: 'Coup Delights Jailed Editor', *New York Times*, 28 May 1960.

196: **'Mine is not a revolutionary party'**: *Istanbul*, 2 June 1960. Also '400 Arrests in Turkey', *The Times*, 2 June 1960.

196: **'innumerable crimes'**: 'What Lies Ahead for Turkey?', *The Times*, 15 June 1960.

196–7: **'reports of the corruption of the old regime . . .'** and **'alleged to have transferred currency . . .'**: G. Lewis, 'Turkey: The End of the First Republic', p. 378.

197: **'the relative modesty of the collection . . .'**: 'Seized Jewels on Show in Ankara', *The Times*, 7 June 1960.

197: **'They were preparing to shoot patriotic youngsters'**: 'Atrocities Laid to Ousted Turks', *New York Times*, 4 June 1960; and *Istanbul*, 9 June 1960.

198: **squads of goons dressed in army uniforms**: FO371/153034, Ankara telegraph No. 23, p. 2.

198: **'heroic and generous student Youth'** and subsequent communiqué quotes: *Istanbul*, 4/5 June 1960. The claims of further atrocities are also covered in *The Times*, 7 June 1960 and *New York Times*, 4 June 1960.

199: **'Can it be, can it be, that one brother kills another?'**: *Istanbul*, 10 June 1960.

199: **'their lives for liberty and whose reward . . .'**: *Istanbul*, 11/12 June 1960.

199: **the martyrs, five in total . . .** : Ali Ihsan Kalmaz, aged twenty-two; Ersan Özey, twelve; Turhan Emeksiz, twenty-one; Nedim Özpulat, eighteen; and Gültekin Sökmen, twenty.

CHAPTER 11

203: **the folly's extensive panelled library**, and **'delightful for a recluse who might have half a dozen visitors'**: Sir Edwin Pears, *Forty Years in Constantinople*, pp. 124ff.

205: **'a sort of Turkish St Helena'**: 'Gen. Gürsel Promises Free Elections', *The Times*, 30 May 1960.

206: **'Your kind letter,' she replied**: From Baysan Aygün's unpublished correspondence in the Bailey family archive, letter of 23 June 1960.

206: **the search for the guns the former mayor was accused of secreting**: The Committee was keen to emphasise Aygün's alleged but unproven links with Istanbul's crime and heroin gangs.

207: **'I know for whom you are worried'**: Baysan Aygün's letter to Baileys, 23 June 1960.

207: **'to shoot anyone who walks out through the garden door'**, **'full of news and details about the corruption of the Democrats . . .'**, and **'We will cut you to pieces'**: Akile Gürsoy, 'The Coup of May 27, 1960', p. 200.

208: **'It cannot happen here'**: Gürsoy, 'The Coup of May 27, 1960', p. 205.

208: **a small square room with bare walls**: all descriptions are from Mehmet Taşdelen's published account of his Yassıada notes, *Yassıada, Menderes ve Muhafızları*, pp. 76ff.

210: **twenty-seven articles in commemoration, it was explained, of 27 May**: Cited in 'Temporary Turkish Constitution', *The Times*, 13 June 1960.

211: **Turkey was not Iraq, as one officer indignantly declared**: G. Lewis, 'Turkey: The End of the First Republic', p. 384.

211: **Menderes was said to have been roughed up**: *Hürriyet* account quoted in *Istanbul*, 28/29 June 1960.

211: **hated interior minister carried off . . . in a dustcart**: 'Dr Namik Gedik', *The Times*, 31 May 1960.

211: **a room with its own bath**: 'General Gürsel Promises Free Elections', *The Times*, 30 June 1960.

211: **'The Fallen on Yassıada'**: Turkish 'Yassıada'da Düşükler', short excerpts of which are available online.

212: **'not only a whole government, but a whole parliamentary majority'**: 'Will Death Sentences Be Pronounced?', *The Times*, 17 August 1961.

212: **'the courts of the obligation to sentence to death . . .'**: 'Turkey's Penal Code Changed', *The Times*, 13 July 1960.

212: **'The peasants,' the Committee explained, 'must learn and understand . . .'**: 'Island Prison of Overthrown Turkish Rulers', *The Times*, 15 July 1960.

213: **Democrat 'almost to a man, except for the village teacher'**: 'Turkish Villagers Bewildered Over the Downfall of Menderes', *New York Times*, 9 June 1960.

213: **'literate thieves'**: Karpat, *Turkey's Politics*, p. 224, footnote.

213: **'to build new mosques, to repair old ones'**: 'Turkish Villagers Bewildered Over the Downfall of Menderes', *New York Times*, 9 June 1960.

214: **'where he would lead the 3rd Army in a march on Ankara'**: 371/153035, RK1015/43.

214: *demir kırat*, **or iron-grey horse**: Leder, 'Party Competition in Rural Turkey', p. 85.

214: **scattered acts of defiance**: Oron (ed.), *Middle East Record 1960*, p. 495, 'July–Dec: Acts of Opposition and Arrests'.

215: **dismissed them as** *kuyruk*: Karpat, 'Recent Political Developments in Turkey and Their Social Background', p. 316.

215: **dealing with the weeds whose unchecked advance . . .**: FO371/153035, 'Some Notes on the Political and Economic Situation in Western Turkey'.

215: **'a sincere and patriotic leader who worked day and night . . .'**: FO371/153035, 'Some Notes on the Political and Economic Situation in Western Turkey'.

215–6: **'I hear gossip that that man will come out again'**: 'Gen. Gursel's Warning to Turks', *The Times*, 6 July 1960.

216: **all shotguns and hunting rifles**: G. Lewis, 'Turkey: The End of the First Republic', p. 385.

223: **At a public event staged at the Dolmabahçe quayside**: 'Yassıada Photos', *Daily News*, 9/10 October 1960.

223: **the most thoroughgoing summation of the Democrats' crimes**: a transcript of the broadcast was published in *Istanbul*, 14 October 1960.

224: **'Cleared, searched and docketed'**: 'The Road to the Island', *Daily News*, 15 October 1960.

225: **officials distributed an educational pamphlet among the passengers**: 'Yassıada Broşürü', published October 1960 by the National Unity Committee's Liaison Office.

CHAPTER 12

228: **'the cruel destruction of their favourites'**: Robert Walsh, *A Residence at Constantinople*, Vol. 2, p. 269.

228: **'a certain quantity of bread . . . daily exported for their support'**: Walsh, *A Residence at Constantinople*, Vol. 2, p. 269.

229: **Georges Goursat, alerted to the dogs' plight . . .** : The incident is covered in Cihangir Gündoğdu, 'The state and the stray dogs in late-Ottoman Istanbul', pp. 555ff.

230: **'a very modern building looking rather like an aircraft hangar . . .'**: 'The Road to the Island', *Daily News*, 9/10 October 1960.

230–1: **'much marching and counter-marching'**: 'Mr Menderes's Outburst at Political Trial', *The Times* 15 October 1950.

231: **'at some official function in Ankara . . .'**: Hotham, *The Turks*, p. 45.

231: **'slow, dignified, elegantly dressed', 'an ancient grey felt hat', 'in a brown suit and gay tie' and 'worn and thin'**: 'Mr Menderes's Outburst at Political Trial', *The Times* 15 October 1950.

231: **'His clothes,' according to one report . . .** : *Milliyet*, quoted in *Istanbul*, 17 October 1960.

231: **'a complete physical wreck' and 'With sunken cheeks and eyes . . .'**: FO371/153038, RK1016/15, No. 1476.

231: **'in a weak and trembling voice, often stammering . . .'**: FO371/153038, RK1016/15, No. 1476.

232: **'One hardly knows whether to laugh or cry'**: 'Tragedy and Comedy in Turkish Trials', *Observer*, 9 October 1960.

232: **'I cannot imagine a more humiliating punishment . . .'**: FO371/153038, RK1016/15, No. 1476.

233: **'the sort of thing which has greater impact on the masses . . .'**: FO371/153038, RK1016/15, No. 1476.

233: **'We needed money for salaries and we were in debt' and 'Besides, we were being offered a crocodile . . .'**: 'Hound Dominates the Turkish Trial', *New York Times*, 16 October 1960.

233: **The businessman's plan for Buster**: 'TL22500 Offered for Bastı', *Daily News*, 18 October 1960.

234: 'the degraded mentality' of the former president: 'Turkish Trials Stir Feelings of Sympathy', *The Times*, 19 October 1960.

234: 'a nice skit on our bad period . . .': Ahmed Emin Yalman writing in *Vatan*, quoted in *Daily News*, 18 November 1960.

239: only for the Committee to insist that it be heard: FO371/153090, RK1741/2 (D), 'Istanbul Press Reviews October 28 1960', p. 4.

239: an envelope marked 'historical documents': 'Menderes Trial Protest', *The Times*, 21 November 1960.; and FO371/153038, RK1016/15 (H), No. 1548.

239: 'the first Muslim prime minister of Turkey': 'Menderes Trial Protest', *The Times*, 21 November 1960.

239: 'who chases women in the street': 'Menderes Trial Protest', *The Times*, 21 November 1960.

240: 'fully fashioned stockings and matching high-heeled shoes' and 'clear and ringing tones': 'True Love Shines Through the Dirt', *Daily News*, 2 November 1960.

240: 'the married Adnan Menderes': Emine Gürsoy Naskali, *Bebek Davası*, p. 27.

240: 'I met Adnan Menderes in 1951 . . .': 'Turkish Court Hears Evidence by Opera Singer', *The Times*, 1 November 1960; FO371/153058 'From Ankara to Turkish Office', 1 November 1960; 'True Love Shines Through the Dirt', *Daily News*, 2 November 1960.

241: 'It takes great courage or a genuine, very deeply rooted love . . .': 'True Love Shines Through the Dirt', *Daily News*, 2 November 1960.

243: the needlepoint of island life: Ülman, Hilal: *Kadınlar Koğuşu Yassıada*.

243: 'was unusually beautiful today, carpeted with spring flowers . . .': '400 Accused in Final Stage of Yassıada Trials', *The Times*, 12 May 1961.

244: Article 17 . . . MPs could not be held legally accountable for their voting decisions: Walter Fritz Weiker and Robert D. Calkins, *The Turkish Revolution*, 1960–61, p. 31.

244: 'lawyer's banquet of Byzantine subtlety' and 'men's heads': 'Will Death Sentences be Pronounced?', *The Times*, 17 August 1961.

247: 'physically shrunken but still well groomed' and 'evasive in his answers but witty and courteous': G. Lewis, 'The Thorny Road to Democracy', p. 188.

247: participated so whole-heartedly in the restoration of Istanbul: Chief Prosecutor Egesel, quoted in Gül, *The Emergence of Modern Istanbul*, p. 145.

248: Announcements that 27 May was to be a national holiday: '21 People Arrested in Turkey', *The Times*, 2 June 1961.

248: 'was born dead, and has merely replaced one dictatorship by another': 'Turks' Concern at Communist Broadcasts', *The Times*, 26 April 1961.

248: public declarations of their devotion to Adnan Bey: 'Arrests in Turkish Restaurant', *The Times*, 5 April 1961. These declarations also disparaged İnönü.

248: 'elaborate courtesies and oriental titles': Hotham, *The Turks*, p. 46.

249: 'I know that revolutions mean that human lives . . .': 'Mr Bayar on Risks of Office', *The Times*, 22 July 1961.

249: 'I have served my country for close on thirty years': 'Final Speeches by Yassıada Prisoners', *The Times*, 28 July 1961.

249: 'So long as there are hundreds of new factory chimneys . . .': 'Reply by Turkish Ex-Minister', *The Times*, 11 August 1961.

249: 'a broken and scarcely audible voice': 'Mr Menderes's Last Chance', *The Times*, 26 July 1961.

249: 'Did you see him?' the taxi driver asked: 'Trial of Leaders Sobers Istanbul', *New York Times*, 17 October 1960.

250: spotted in the early hours at Eyüp mosque: Hotham, *The Turks*, p. 47. 'Foreign Affairs', *New York Times*, 18 September 1961.

251: 'I cannot guess at the decision': Ahmet Kocabiyikoğlu letter; Erhan Kocabiyikoğlu's private collection.

251: 'Today is decision day,' wrote Hasan Polatkan: The last letters of Polatkan, Zorlu and Menderes are quoted in Taşdelen, *Yassıada, Menderes ve Muhafızları*, pp. 161ff.

251: 'yellow blooms danced in the barbed wire'. As gunboats circled the island and 'jet aircraft streamed overhead . . .': 'Menderes to Die; Bayar Gets Life', *New York Times*, 16 September 1961.

252: 'stoic and exemplary courage': 'Fifteen Death Sentences Passed on Men of the Menderes Regime', *The Times*, 16 September 1960.

252: 'escaped with a lighter sentence than had been expected': Hotham, *The Turks*, p. 46.

CHAPTER 13

253: 'We know that Adnan Bey wavered towards the end': Başgil, *La Révolution Militaire*, p. 148.

254: Two days after the coup an army major . . . : Orhan Erkanlı, quoted in Ahmad, *The Turkish Experiment in Democracy*, p. 162.

256: 'such different ideas, such disagreements . . .': Weiker and Calkins, *The Turkish Revolution, 1960–1961*, p. 131.

258: the duty slot which exactly served his purposes: Taşdelen: *Yassıada, Menderes ve Muhafızları*, pp. 176ff.

261: 'and a 80/20 chance against executions': Behcet Yeşilbursa, 'The "Revolution" of 27 May 1960', p. 137.

261: 'In all my service,' wrote US Ambassador Warren: Pelt, *Military Intervention*, p. 198.

262: 'oriental enough to enjoy standing on their honour . . .' and 'largely be judged abroad . . .': Behcet Yeşilbursa, 'The "Revolution" of 27 May 1960 in Turkey', p. 139. FO317/153037, RK1018/1, Burrows dispatch, 21 October 1961.

262: 'an old friend of several of the leading Turkish soldiers': FO371/160791, Burrows to Tompkins, 29 July 1961.

262: 'inconsistent with the high ideals of the Western community . . .': FO371/160791: 'Draft Personal Message from the Prime Minister to President Gürsel'.

262-3: 'also confident of the votes of five other Committee members . . .', 'shadow committee' in the Turkish army, 'express to the Committee the views of the armed services' and 'still fanatically supported the view . . .': FO371/160791, CT1017/17. Burrows dispatch, 5 August 1961.

263: 'eight in favour of clemency, eight in favour of executions', 'some thirty or forty officers in the army outside the Committee . . .', 'whether the efforts being made by this group . . .', 'the Committee were to some extent no longer . . .', and 'considerable influence over the Committee . . .': FO371/160791, CT1016/15. Burrows dispatch, 8 September 1961.

263: 'fairly reliably' and 'never get out of Yassıada alive . . .': FO371/ 160791, CT1015/5, Burrows dispatch, 2 September 1961.

264: 'a greyish-blue colour', with an oxygen tube . . .': 'Fifteen Death Sentences Passed on Men of the Menderes Regime', The Times, 16 September 1961.

264: 'pitiful, deathly-marble colour': 'Menderes Waits in Coma for Hangman', Daily Express, 16 September 1961.

264: 'I'm letting you see him so that . . .': 'Menderes to Die; Bayar Gets Life', New York Times, 16 September 1961.

264: whose governor had lately received instructions . . . : Ahmet Acarol, quoted in Demirkırat, part 10.

267: 'the beneficial effect it would have on all who wish you well . . .': FO371/160792, No. 1914, 6.20 p.m., 15 September 1961.

267: 'where he says any executions, however few . . .': I have paraphrased Ismet Inönü's letter given in Metin Heper, Ismet Inönü: Turkish Democrat and Statesman, p. 219.

269: 'We had hoped that in the end Mr Menderes would be set free': Daily Express, 16 September 1961.

270: 'If Menderes and his colleagues are executed . . .': Heper, Ismet Inönü: Turkish Democrat and Statesman, p. 219.

270: The 'men with guns': FO371/160792 1018/1/100, Burrows dispatch, 23 September 1961, p. 8.

271: Room 2's occupant set about strangling himself: For Bayar's suicide attempt, Daily News, 28 September 1960.

271: the prisoner's Quran had been steeped in a poison so powerful: Military memorandum, 2 June 1960, Mehmet Taşdelen's private archive.

272: First they came for Zorlu: 'les derniers moments des condamnés', Istanbul, 19 September 1961.

275: 'I'm worried about my son entering politics': 'Les derniers moments des condamnés', Istanbul, 19 September 1961.

CHAPTER 14

277: 'the people's courts in Bulgaria': 'Fifteen Death Sentences Passed on Men of the Menderes Regime', *The Times*, 16 September 1961.

277 'the savage and bloody dawn of the new Turkey': *Il Messagero* (Rome), 18 September 1961, quoted in FO371/160792, 'From Rome to Foreign Office'.

277: 'tragic and barbarous end . . .': *I Katherimini*, 20 September 1961; FO371/160972, 1021/61/61.

277: the 'greatest murder story of the last years': Baysan Aygün letter to Baileys, 11 October 1961.

277: 'a living corpse' and subsequent quotes: Baysan Aygün letter to Baileys, 11 October 1961.

278: 'where the old democrats and Menderes lovers are': Baysan Aygün letter to Baileys, 11 October 1961.

278: 'with a gleaming new red-brick minaret': '13 Million Go to Polls in Turkey', *The Times*, 16 October 1961.

279: 'an offence calling for vengeance . . .': 'Behind the Death Sentences in Turkey', *New York Times*, 24 September 1961.

279: 'A whole week,' Baysan told the Baileys: Baysan Aygün letter to Baileys, 25 April 1963.

280: On a July night in 1960 army units . . . : Vahide, *Islam in Modern Turkey*, pp. 344ff.

281: Newspapers were suspended: After running photographs of the Imralı graves to mark the fifth anniversary of the executions, *Adalet*'s print run was confiscated ('Turks Hold Rite for Gen. Gursel', *New York Times*, 16 September 1966).

281: running a photograph of Margaret Bailey: This photograph was originally published in *Daily Express*, 16 September 1961.

281: 'the inclination of the Turkish people to rejoice . . .': 'Turks Hold Rite for Gen. Gursel', *New York Times*, 16 September 1966.

282: 'the name of the action by which the Republican Peoples Party . . .': Hale, *Turkish Politics and the Military*, p. 112.

282: The general's son condemned the downgrade . . . : *Milliyet*, 25 August 1988.

283: radical officers under Colonel Talat Aydemir: The Aydemir coup attempts are covered in David Hotham, *The Turks*, pp. 48–51.

285: the state funerals their families had been seeking: 'Hanged PM gets a state funeral', *Guardian*, 18 September 1990.

List of Illustrations

Maps by Jane Randfield
All photographs are the author's own, unless otherwise stated

Every effort has been made by the publishers to trace the holders of copyright. Any inadvertent omissions of acknowledgement or permission can be rectified in future editions.

Index

Abraham, Prophet 167
academics, and professors 5, 60, 120, 173, 174, 194, 199
Academics for Peace 147–8, 293
Adnan Bey, *see* Menderes, Adnan
Abdul Hamid II, Sultan 66, 93, 116, 153, 225
Abdülaziz, Sultan 38
Afghanistan, king of 232
Afyon, Turkey 15, 124, 280
agriculture 32, 35
America, and Americans, *see* United States
Anıtkabir Mausoleum, Ankara 6, 87–9, 123, 126, 132–5, 138, 195, 199–200, 282
Ankara, Turkey 4, 5, 14, 17, 23, 29, 31, 40, 42, 46, 48, 57, 59, 60, 61, 62, 68, 95, 99, 109, 110, 111–2, 114, 119–21, 122–6, 137, 143, 146, 149, 158, 160, 165, 174, 176, 180–1, 182, 186, 188, 189, 190, 196, 199, 211, 213, 214, 219, 231, 237, 238, 245, 254–5, 256, 262, 273, 278, 282, 286, 289, 291, 296
Ankara railway station 5–10, 11, 12, 142–4
Ankara University 174, 191
Armenians 39, 58, 81, 85, 201, 221
army, and army officers 5, 60, 123, 124, 132, 133–5, 154, 156, 160, 171, 174–5, 176, 180–8, 190–4, 196, 197, 199, 200, 248, 254–6, 260, 263, 266, 267–8
Aslanhane Mosque, Ankara 121, 124, 128, 130
As Said, Nuri 149, 150, 152–3, 154
Atabey, Fahri 238–40

Atatürk, Mustafa Kemal 6, 9, 11, 13, 15, 19, 27, 31, 32, 36, 38, 39–41, 42, 44–8, 50, 56, 57, 58, 60, 61, 62, 66, 68, 73, 76, 87–9, 97, 98, 105, 114, 116, 121, 123, 125, 132, 137, 147, 151, 154, 155, 170, 171, 172, 173, 176, 185, 186, 191, 194, 195, 199, 200, 222, 225, 230, 256
Athens, Greece 5, 95
Atıf Hoca 47–8, 114
Austria 44, 125
Aya Sofya Basilica, Istanbul 43, 70, 81
Aydan, Ayhan 236–242, 247
Aydemir, Talat 283
Aydın, Turkey 25, 28, 52, 57, 71, 86, 184, 214, 215, 281, 284
Aygün, Baysan 161–3, 183–4, 205–7, 277–8, 279–80
Aygün, Kemal, mayor of Istanbul 15, 22, 162, 183–4, 243, 252, 277–8, 279–80
Ayvansaray, Istanbul 77

Baghdad, Iraq 146, 149, 150, 152–3, 219
Baghdad Pact 149
Bailey, Margaret 1–4, 8, 14–6, 21–4, 268–9, 281
Bailey, Tony 2–4, 14–6, 22
Bailey family, and holiday in Turkey 21–3, 29, 70, 162, 205–7, 277–8
Bailey, Elizabeth 24
Başgil, Ali Fuad 172–4, 244
Bayar, Celal 27, 28, 31, 36, 67, 88–9, 91, 93, 99–103, 127, 130, 149, 174, 181–2, 195, 225, 230–1, 232–4, 243, 245, 249, 253, 264, 271
Bayar, Celal, family of 197, 207, 212
beauty contests 69, 128,

250, 254, 255, 260, 284, 285, 289, 294–6

Istanbul (Atatürk) Airport 29, 97, 149–50, 162, 180, 289, 291

Istanbul University 164, 166, 172, 174, 203, 239

Istiklal Caddesi, Istanbul, *see* Independence Street

Italy 38, 40, 42, 211

Izmır (Smyrna), Turkey 15, 22, 39, 40, 52, 56–7, 133, 155, 159, 185, 189, 197, 207, 214, 219, 234, 282, 285, 296

Janissaries 81, 82

Jews 81, 85, 201

journalism, journalists 14, 23, 47, 58–60, 66, 96, 97, 117, 119–20, 130–2, 155, 165–6, 168, 169, 172, 174, 175, 194, 196–9, 213, 224, 229–30, 268, 275, 281, 294

judiciary 60, 90, 169, 294

Justice Party, Turkey 278–9, 282, 283

Kadıköy, Istanbul 58, 70, 167, 253

Kargıcak, Turkey 18–9

Kayseri, Turkey 124, 158, 160, 161, 171, 187, 231, 251, 277, 279

Kemalism, Kemalists 11, 67, 75, 133, 185, 283

Kennedy, John F. 242, 267, 270

Knebworth, England 203

Koç Transport Museum, Istanbul 245

Kocabiyikoğlu, Ahmet 242, 251

Kocabiyikoğlu, Erhan 244–2

Kocatepe, Ankara, and Mosque 122, 124, 126, 128–30, 132, 162, 177

Konya, Turkey 124, 165

Koraltan, Refik 162, 174

Korea, and war 4, 64, 66, 67, 94, 168, 172, 217, 255, 284

Kurds, Kurdish region 21, 39, 58, 60, 105, 112, 147, 177, 289

Kütahya, Turkey 15, 184, 189

Labraunda 18

Lausanne, Treaty of 74, 86, 97, 170

lawyers, legal professors 189–94, 210, 212

Lemnos, Greece 38

Lewis, Bernard 149

Linke, Lilo 48, 55

Lloyd George, David 85

London, England 3, 4, 5, 13, 14, 16, 51, 96, 97, 100, 102, 219

Maclean, Fitzroy 34

Macmillan, Harold 4, 262

Mahmut II, Sultan 37–8

Makal, Mahmut 32, 33

Makarios, Archbishop; Greek Cypriot leader 7, 95, 96

Malatya, Turkey 15, 65–6, 69, 151, 152

martial law 102, 103, 174, 187

Meander, River 57, 284

Mecca, Saudi Arabia 7, 127

Mehmet the Conqueror (Fatih Sultan Mehmet) 37, 55, 76–82, 85, 92–3, 104, 227, 250

Mehmet VI, Sultan 41

Menderes, Adnan 4, 5, 6, 7–16, 19, 22, 23, 25–8, 30, 34, 49, 50–3, 55–7, 58, 60, 65–70, 71, 72, 86, 87, 88–9, 90–1, 93, 96, 99–103, 113, 114, 115, 118, 119, 126, 127, 128, 130, 139–41, 144–6, 149–50, 151–2, 153, 154, 155–6, 157, 161, 162, 166, 167–8, 169, 170, 171, 173, 174–6, 178–9, 183, 184, 186, 189, 190, 191, 196, 197, 207, 208–10, 211, 212, 213, 214, 215, 216–7, 225–6, 230–1, 234, 236, 237, 238–42, 243, 245, 247, 248, 249–50, 251, 253–4, 257–9, 262, 264–5, 269, 270, 271–2, 273–6, 277, 278, 280, 281, 282, 284–5, 286, 296, 297

Menderes, Adnan (Dr) 285–7

Menderes, Aydın 181, 285, 286

Menderes, Berin 22, 55–57, 101, 115–16, 117, 181, 209, 215, 237, 241, 251, 269, 270, 286

Menderes, Dunyam 236, 238

Menderes, Mutlu 241, 285, 286

Military Academy, and Cadets, Ankara 176, 181, 187, 197, 200, 205, 270